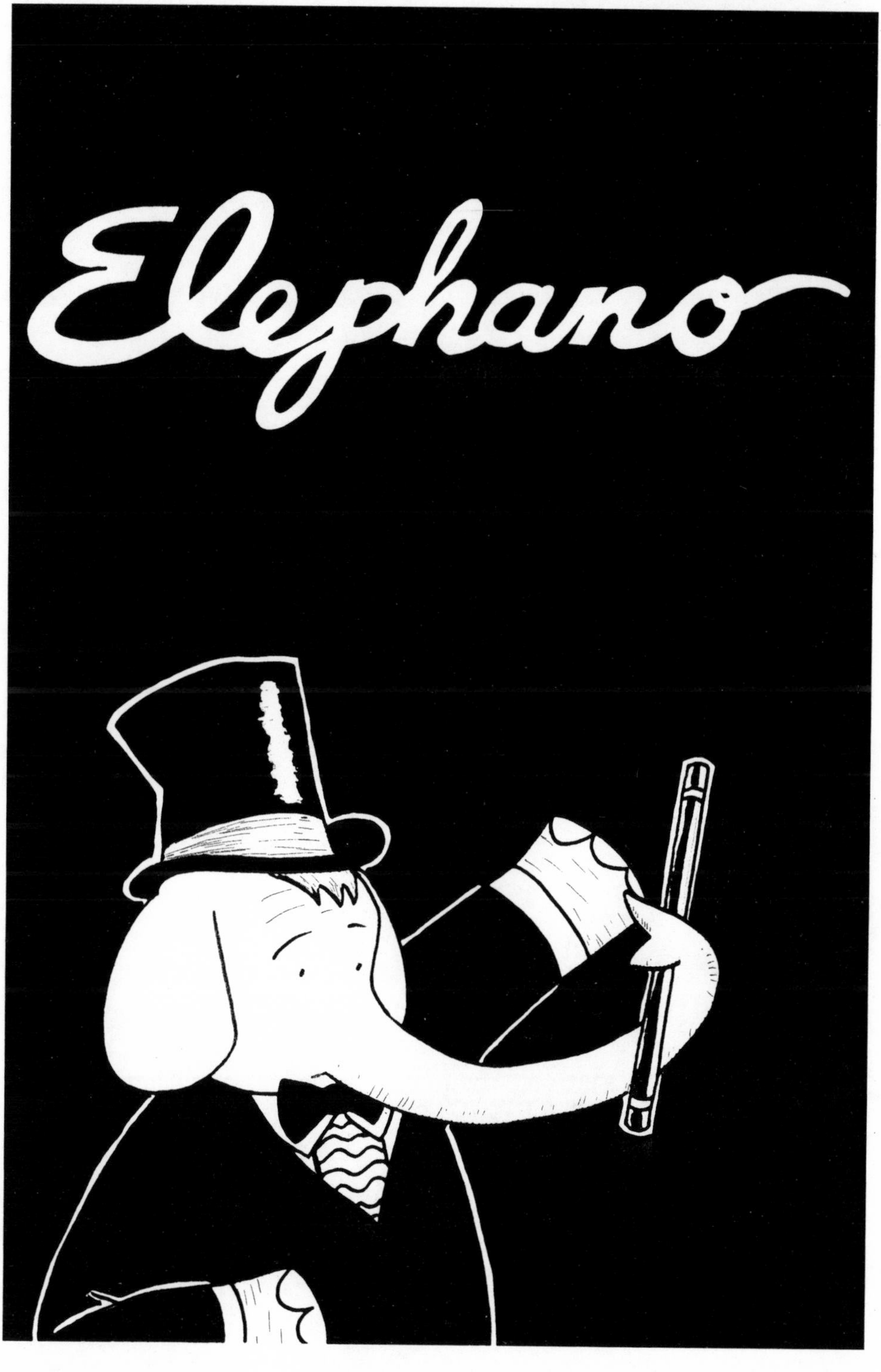
Elephano

Elephano the Magician: A Comics Anthology
ISBN 978-0557-01798-0

Special thanks to Linda Medley for helping me coming up with
the character.

Editor David Yoder

TABLE ⚬f CONTENTS

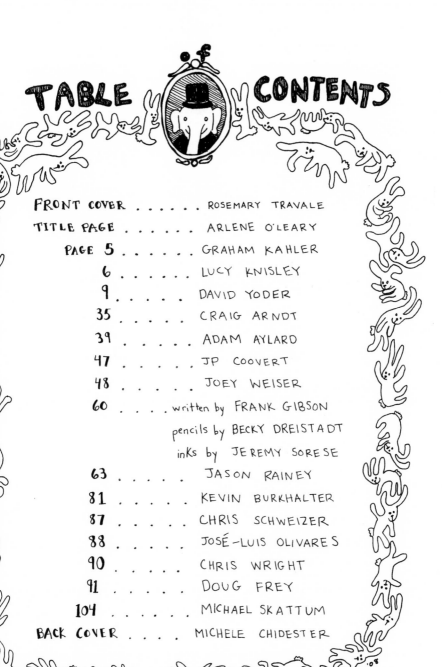

MELISSA MENDES '08

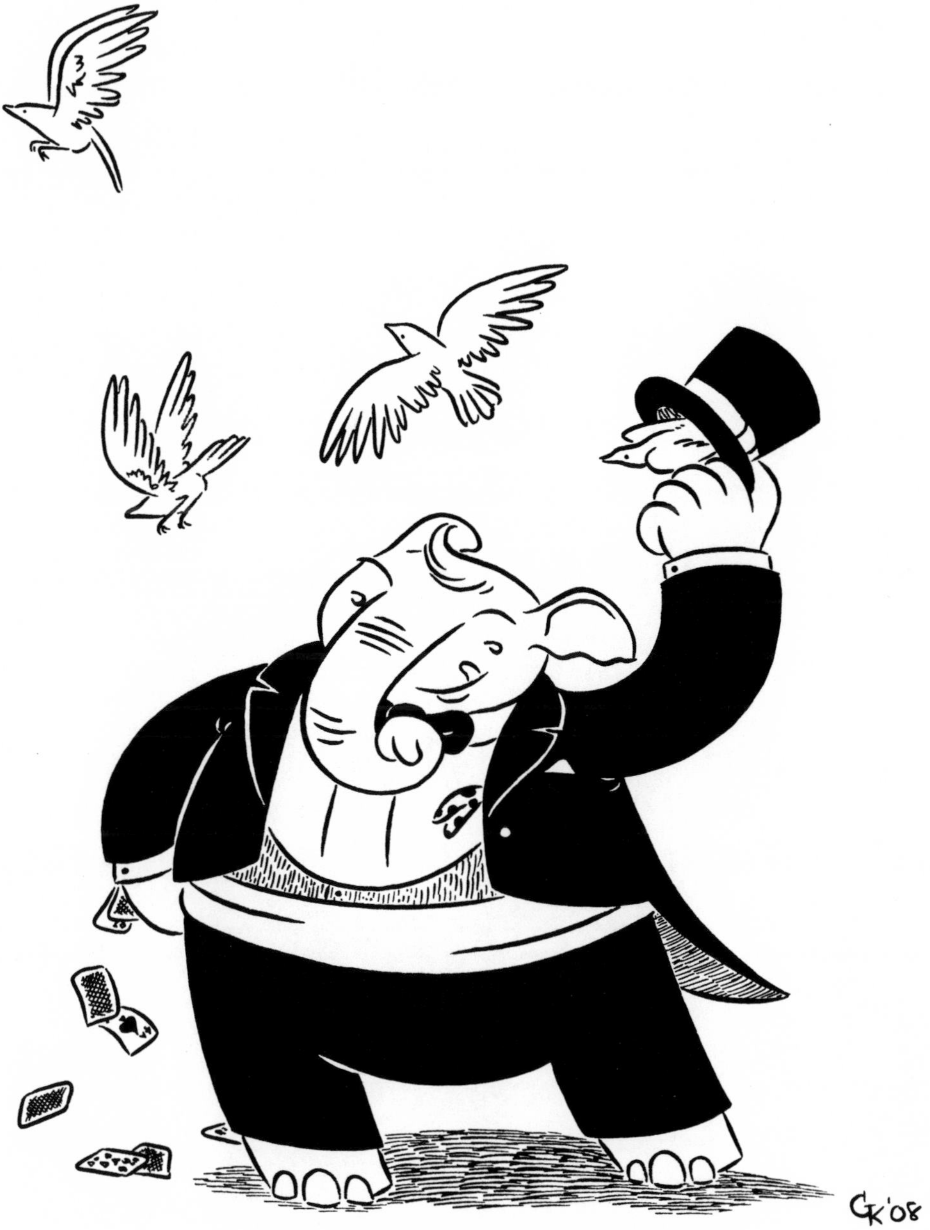
GK'08

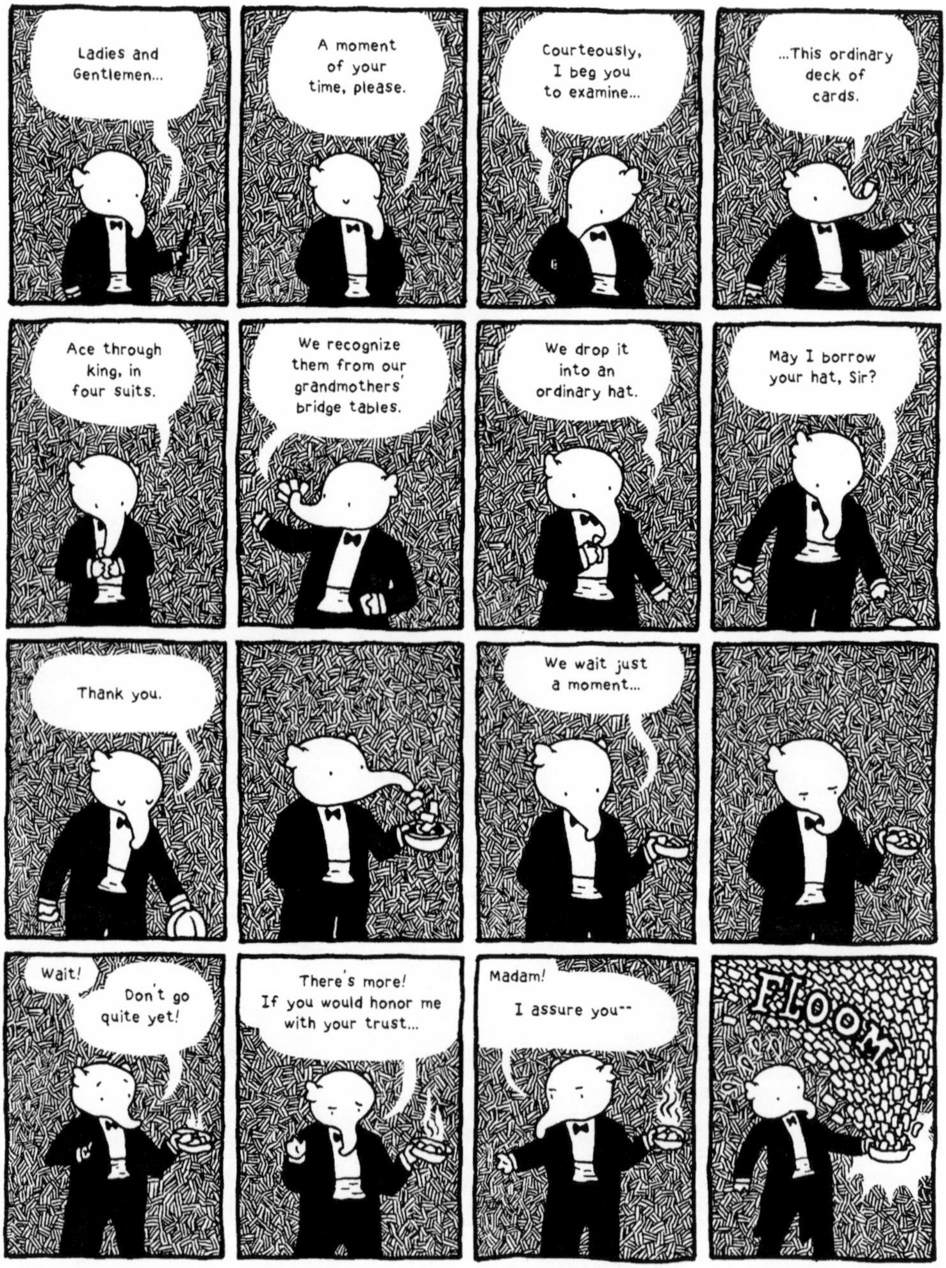

Ladies and Gentlemen...
A moment of your time, please.
Courteously, I beg you to examine...
...This ordinary deck of cards.
Ace through king, in four suits.
We recognize them from our grandmothers' bridge tables.
We drop it into an ordinary hat.
May I borrow your hat, Sir?
Thank you.
We wait just a moment...
Wait!
Don't go quite yet!
There's more! If you would honor me with your trust...
Madam!
I assure you--
FLOOM

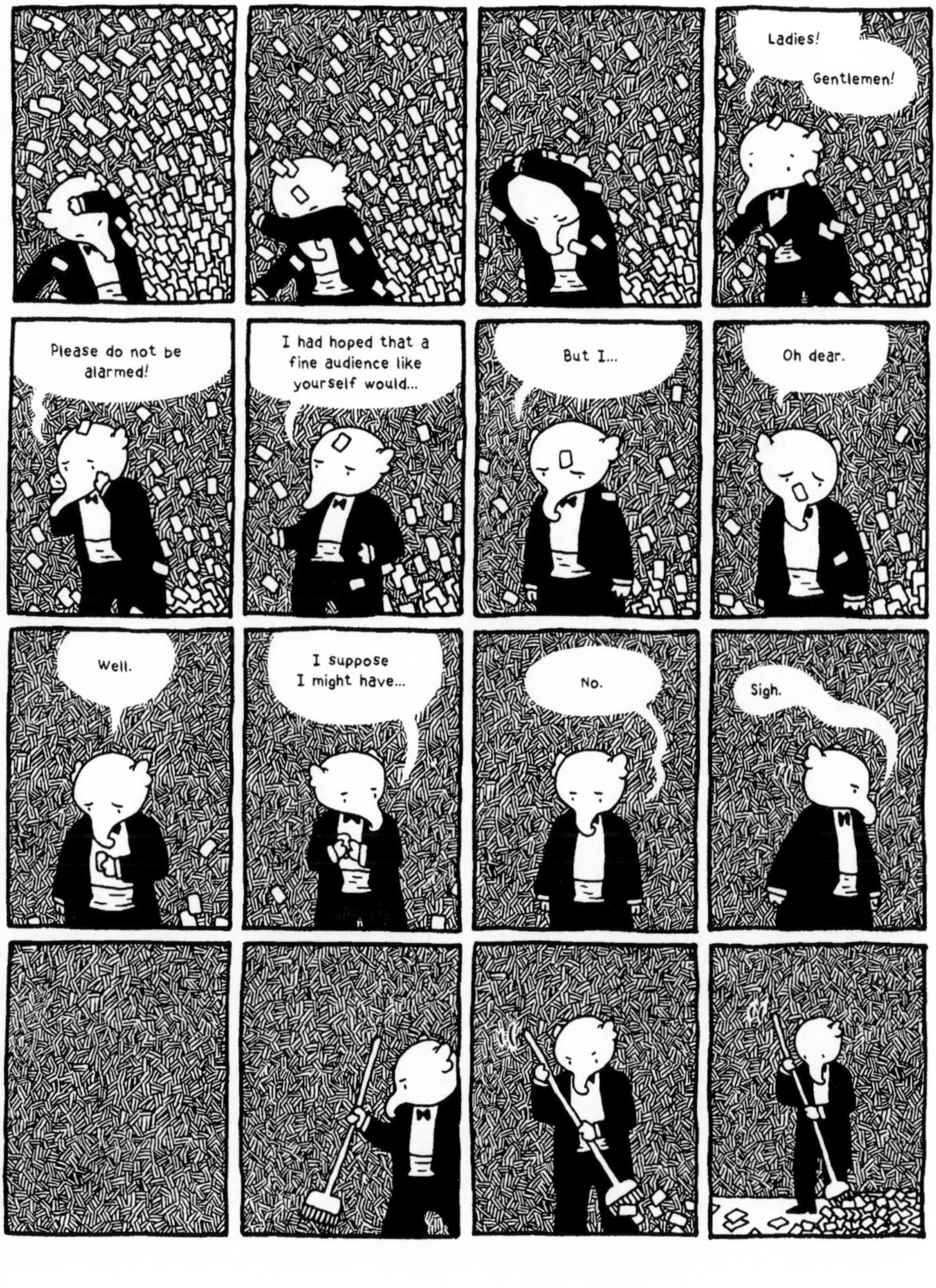
Ladies!
Gentlemen!
Please do not be alarmed!
I had hoped that a fine audience like yourself would...
But I...
Oh dear.
Well.
I suppose I might have...
No.
Sigh.

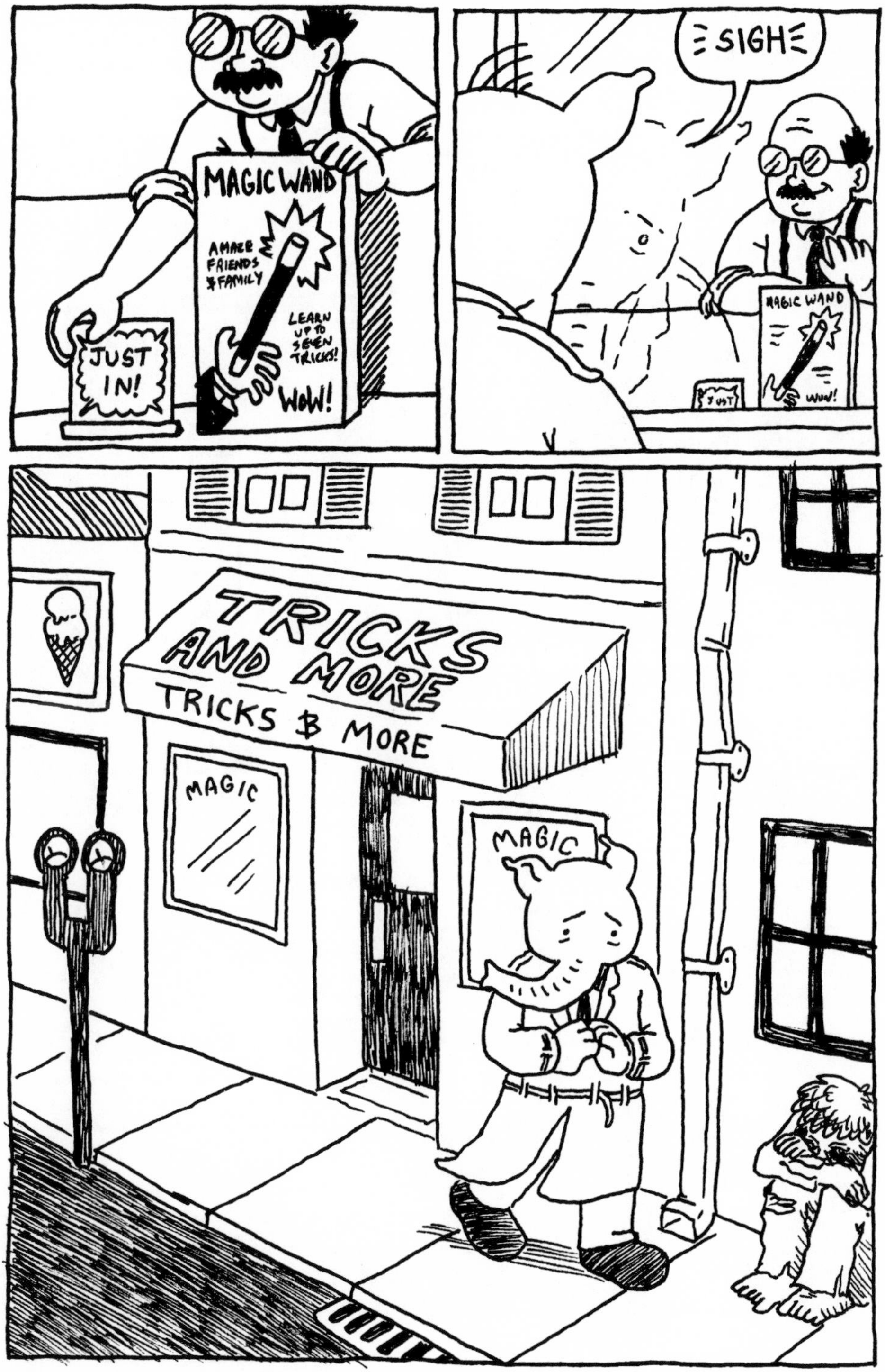
MAGIC WAND
AMAZE FRIENDS & FAMILY
LEARN UP TO SEVEN TRICKS!
WOW!
JUST IN!
SIGH
MAGIC WAND
TRICKS AND MORE
TRICKS & MORE
MAGIC
MAGIC

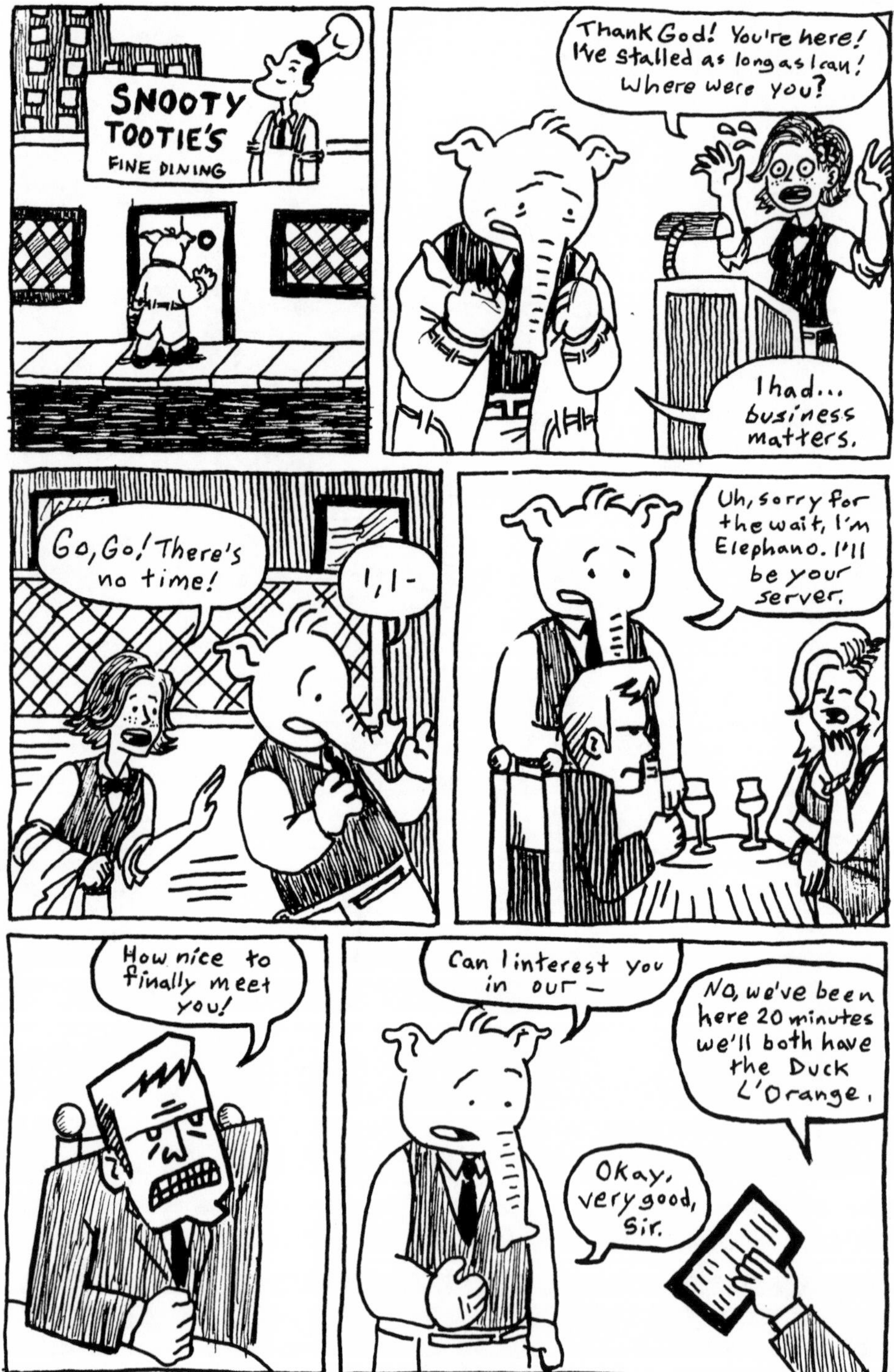
SNOOTY TOOTIE'S FINE DINING
Thank God! You're here! I've stalled as long as I can! Where were you?
I had... business matters.
Go, Go! There's no time!
I, I-
Uh, sorry for the wait, I'm Elephano. I'll be your server.
How nice to finally meet you!
Can I interest you in our—
No, we've been here 20 minutes we'll both have the Duck L'Orange.
Okay, very good, Sir.

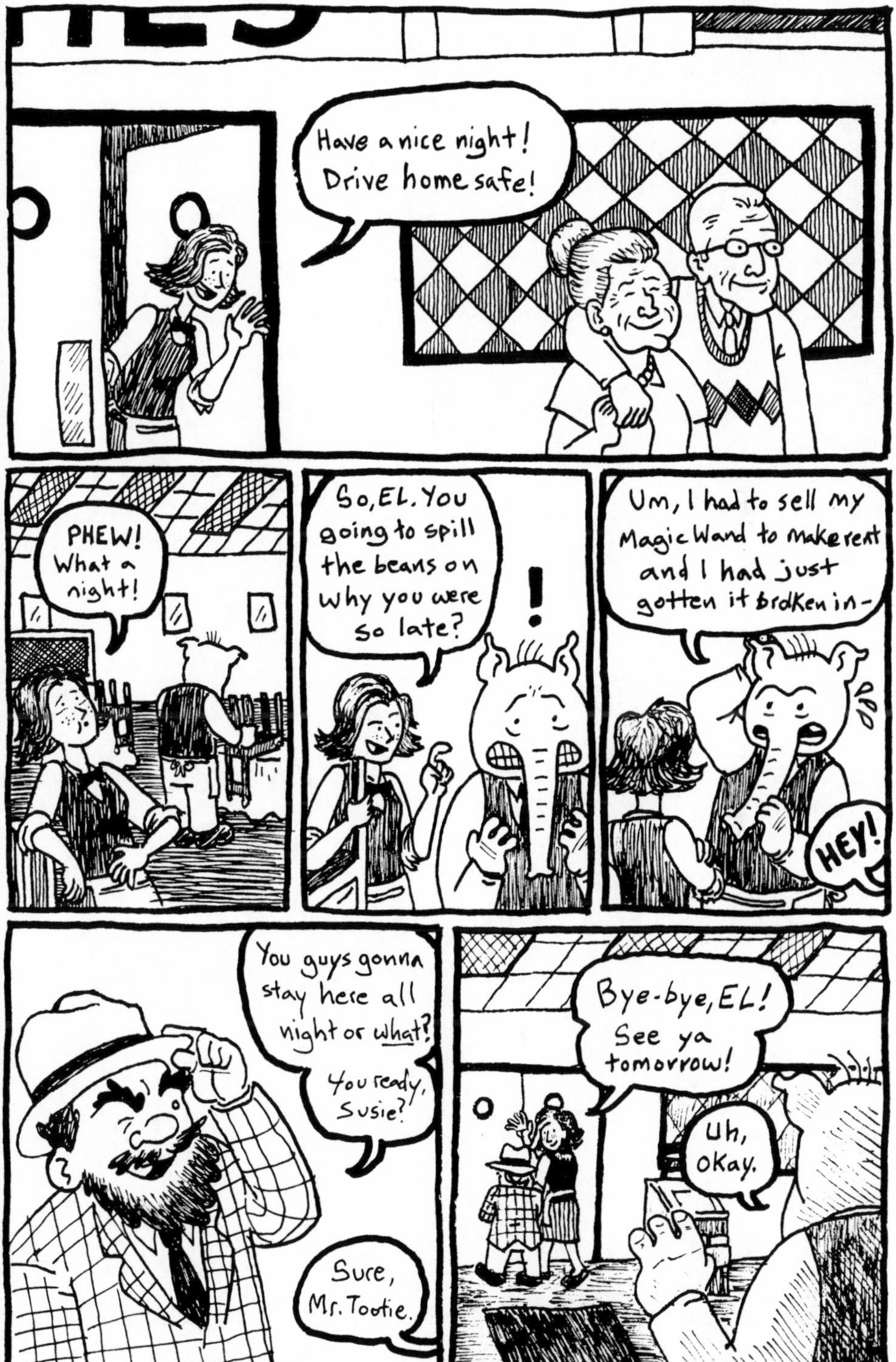
Have a nice night!
Drive home safe!
PHEW! What a night!
So, EL. You going to spill the beans on why you were so late?
!
Um, I had to sell my Magic Wand to make rent and I had just gotten it broken in-
HEY!
You guys gonna stay here all night or what?
You ready, Susie?
Sure, Mr. Tootie.
Bye-bye, EL! See ya tomorrow!
Uh, okay.

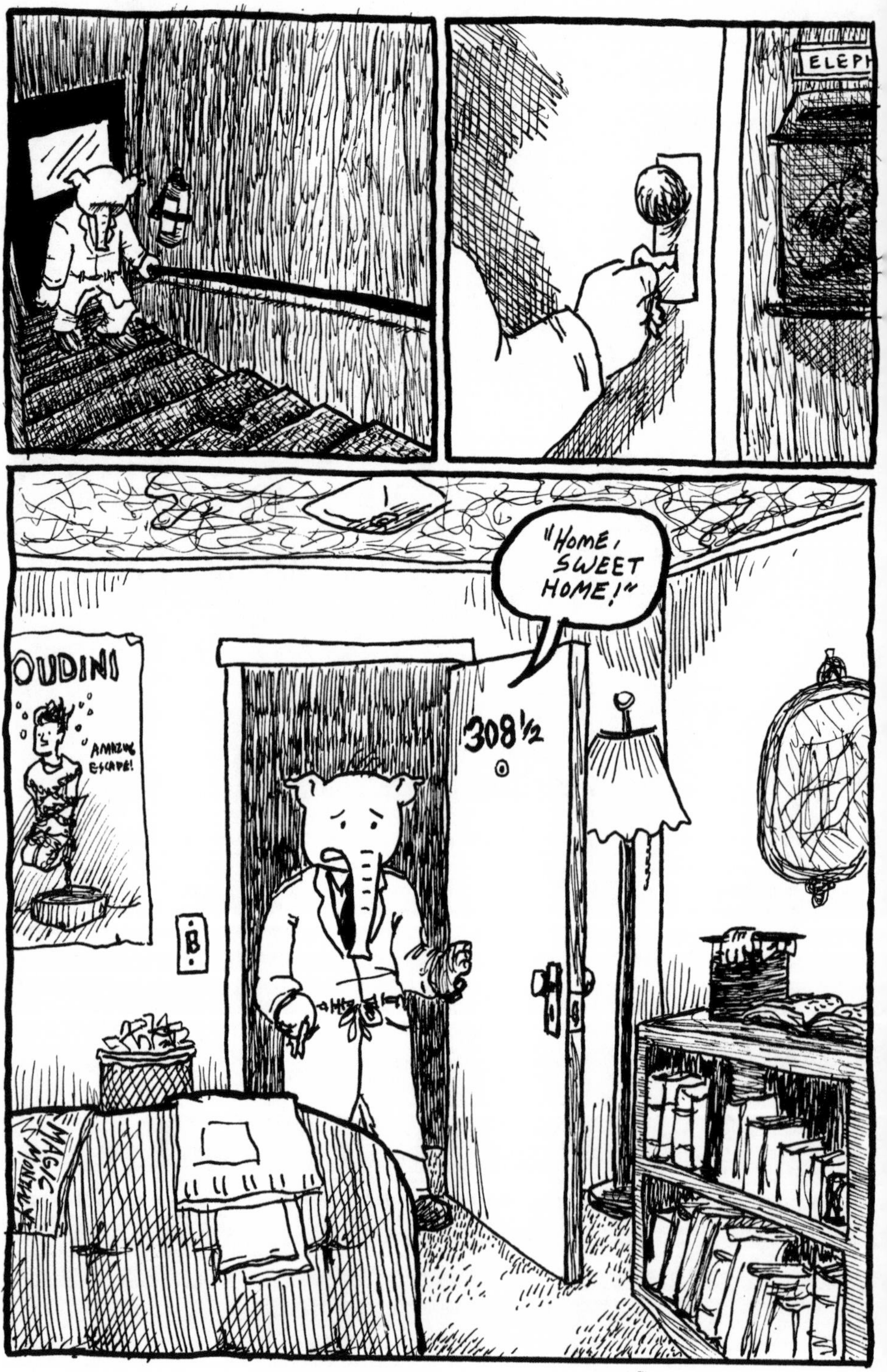
ELEPH
"HOME, SWEET HOME!"
OUDINI
AMAZING ESCAPE!
308½
B

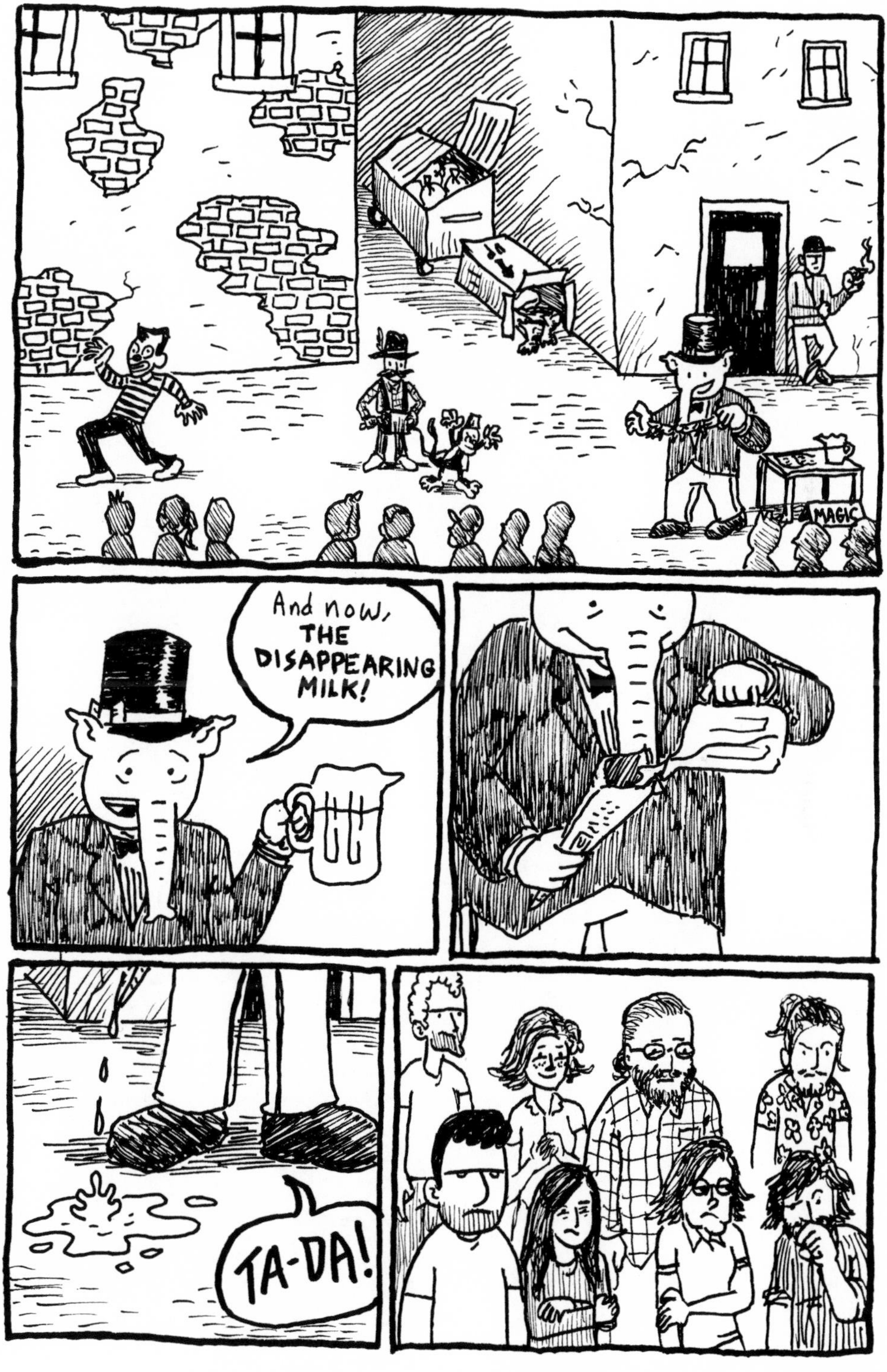
MAGIC
And now, THE DISAPPEARING MILK!
TA-DA!

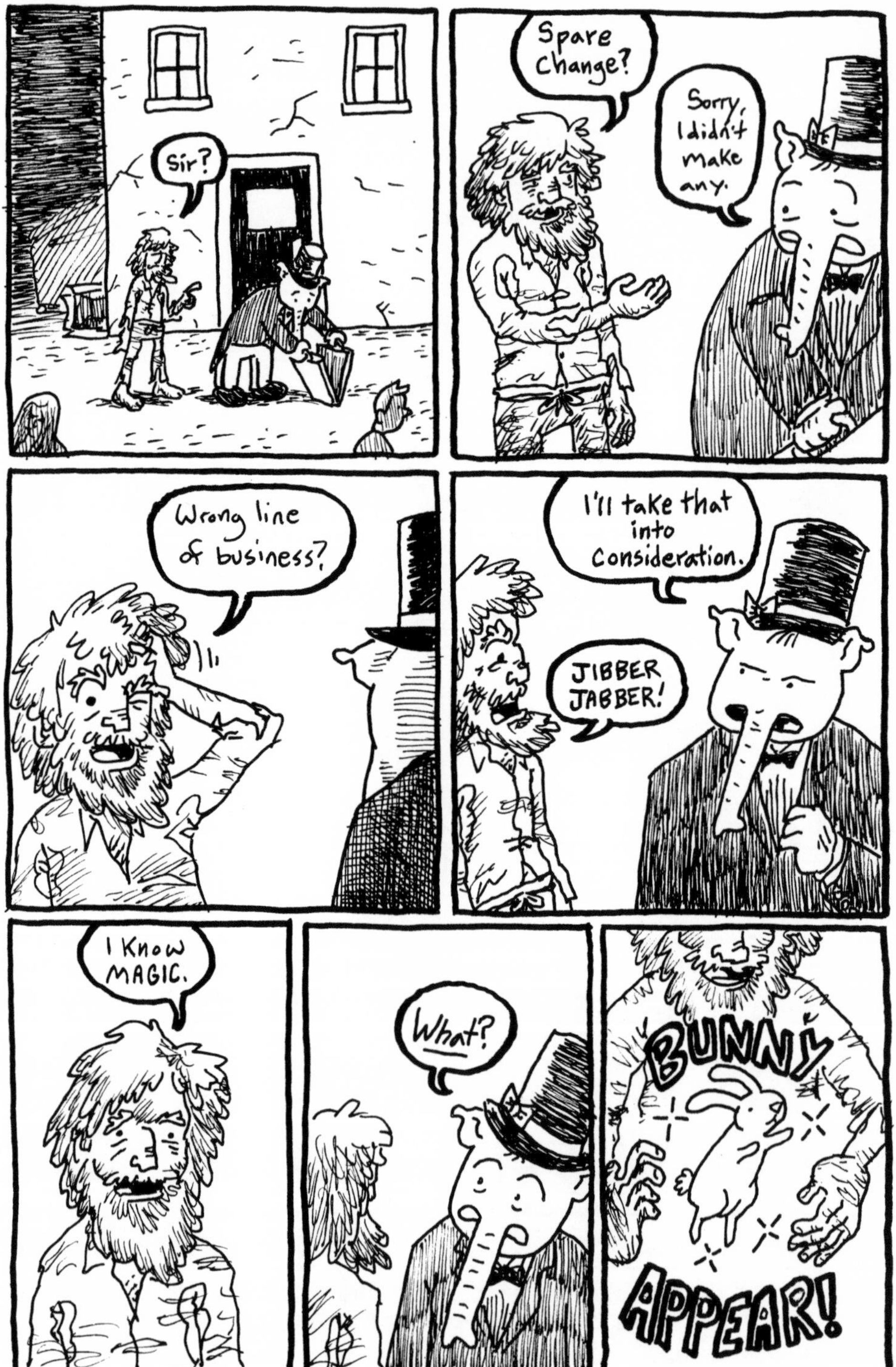
Sir?
Spare Change?
Sorry, I didn't make any.
Wrong line of business?
I'll take that into consideration.
JIBBER JABBER!
I Know MAGIC.
What?
BUNNY
APPEAR!

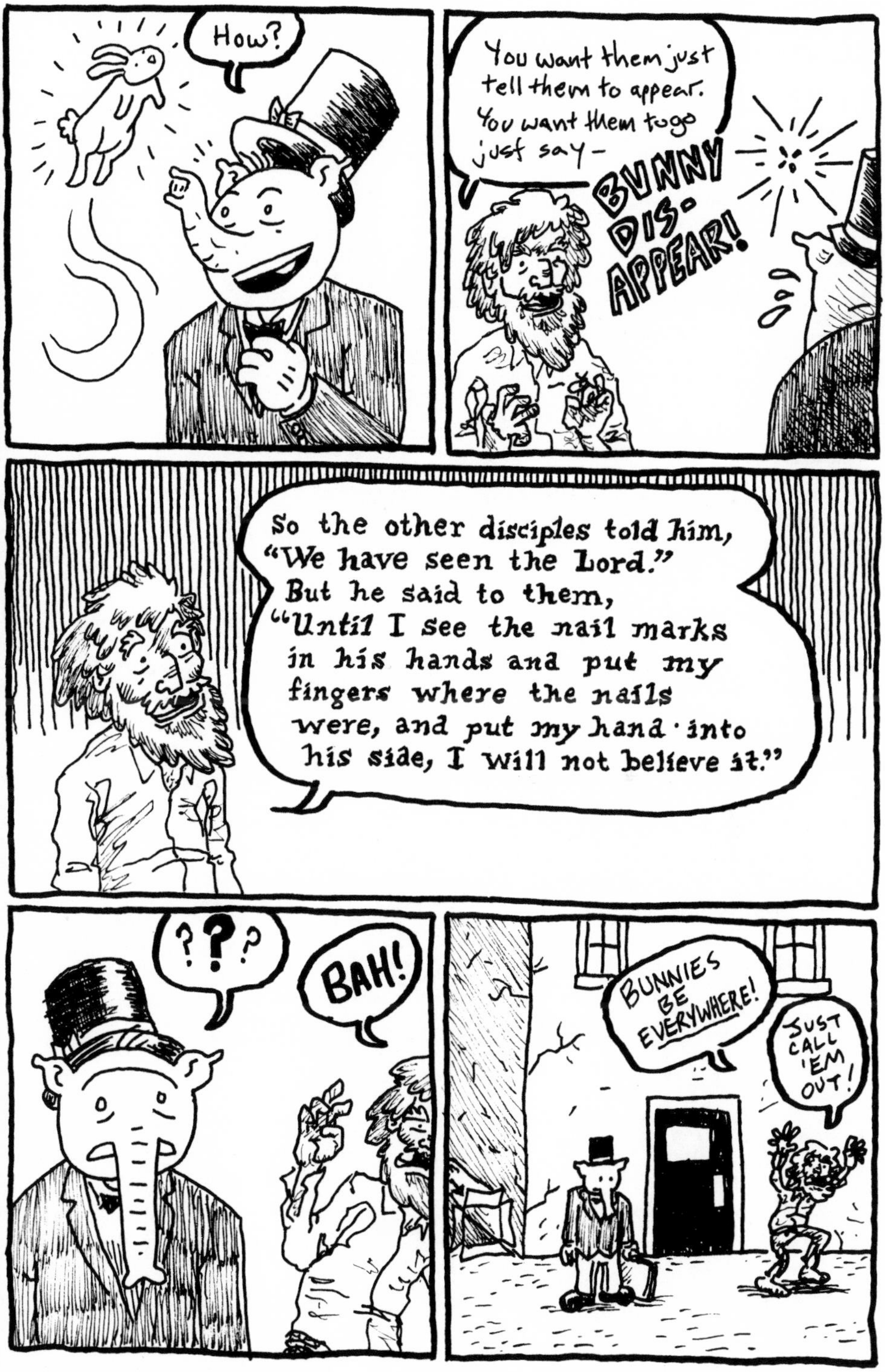
How?
You want them just tell them to appear. You want them to go just say -
BUNNY DIS-APPEAR!
So the other disciples told him, "We have seen the Lord." But he said to them, "Until I see the nail marks in his hands and put my fingers where the nails were, and put my hand into his side, I will not believe it."
???
BAH!
BUNNIES BE EVERYWHERE!
JUST CALL 'EM OUT!

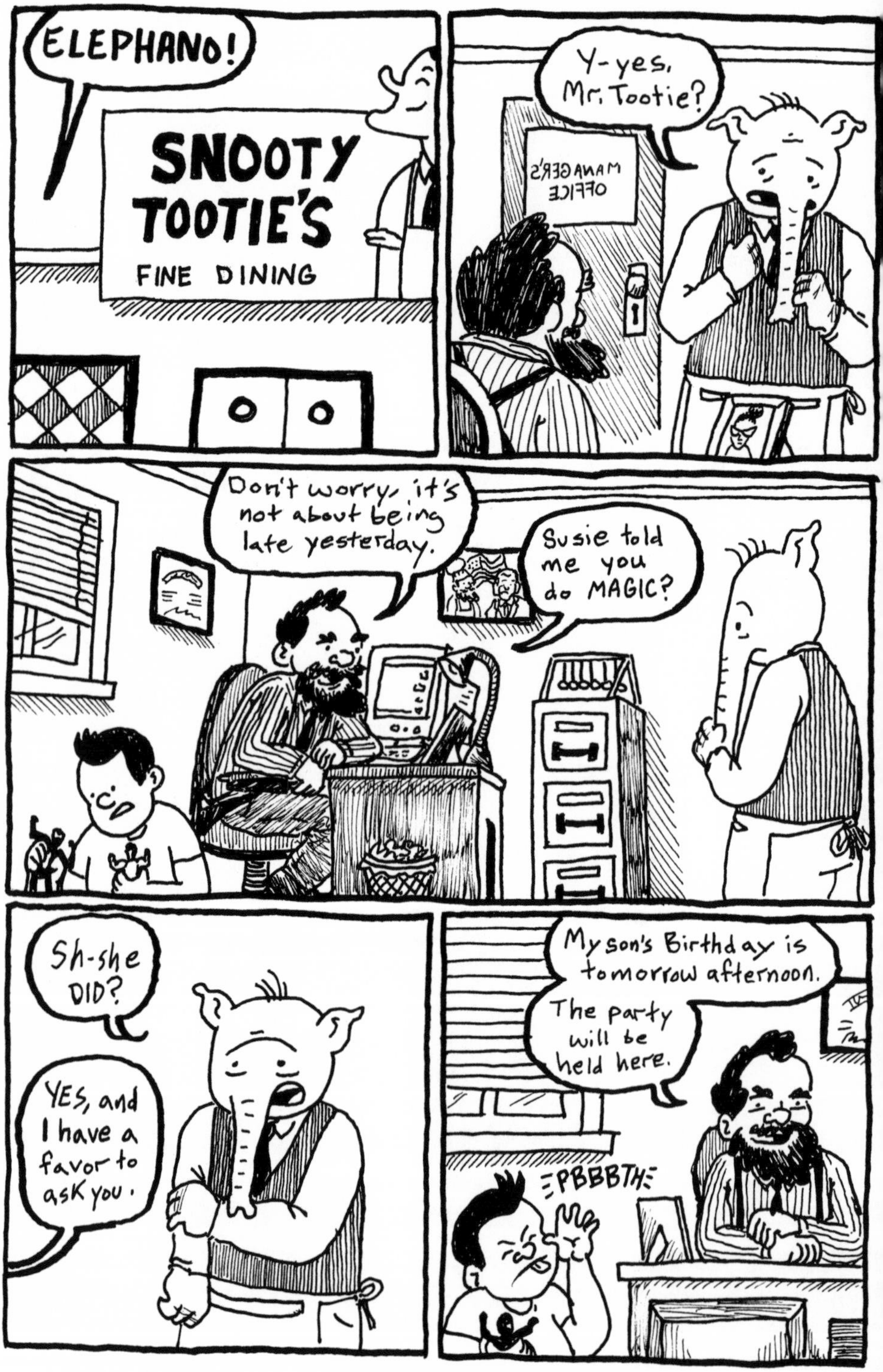
ELEPHANO!
SNOOTY TOOTIE'S
FINE DINING
Y-yes, Mr. Tootie?
MANAGER'S OFFICE
Don't worry, it's not about being late yesterday.
Susie told me you do MAGIC?
Sh-she DID?
YES, and I have a favor to ask you.
My son's Birthday is tomorrow afternoon.
The party will be held here.
PBBBTH

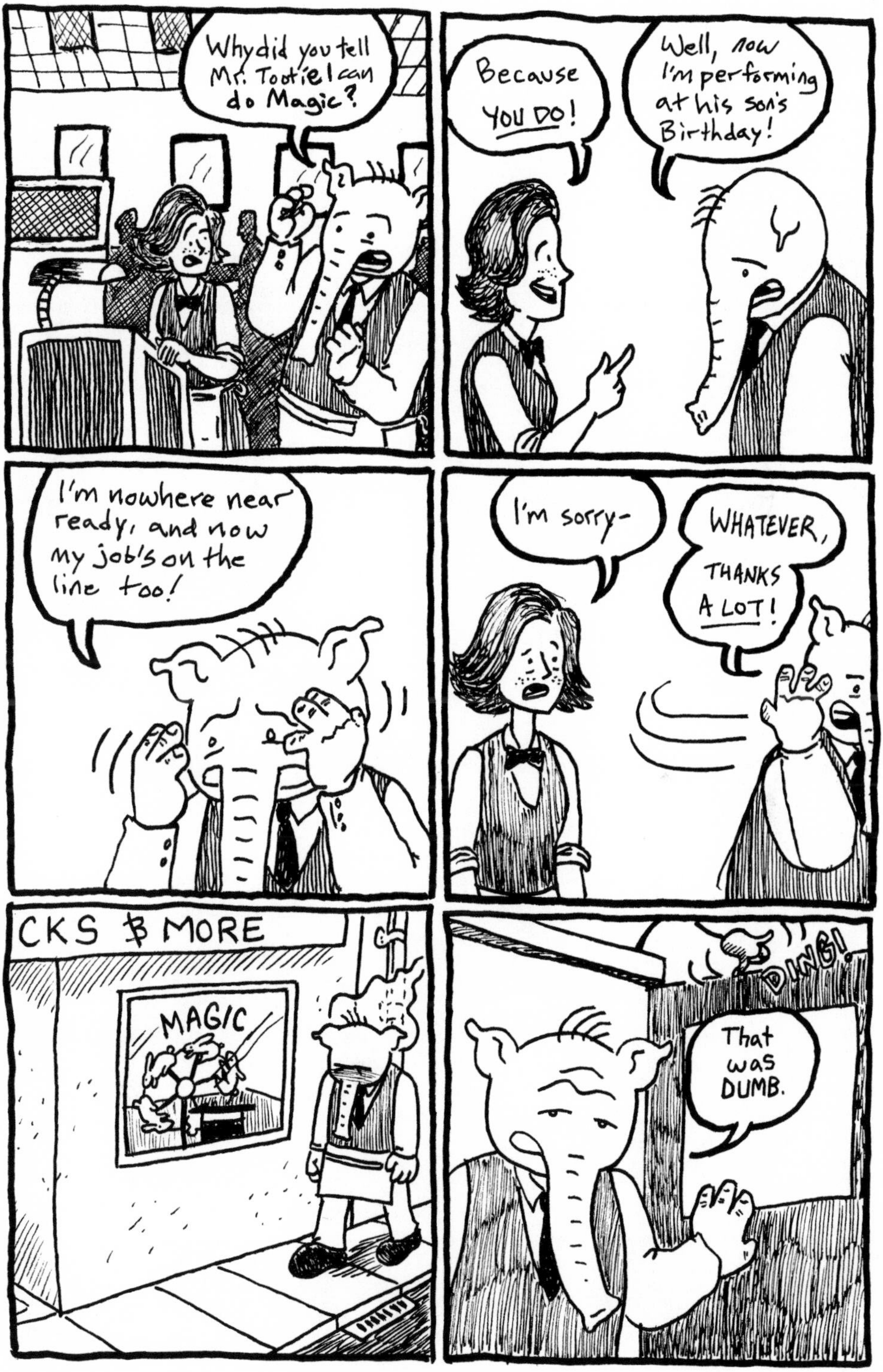
Why did you tell Mr. Tootie I can do Magic?
Because YOU DO!
Well, now I'm performing at his son's Birthday!
I'm nowhere near ready, and now my job's on the line too!
I'm sorry-
WHATEVER, THANKS A LOT!
CKS $ MORE
MAGIC
DING!
That was DUMB.

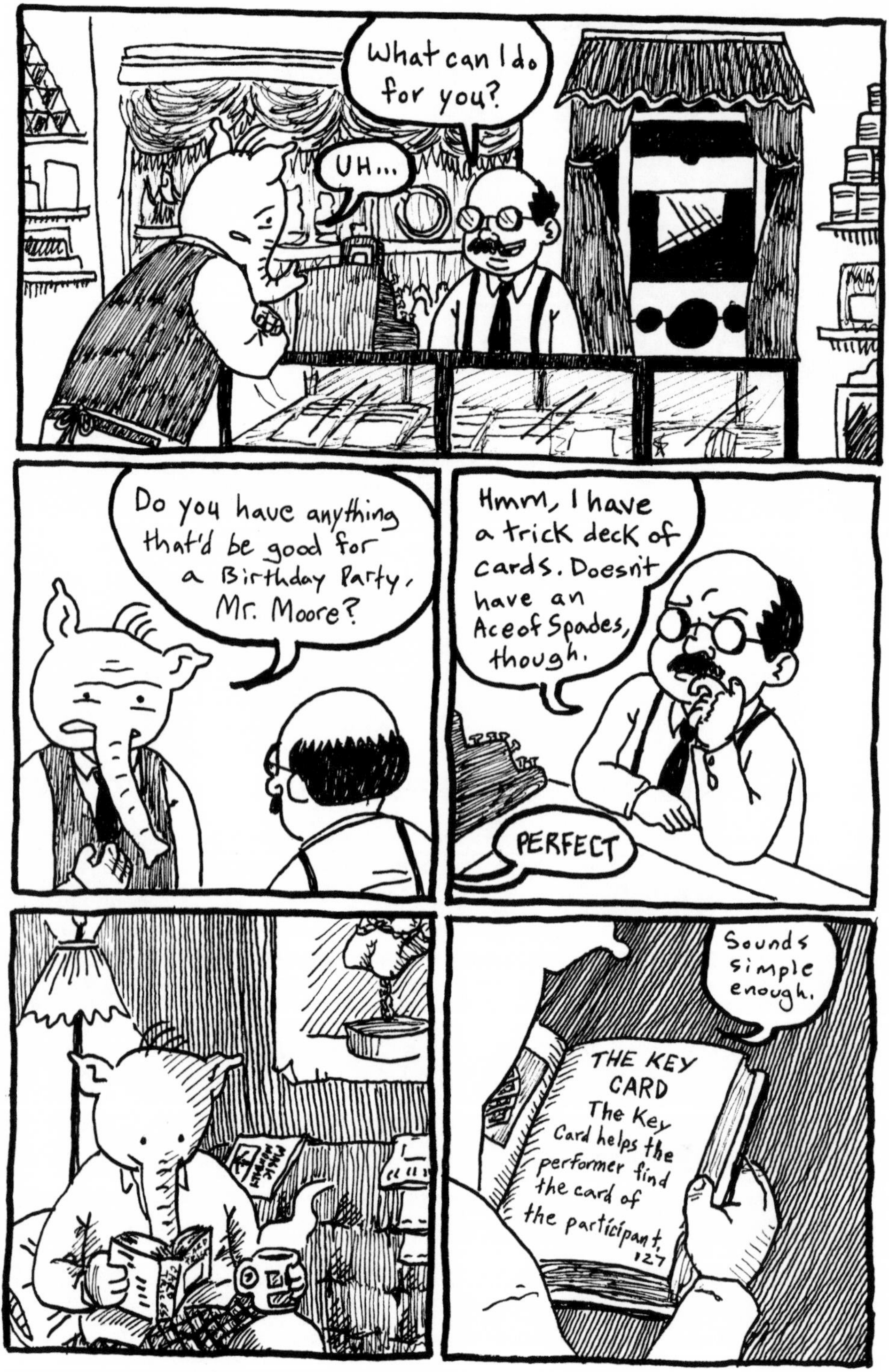
What can I do for you?
UH...
Do you have anything that'd be good for a Birthday Party, Mr. Moore?
Hmm, I have a trick deck of cards. Doesn't have an Ace of Spades, though.
PERFECT
Sounds simple enough.
THE KEY CARD
The Key Card helps the performer find the card of the participant.
127

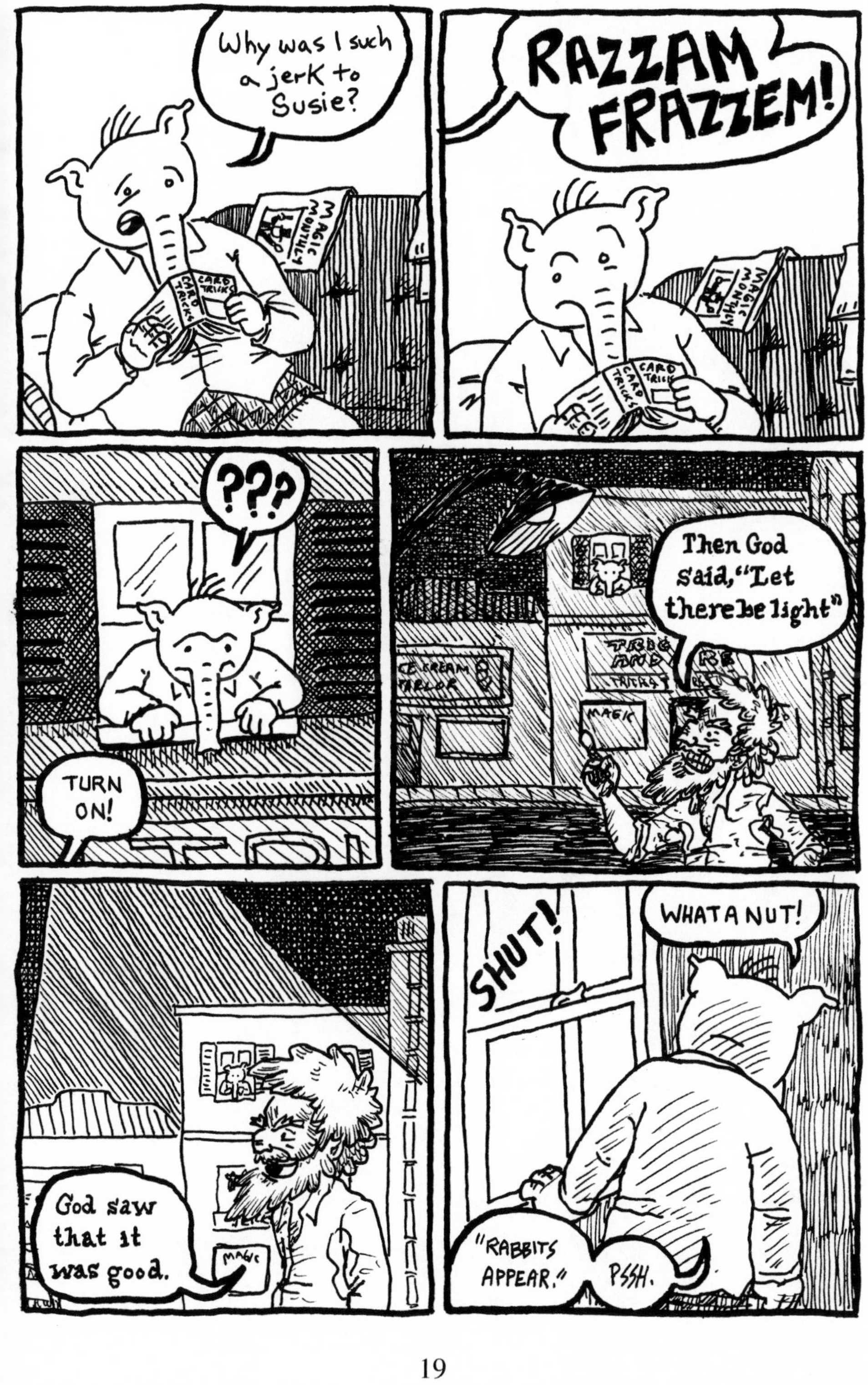
Why was I such a jerk to Susie?
MAGIC MONTHLY
CARD TRICKS
RAZZAM FRAZZEM!
MAGIC MONTHLY
CARD TRICKS
???
TURN ON!
Then God said, "Let there be light"
MAGIC
God saw that it was good.
MAGIC
SHUT!
WHAT A NUT!
"RABBITS APPEAR."
PSSH.

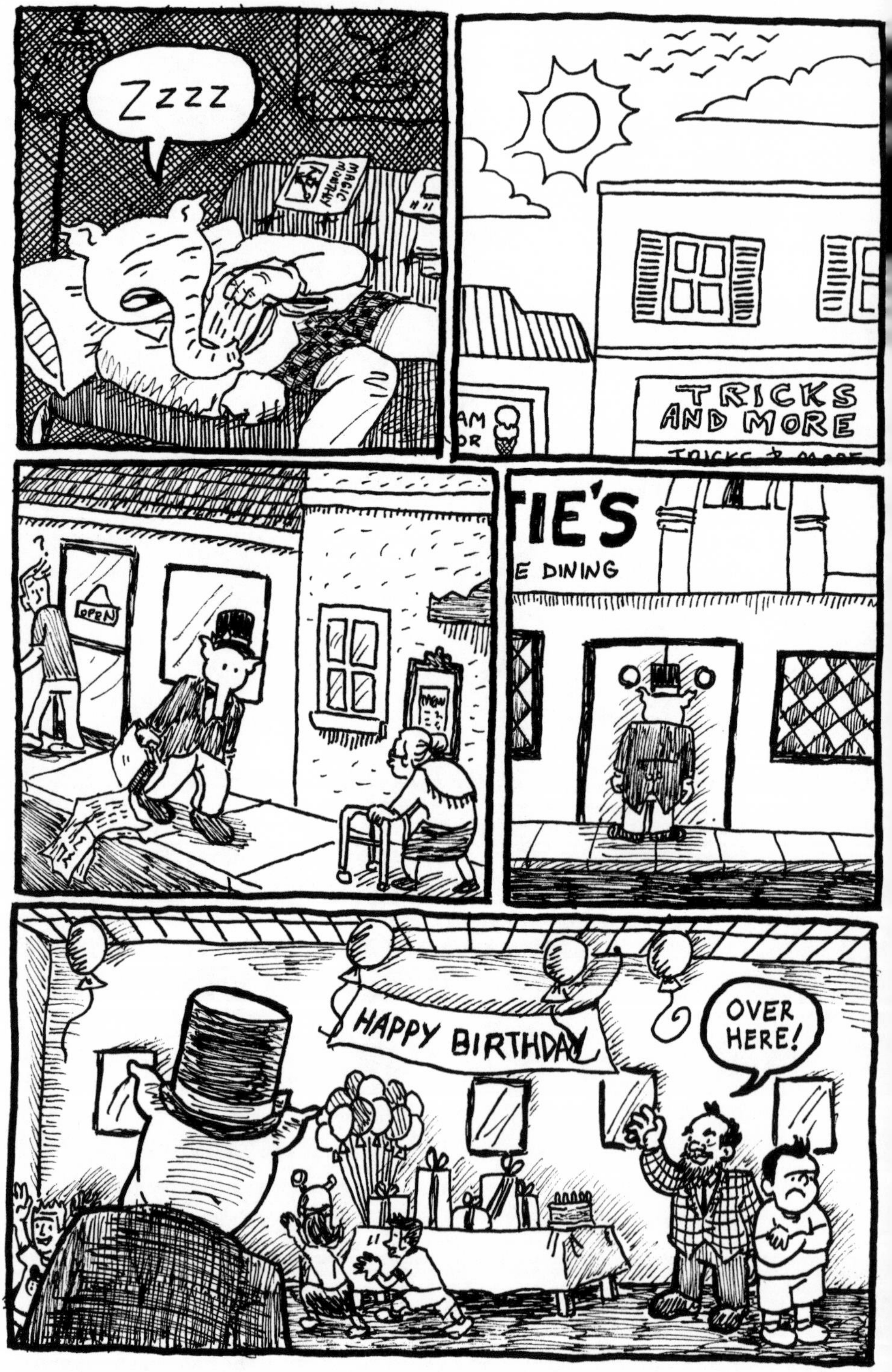
Zzzz
MAGIC MONTHLY
TRICKS AND MORE
OPEN
HAPPY BIRTHDAY
OVER HERE!

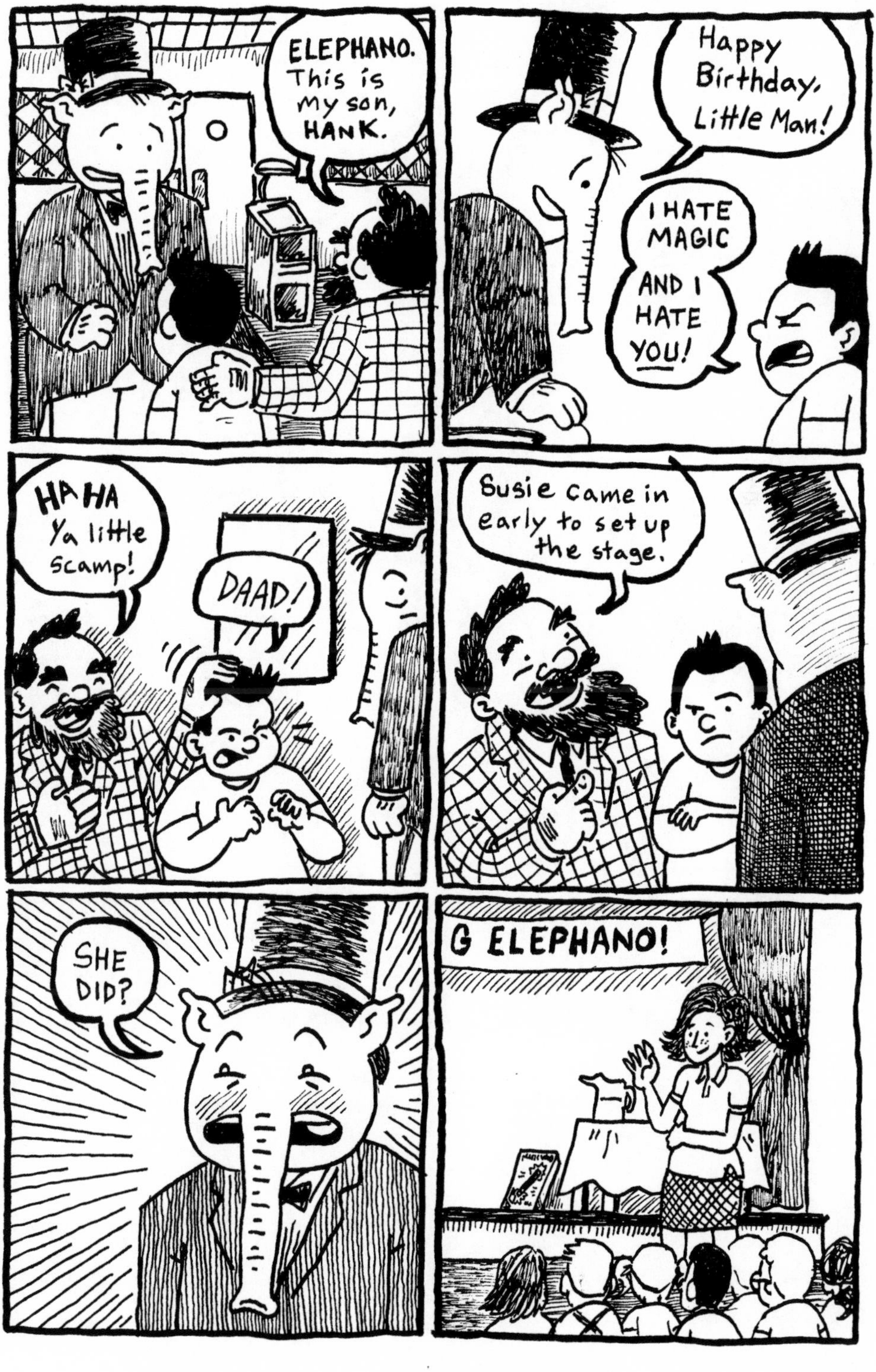
ELEPHANO. This is my son, HANK.
Happy Birthday, Little Man!
I HATE MAGIC
AND I HATE YOU!
HA HA Ya little scamp!
DAAD!
Susie came in early to set up the stage.
SHE DID?
G ELEPHANO!

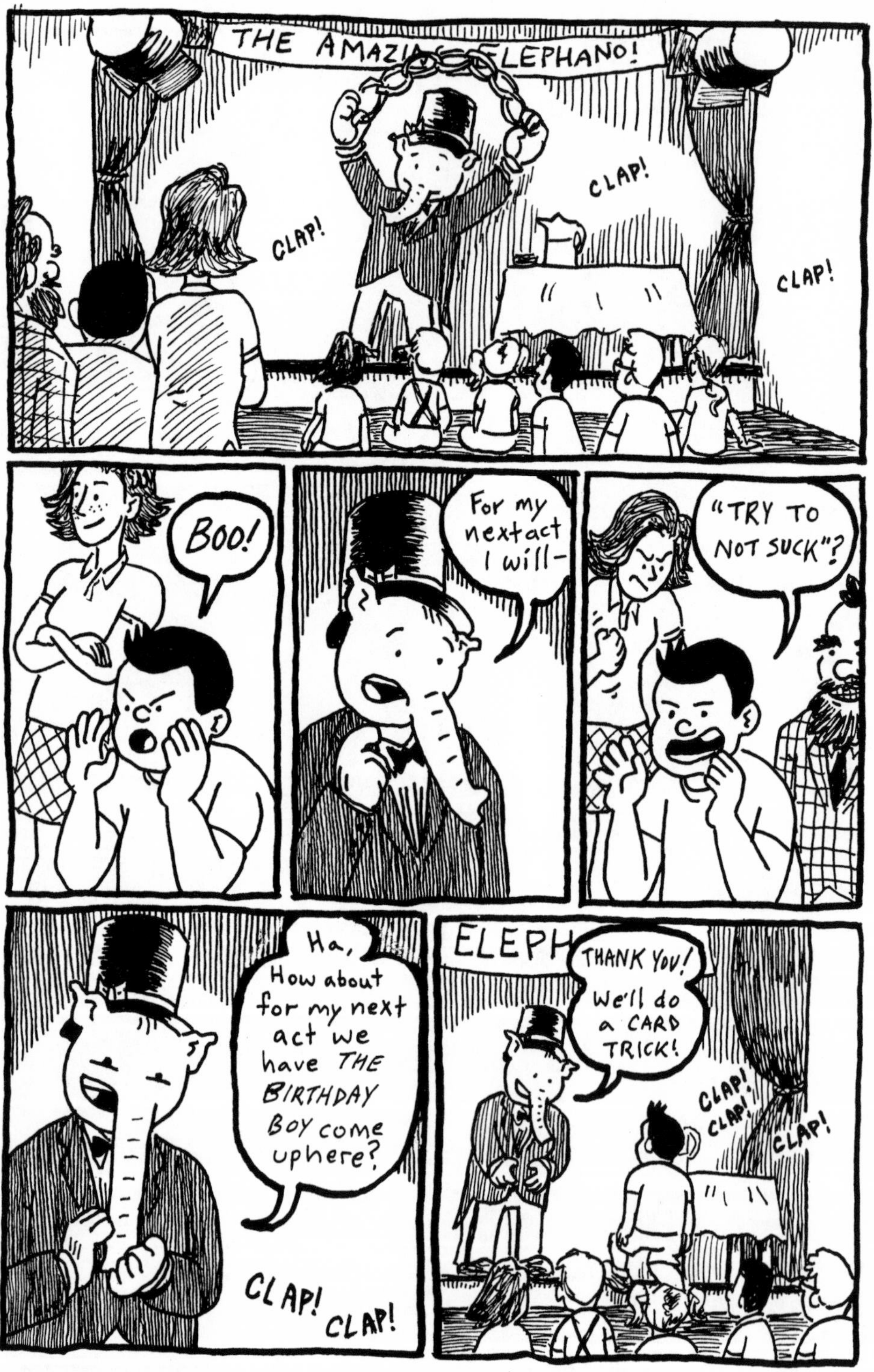
THE AMAZING ELEPHANO!
CLAP!
CLAP!
CLAP!
Boo!
For my nextact I will-
"TRY TO NOT SUCK"?
Ha, How about for my next act we have THE BIRTHDAY BOY come uphere?
CLAP! CLAP!
ELEPH
THANK YOU! We'll do a CARD TRICK!
CLAP! CLAP!
CLAP!

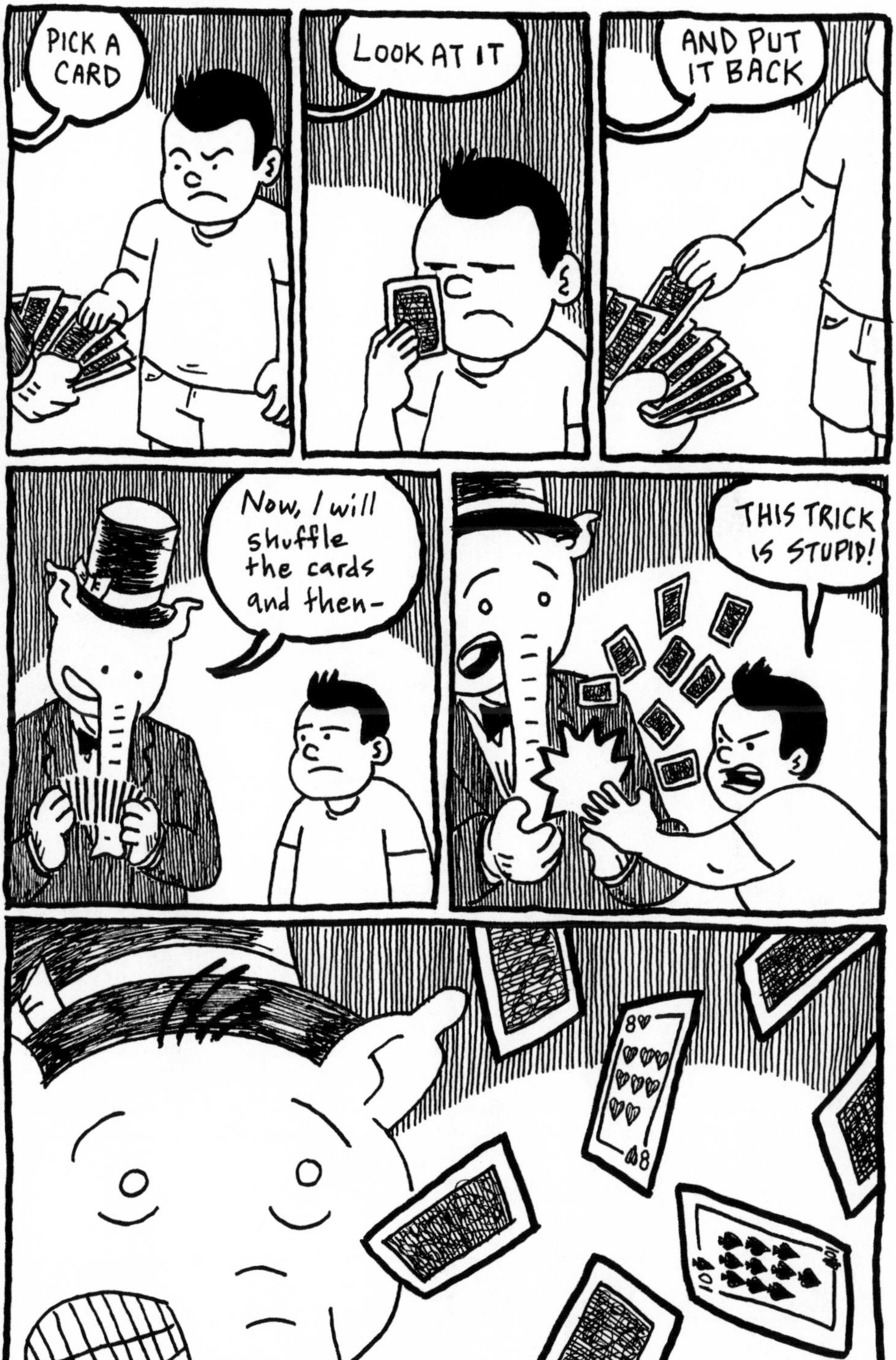
PICK A CARD
LOOK AT IT
AND PUT IT BACK
Now, I will shuffle the cards and then-
THIS TRICK IS STUPID!

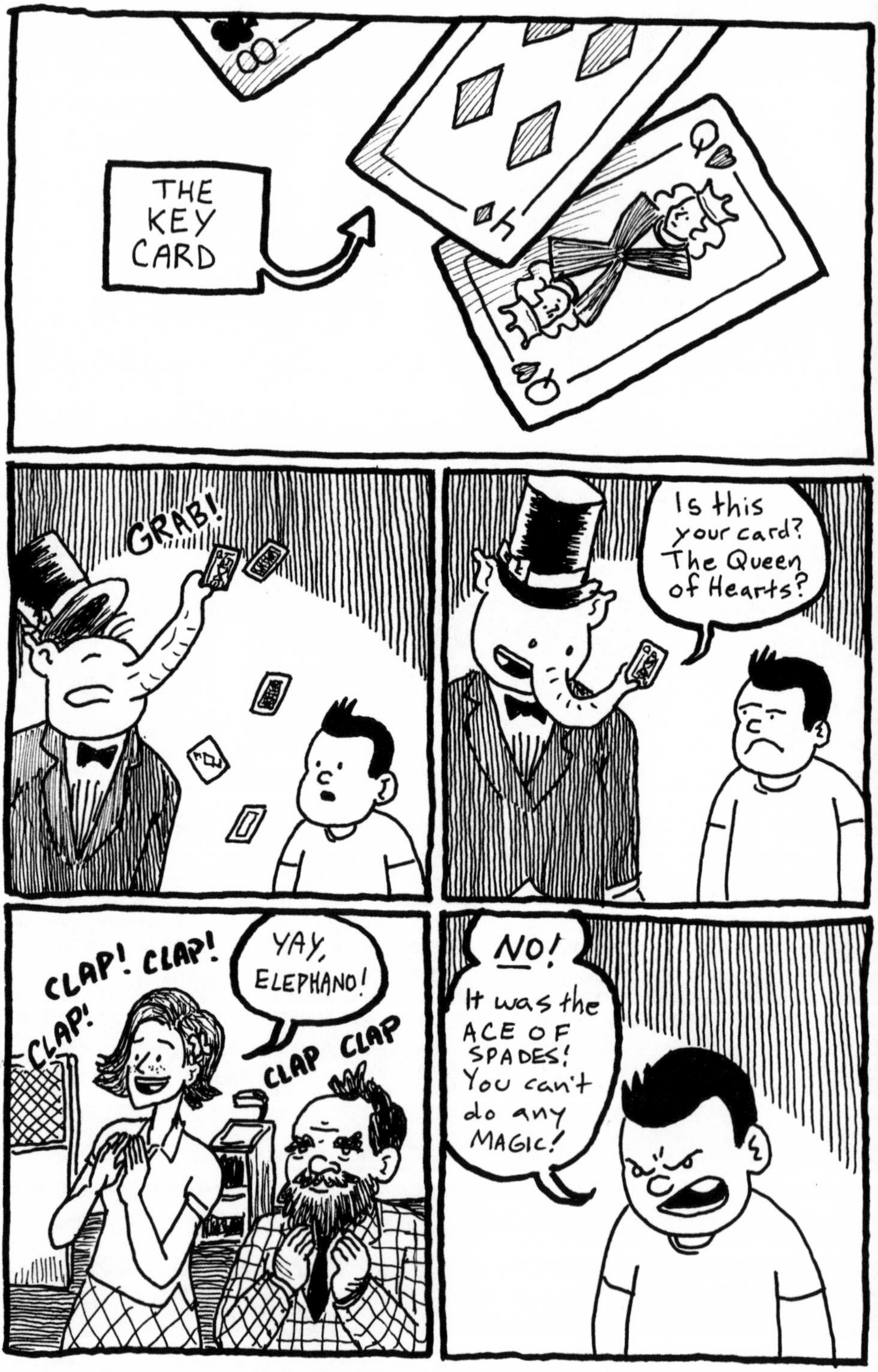
THE KEY CARD
GRAB!
Is this your card? The Queen of Hearts?
CLAP! CLAP! CLAP!
YAY, ELEPHANO!
CLAP CLAP
NO! It was the ACE OF SPADES! You can't do any MAGIC!

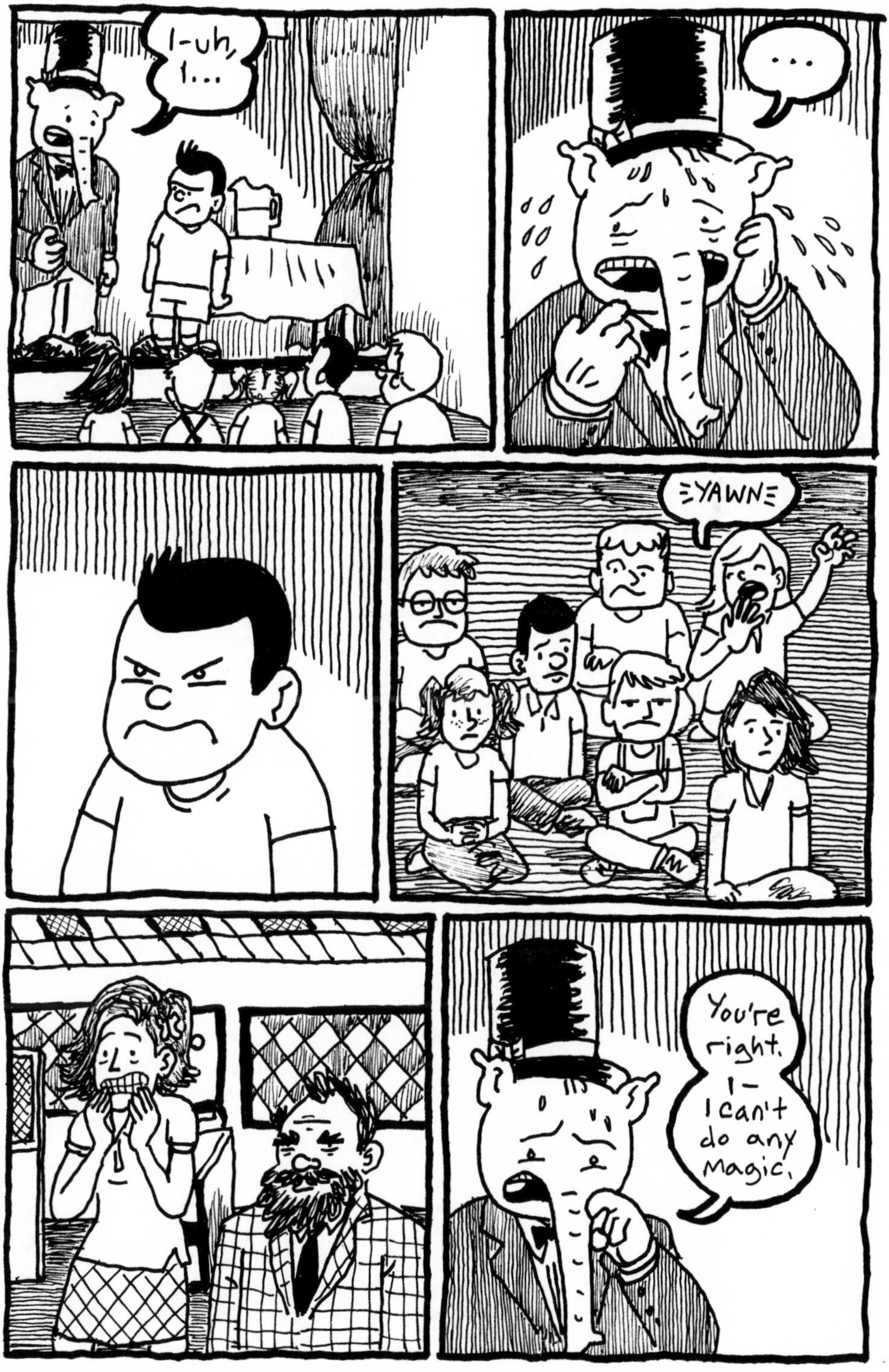
I-uh, I...
...
YAWN
You're right. I— I can't do any Magic.

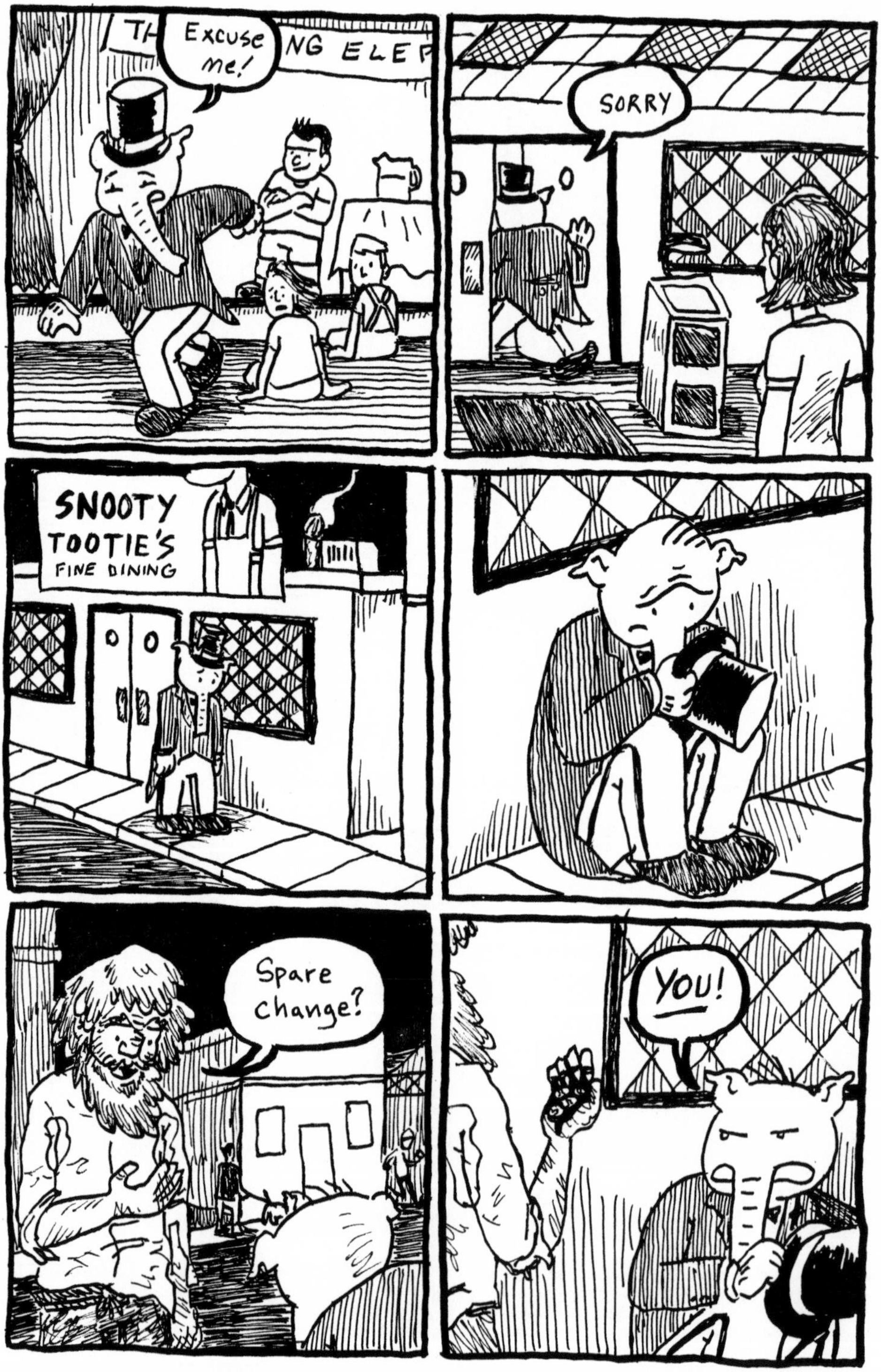
TH
NG ELEP
Excuse me!
SORRY
SNOOTY TOOTIE'S FINE DINING
Spare change?
YOU!

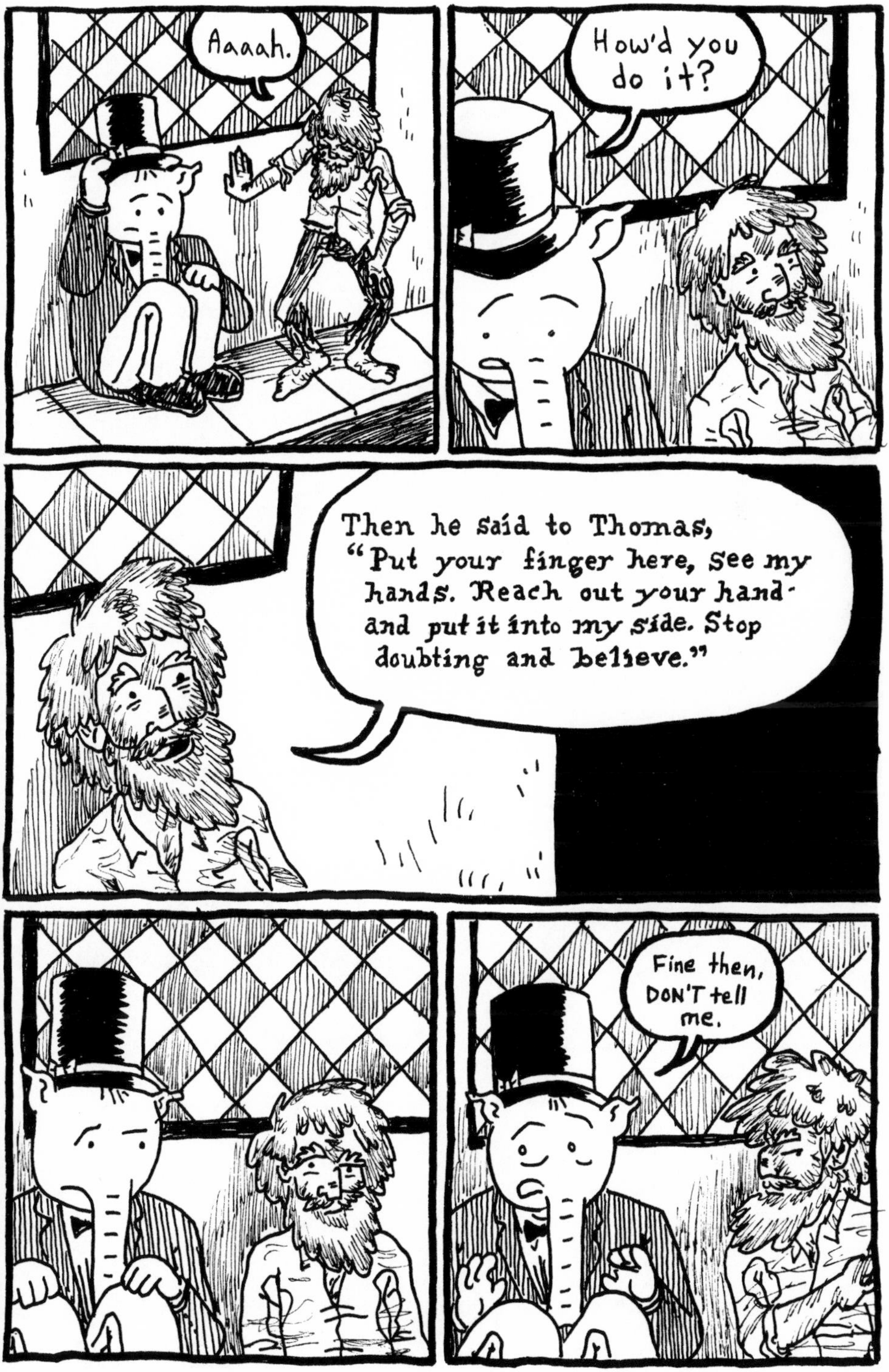
Aaaah.
How'd you do it?
Then he said to Thomas, "Put your finger here, see my hands. Reach out your hand and put it into my side. Stop doubting and believe."
Fine then, DON'T tell me.

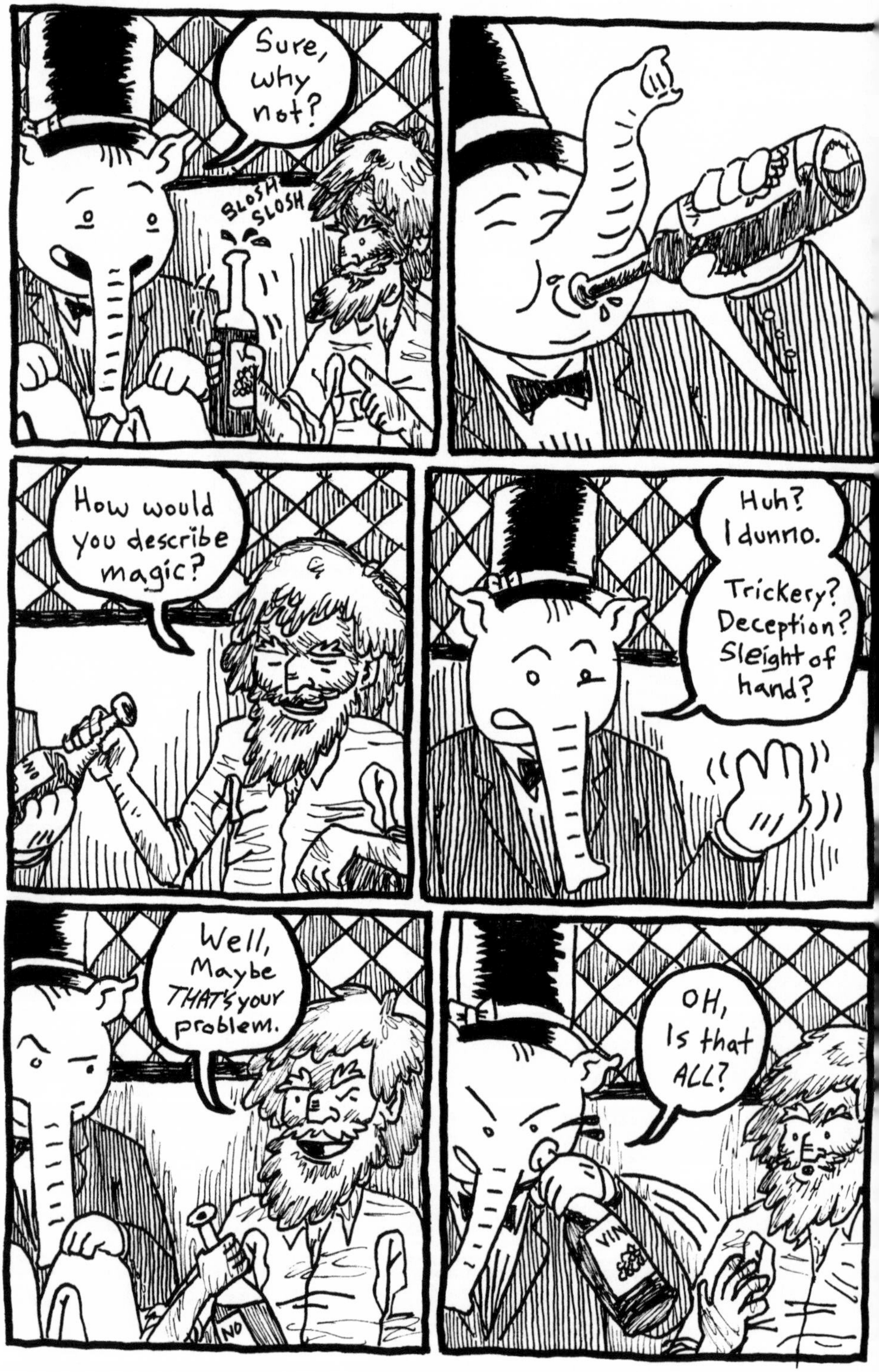
Sure, why not?
SLOSH SLOSH
How would you describe magic?
Huh? I dunno.
Trickery? Deception? Sleight of hand?
Well, Maybe THAT'S your problem.
NO
OH, Is that ALL?
VIN

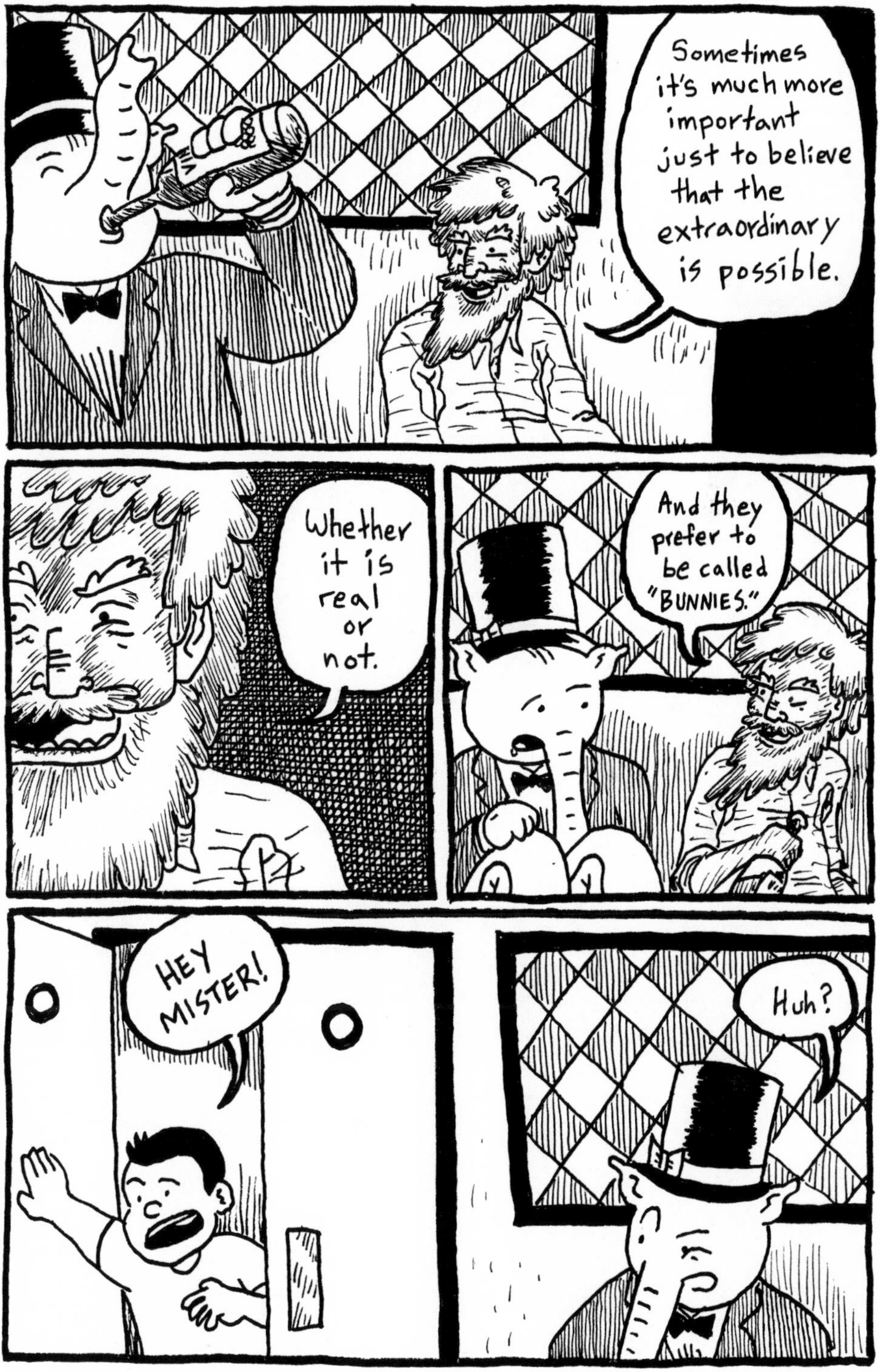
Sometimes it's much more important just to believe that the extraordinary is possible.
Whether it is real or not.
And they prefer to be called "BUNNIES."
HEY MISTER!
Huh?

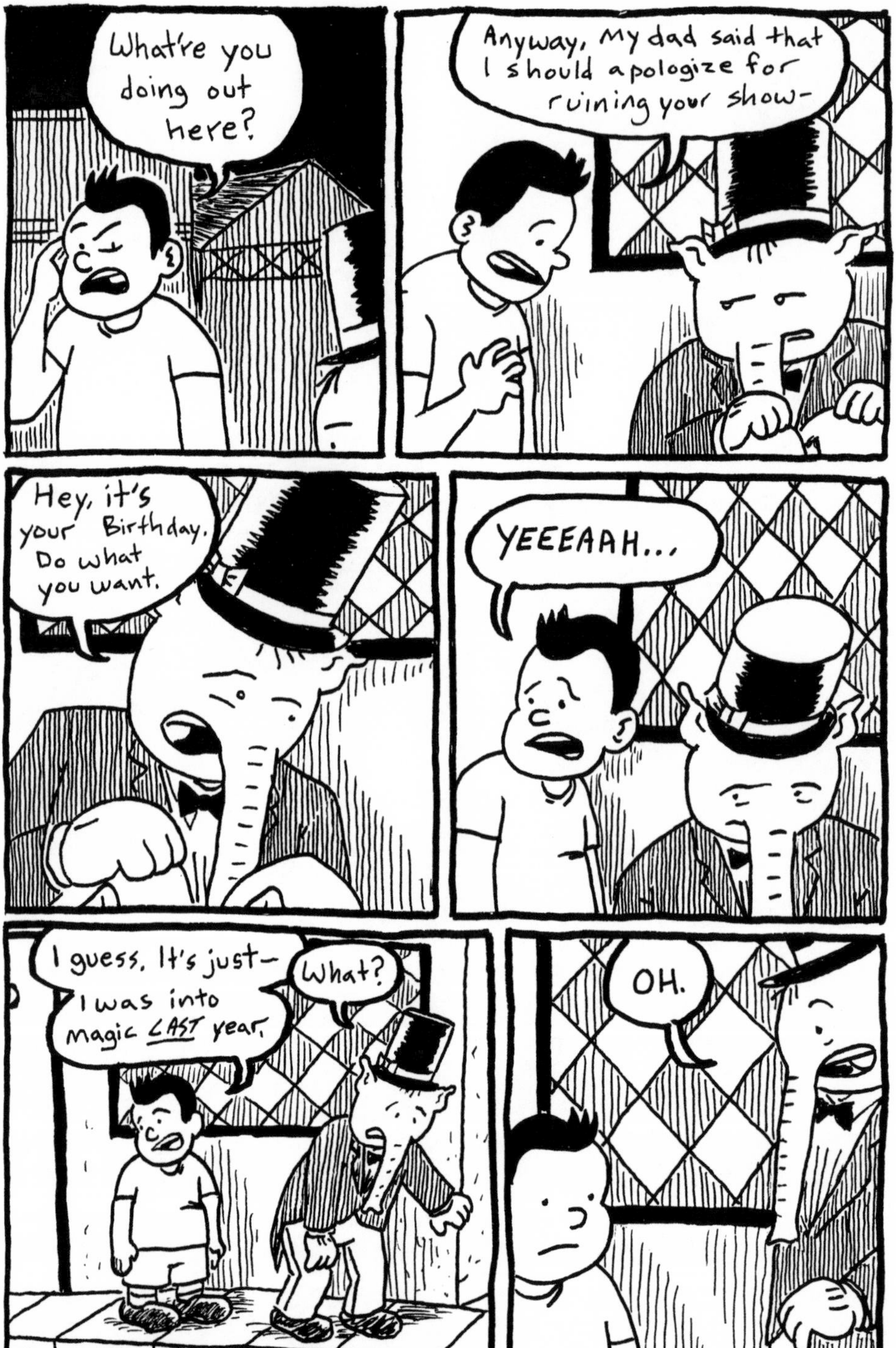
What're you doing out here?
Anyway, My dad said that I should apologize for ruining your show-
Hey, it's your Birthday. Do what you want.
YEEEAAH...
I guess. It's just- I was into magic LAST year.
What?
OH.

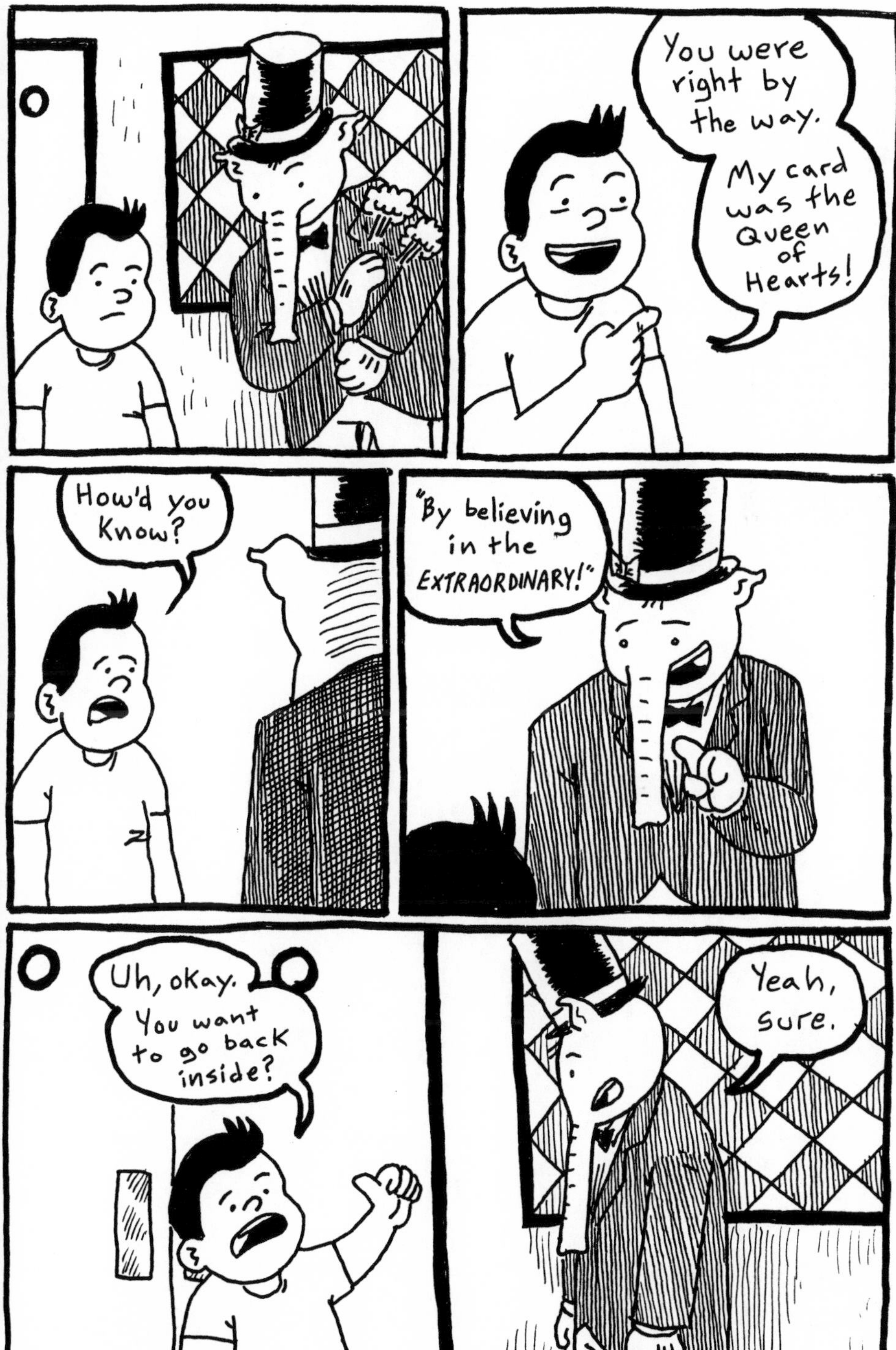
You were right by the way.
My card was the Queen of Hearts!
How'd you Know?
"By believing in the EXTRAORDINARY!"
Uh, okay.
You want to go back inside?
Yeah, sure.

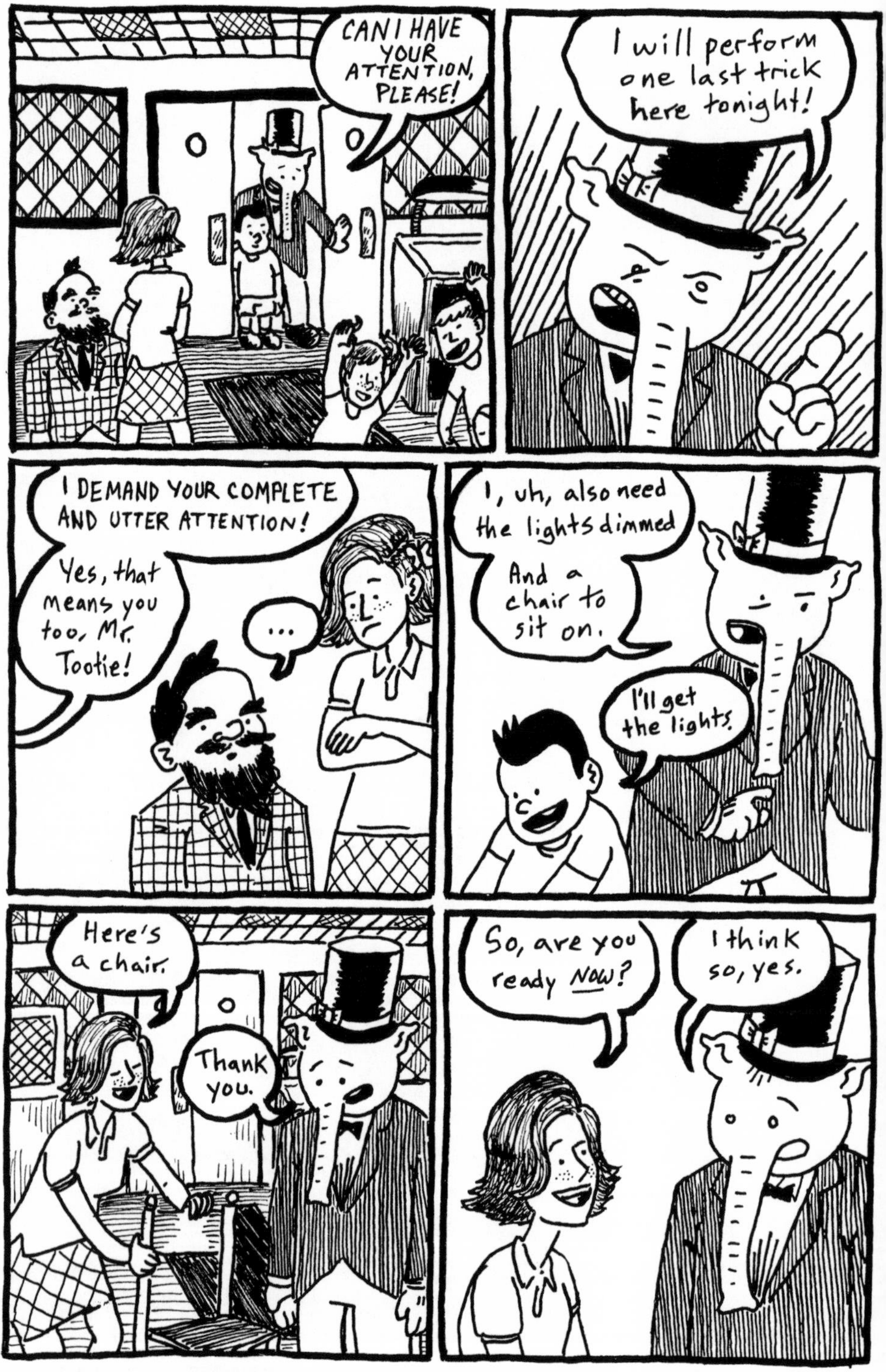
CAN I HAVE YOUR ATTENTION, PLEASE!
I will perform one last trick here tonight!
I DEMAND YOUR COMPLETE AND UTTER ATTENTION!
Yes, that means you too, Mr. Tootie!
...
I, uh, also need the lights dimmed
And a chair to sit on.
I'll get the lights.
Here's a chair.
Thank you.
So, are you ready NOW?
I think so, yes.

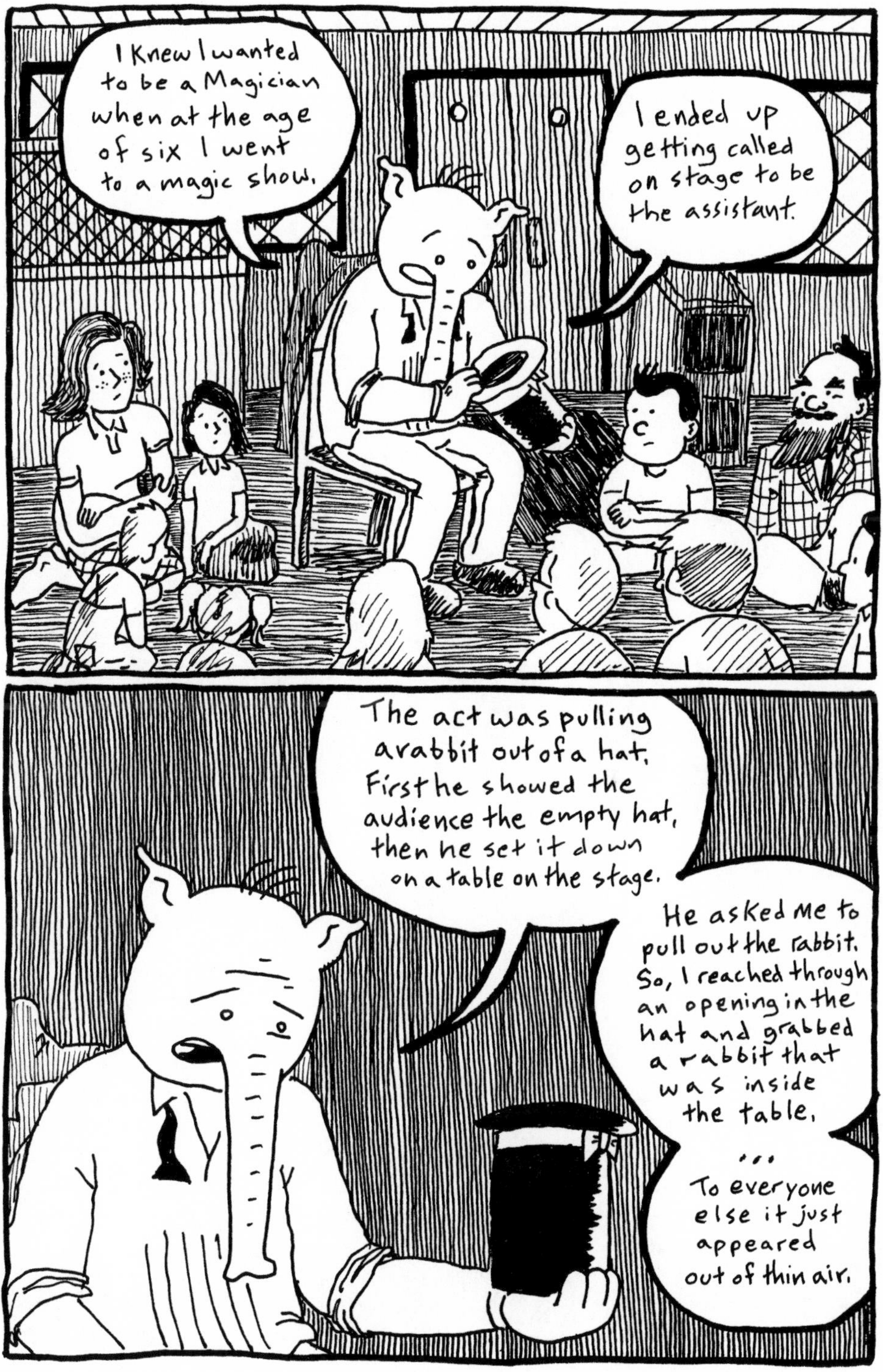
I Knew I wanted to be a Magician when at the age of six I went to a magic show.
I ended up getting called on stage to be the assistant.
The act was pulling a rabbit out of a hat. First he showed the audience the empty hat, then he set it down on a table on the stage.
He asked me to pull out the rabbit. So, I reached through an opening in the hat and grabbed a rabbit that was inside the table.
... To everyone else it just appeared out of thin air.

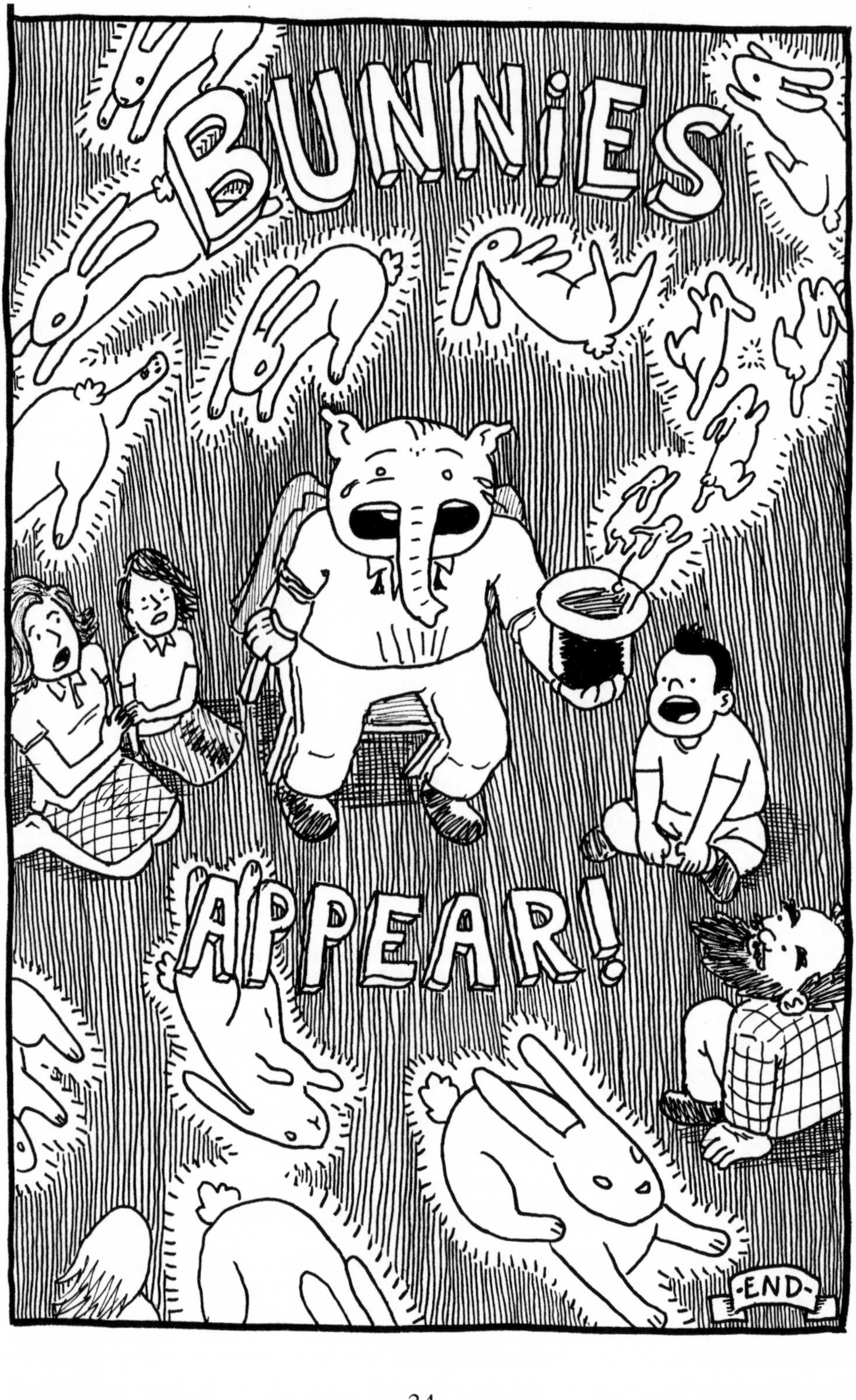
BUNNIES
APPEAR!
-END-

wednesdays...

by craig arndt

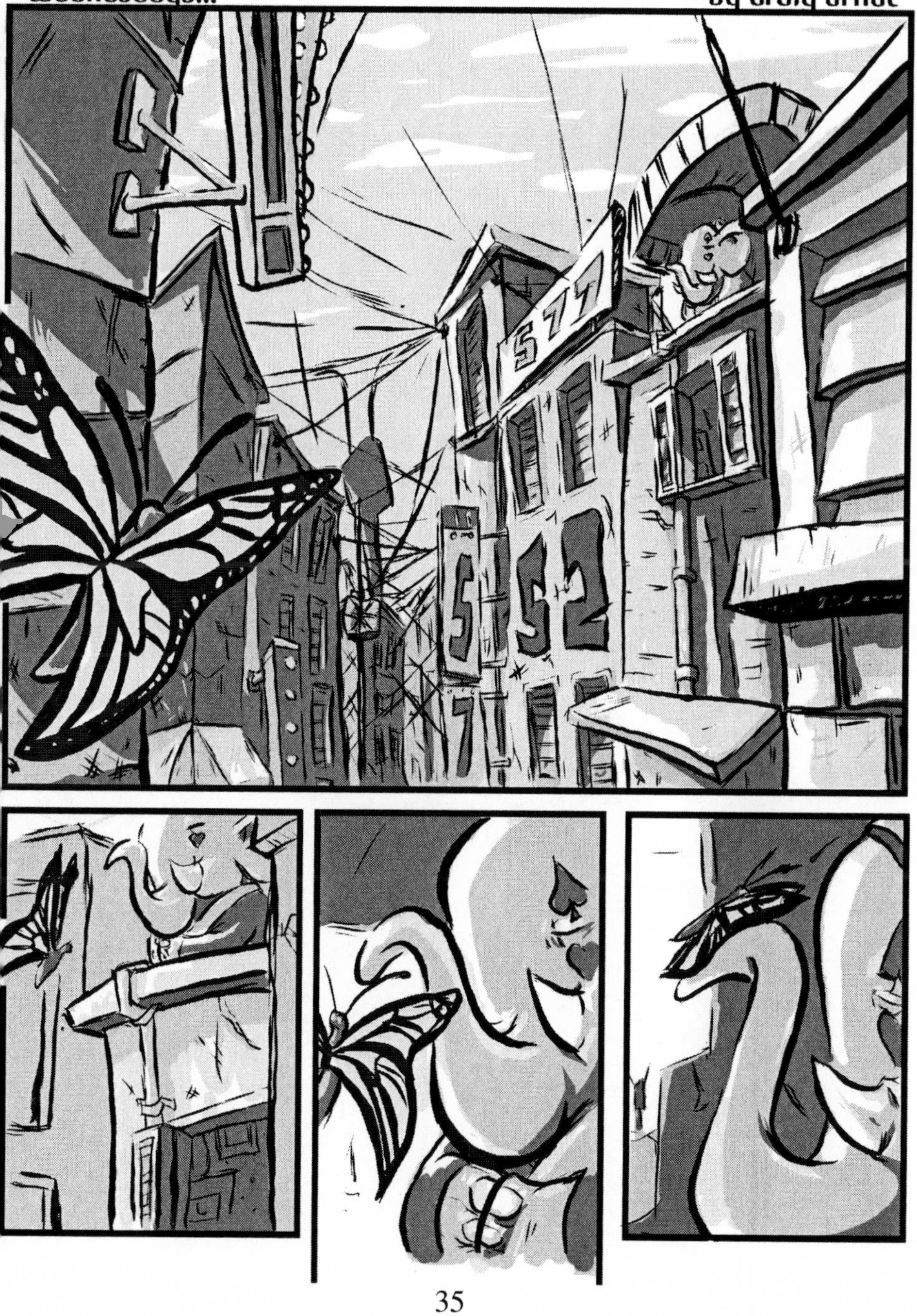

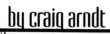

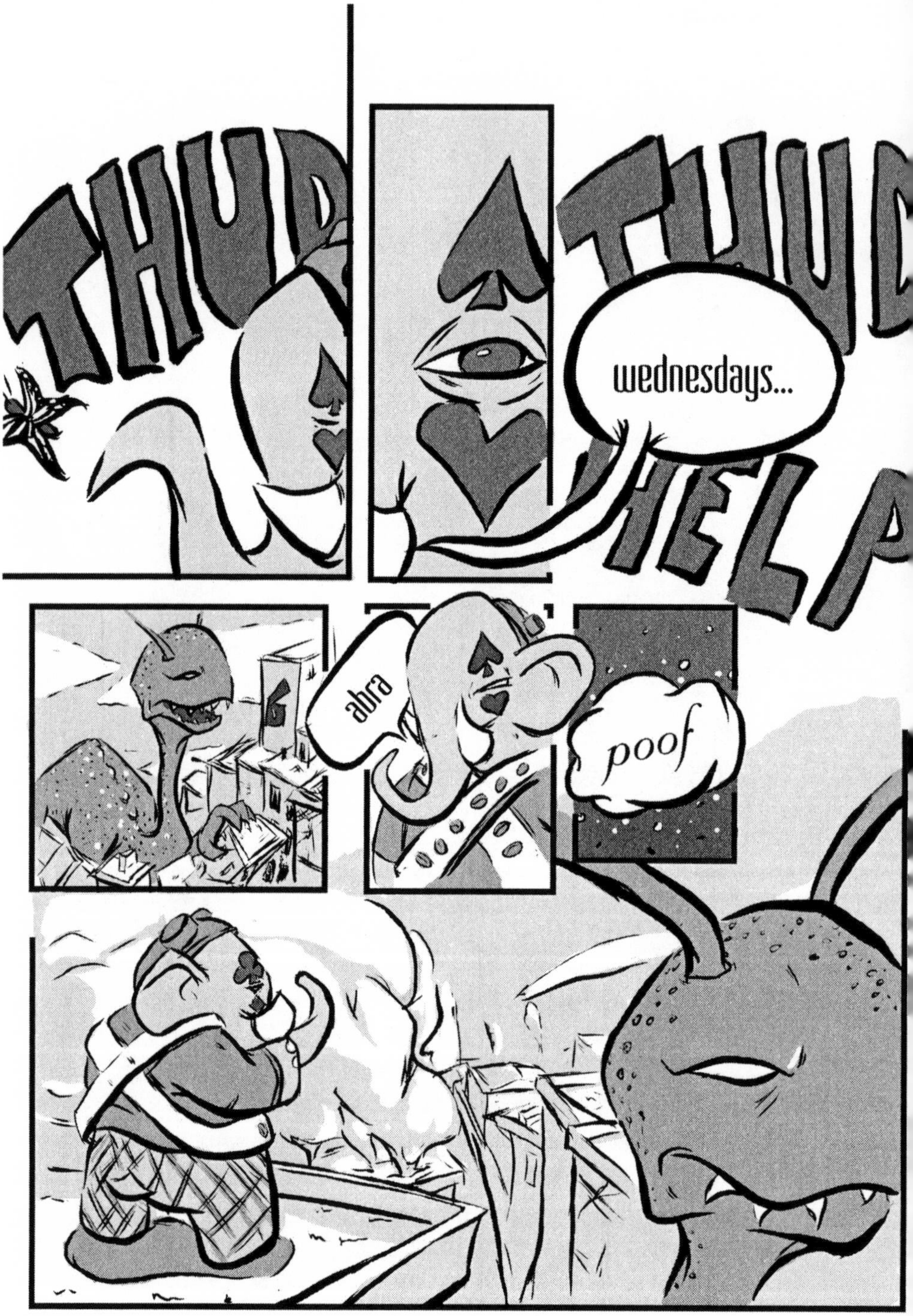
THUD
THUD
wednesdays...
HELP
abra
poof

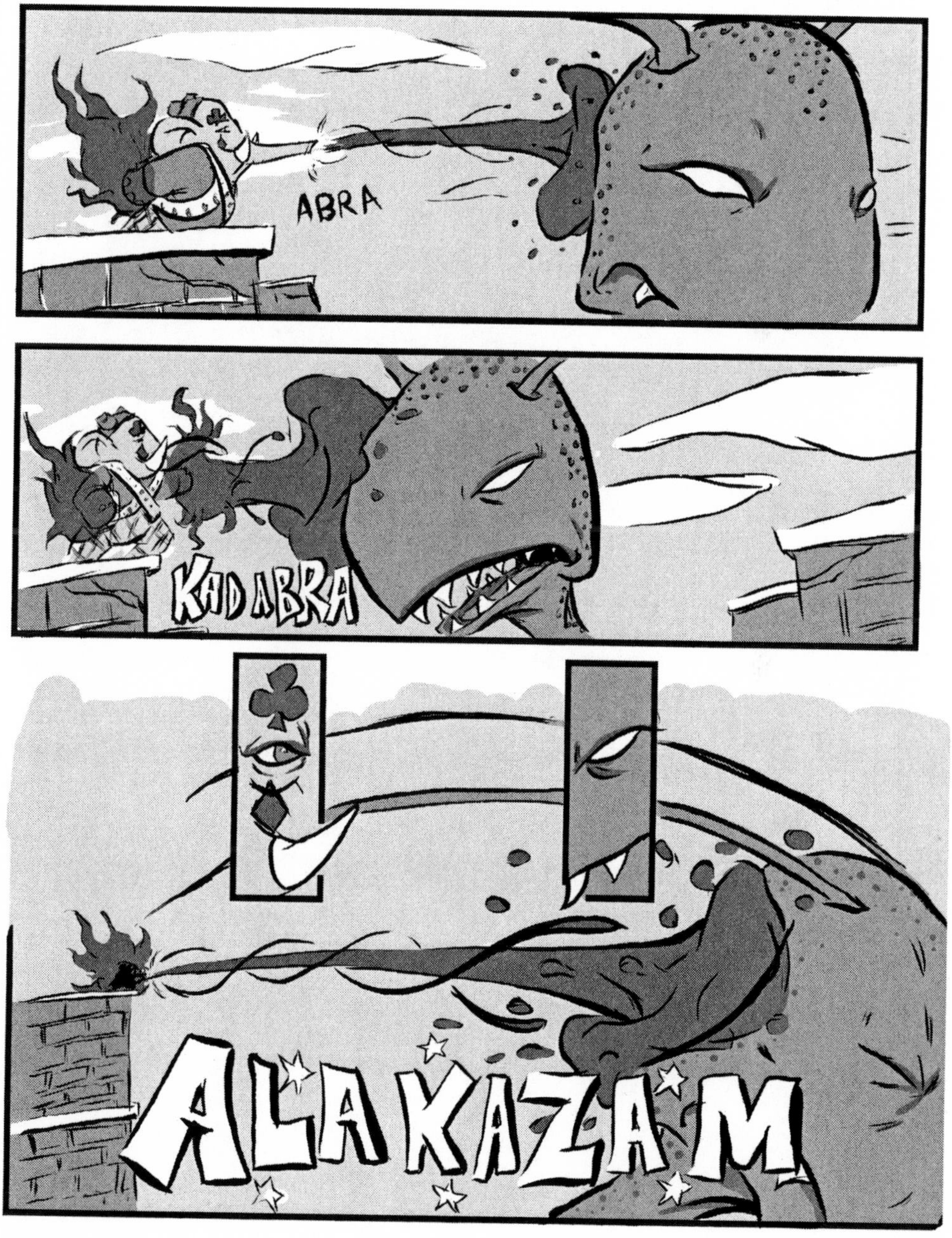
ABRA
KADABRA
ALAKAZAM

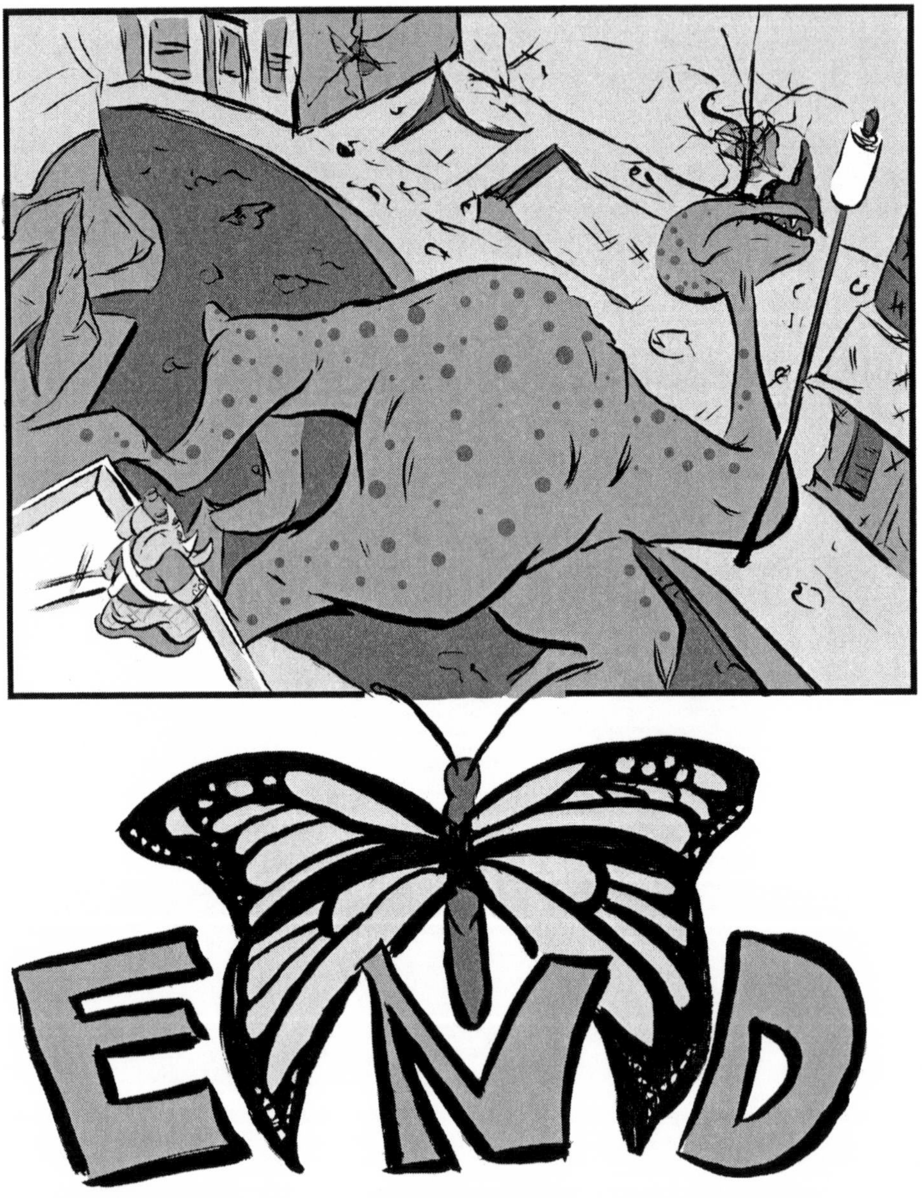
END

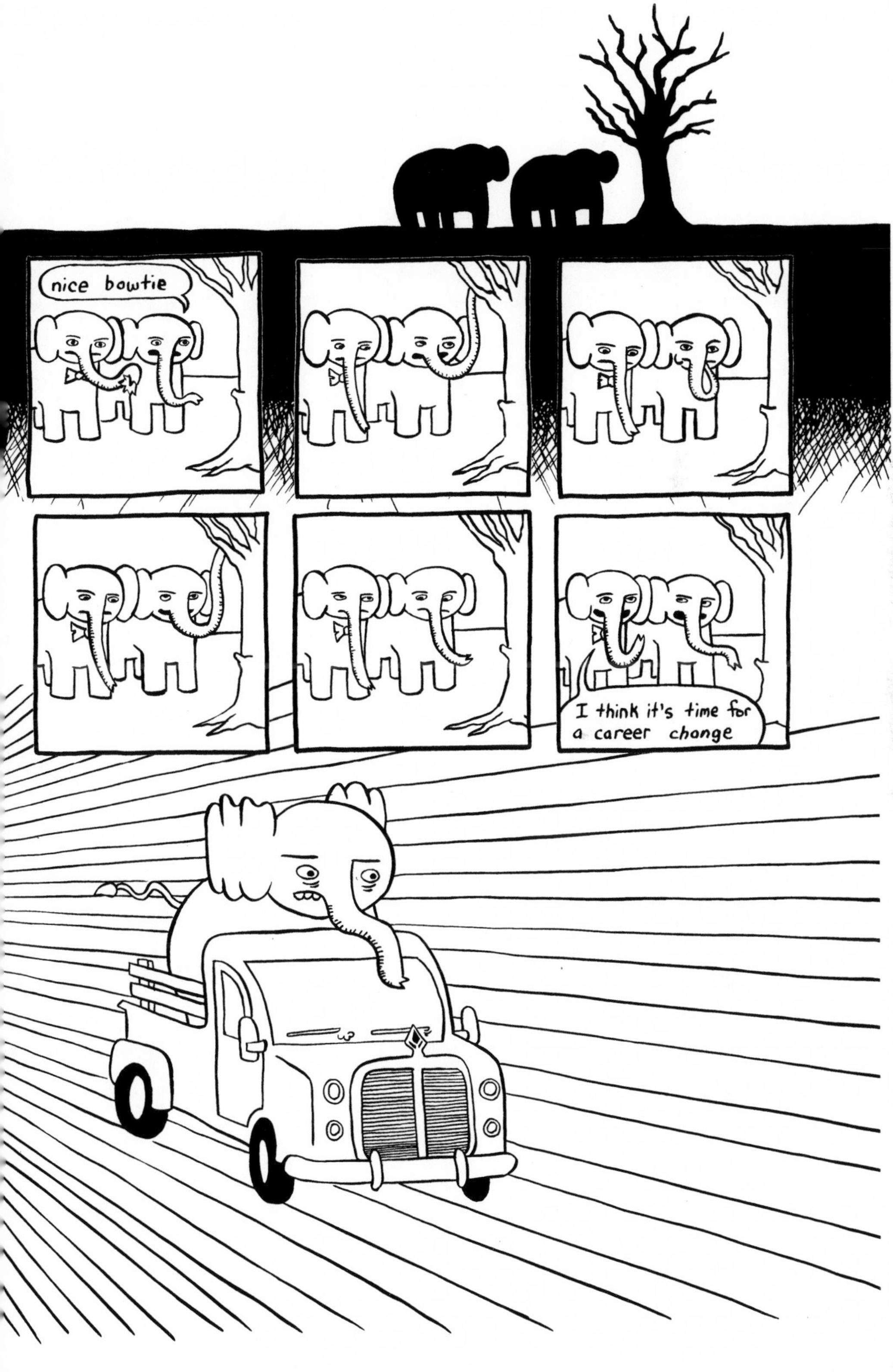
nice bowtie
I think it's time for a career change

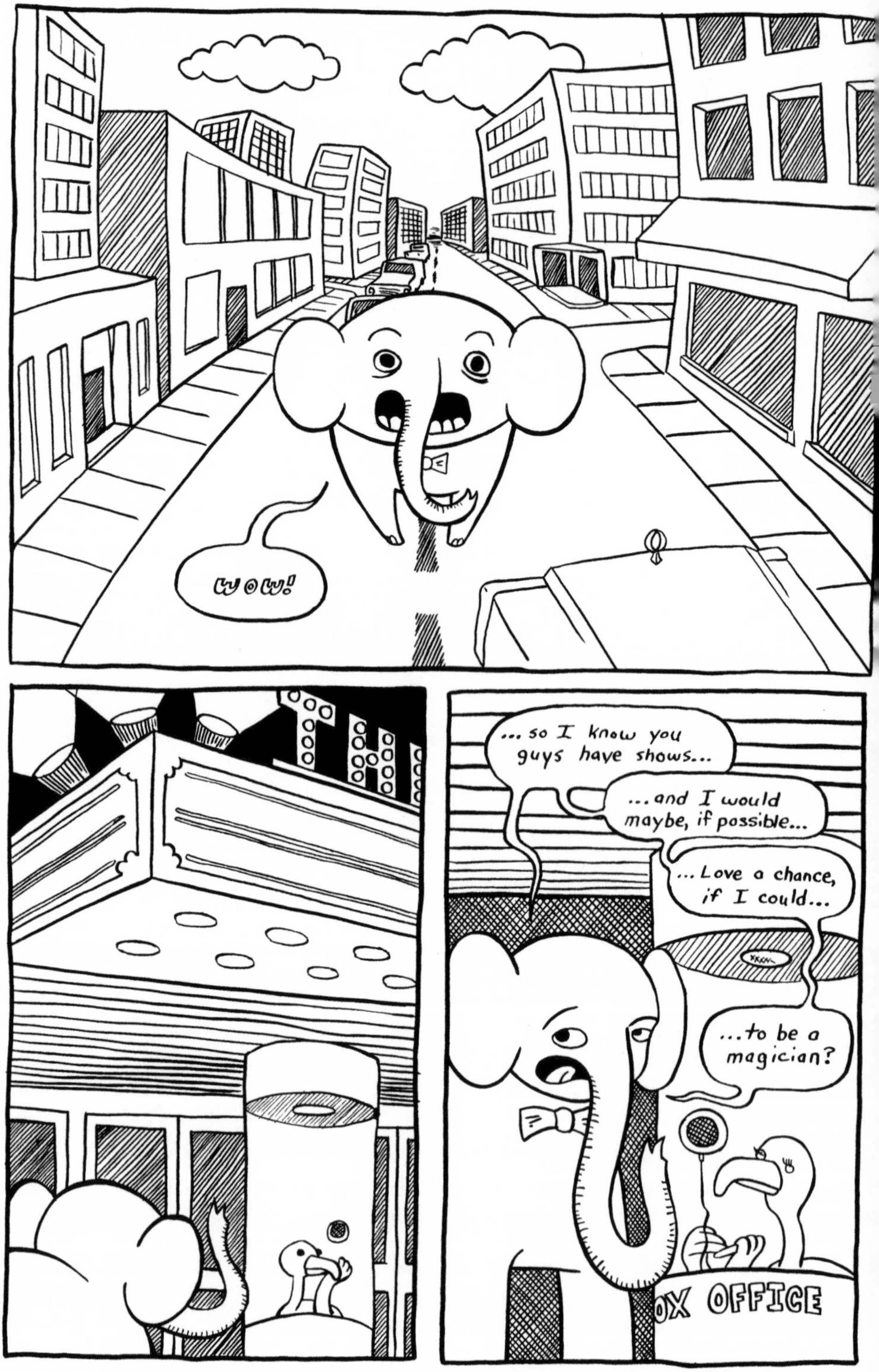
WOW!
THE
... so I know you guys have shows...
... and I would maybe, if possible...
... Love a chance, if I could...
... to be a magician?
OX OFFICE

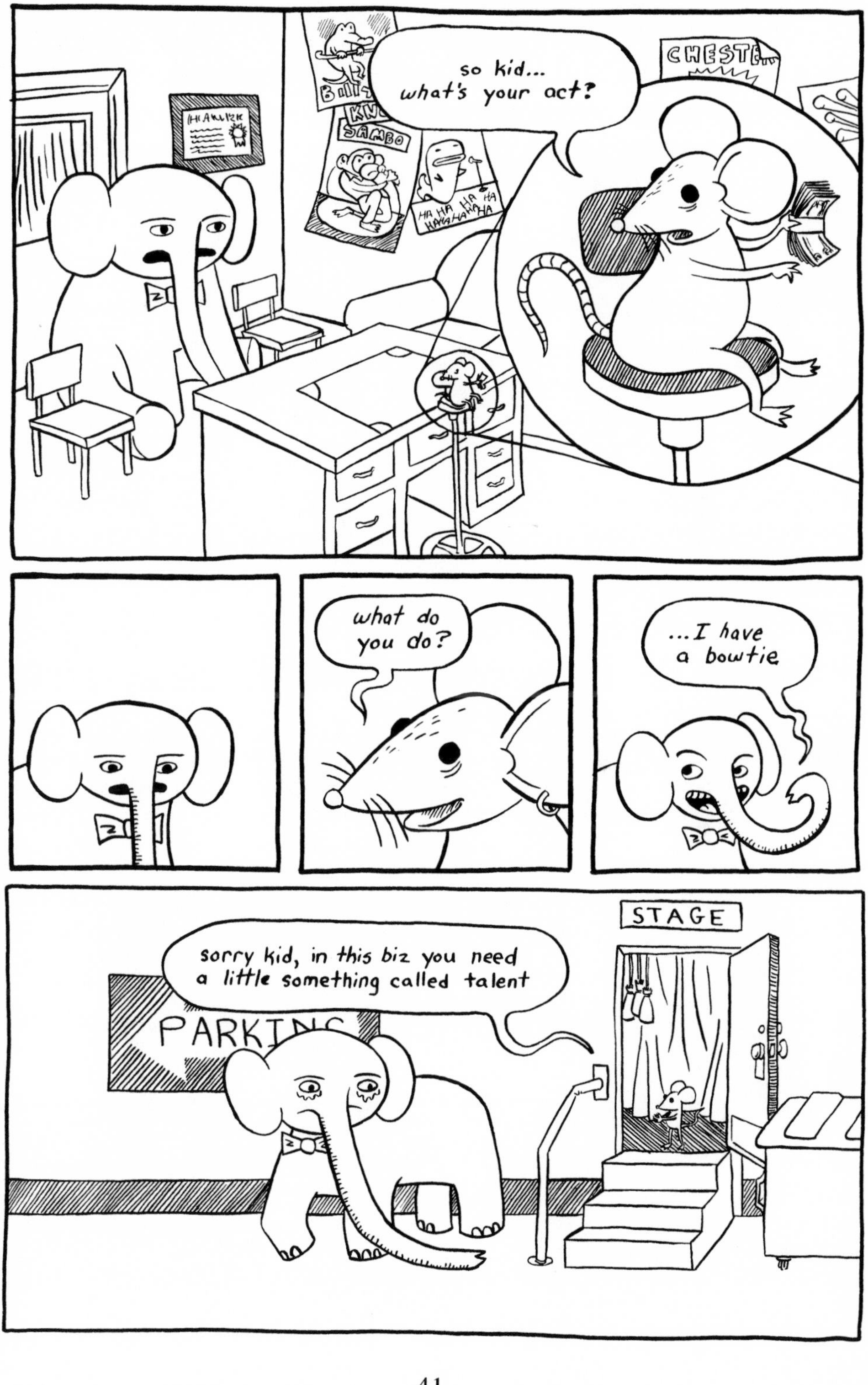
SAMBO
so kid...
what's your act?
what do
you do?
...I have
a bowtie
STAGE
sorry kid, in this biz you need
a little something called talent

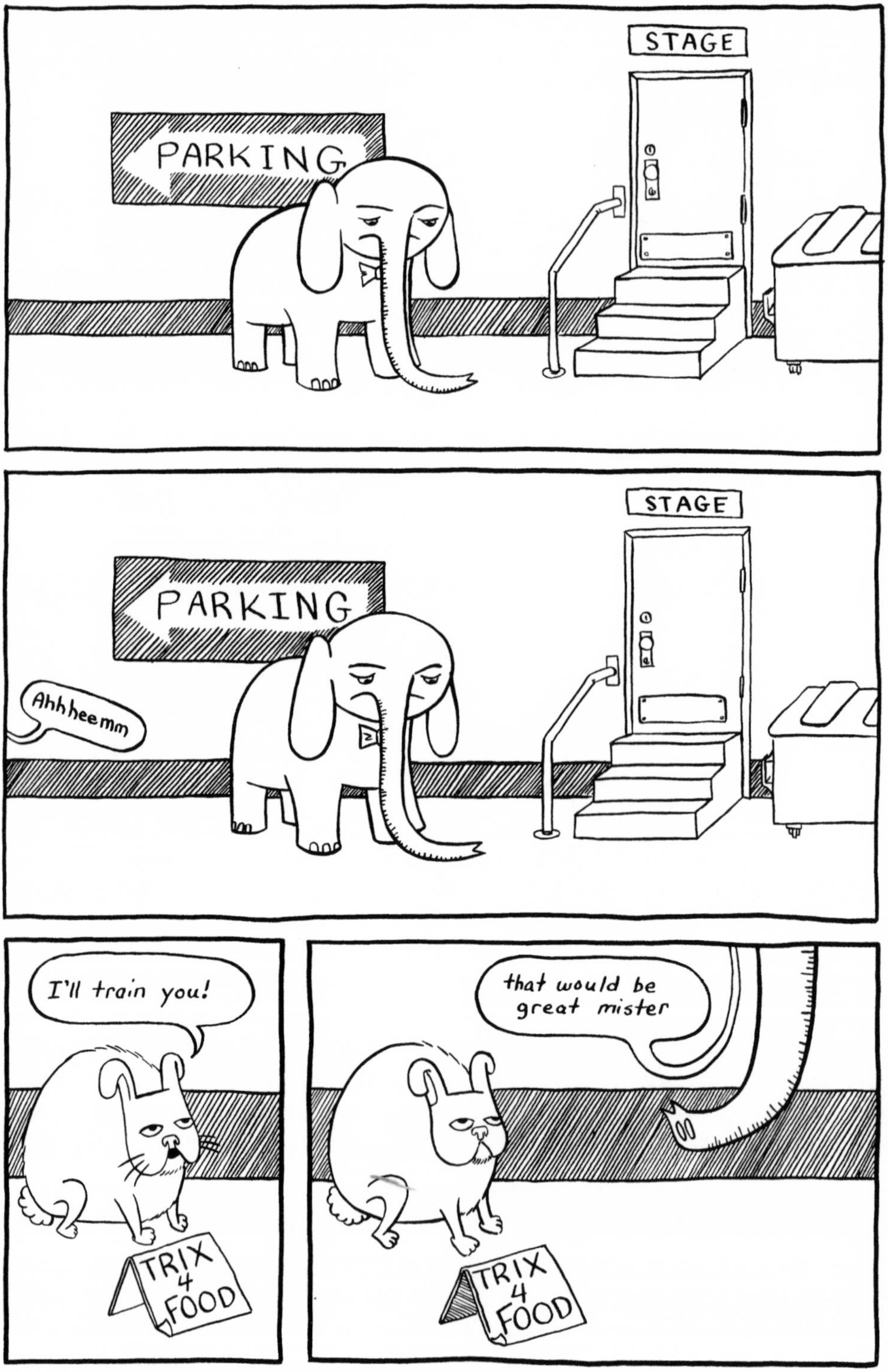
STAGE
PARKING
STAGE
PARKING
Ahhheemm
I'll train you!
TRIX 4 FOOD
that would be great mister
TRIX 4 FOOD

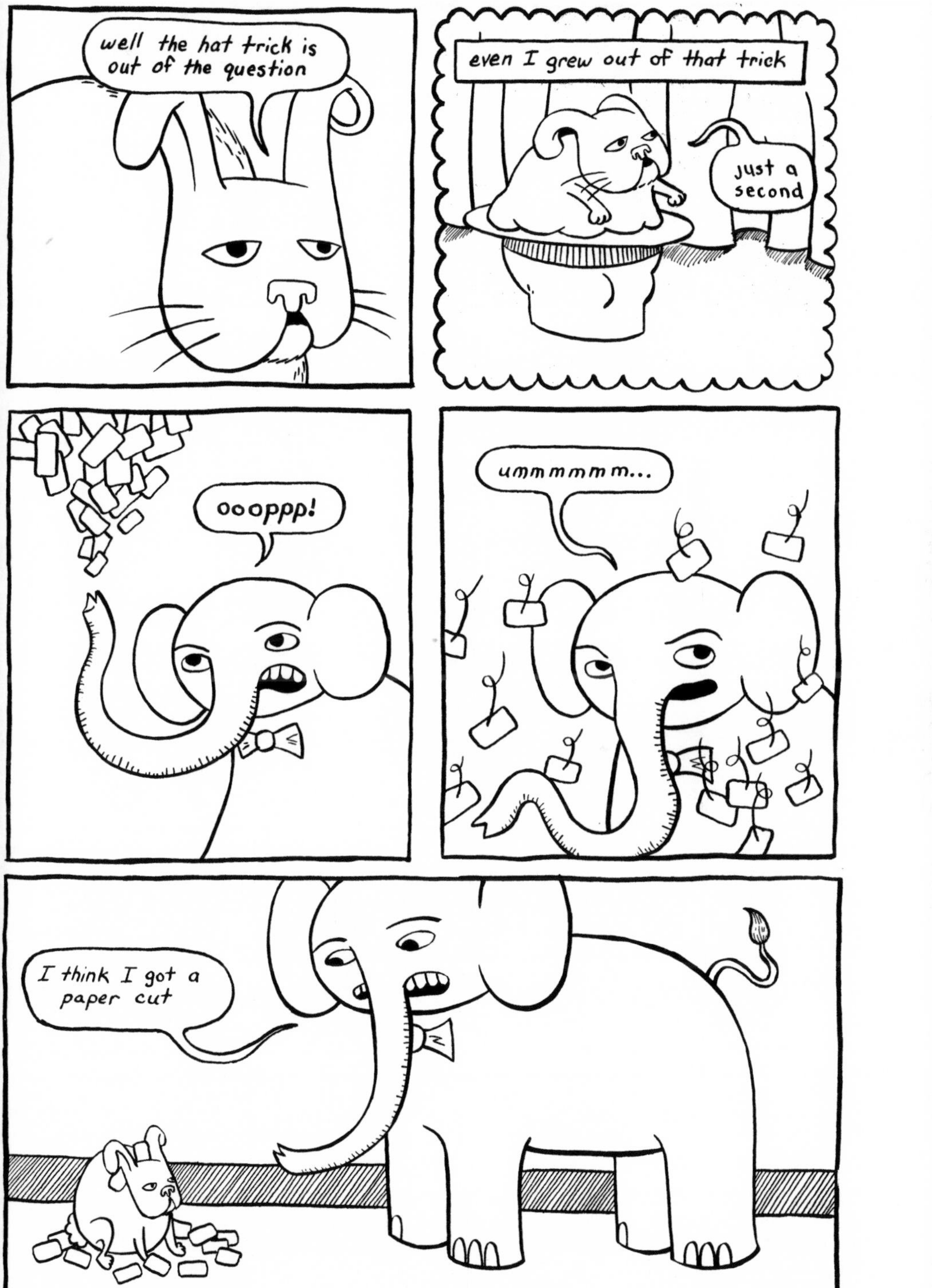
well the hat trick is out of the question
even I grew out of that trick
just a second
oooppp!
ummmmmm...
I think I got a paper cut

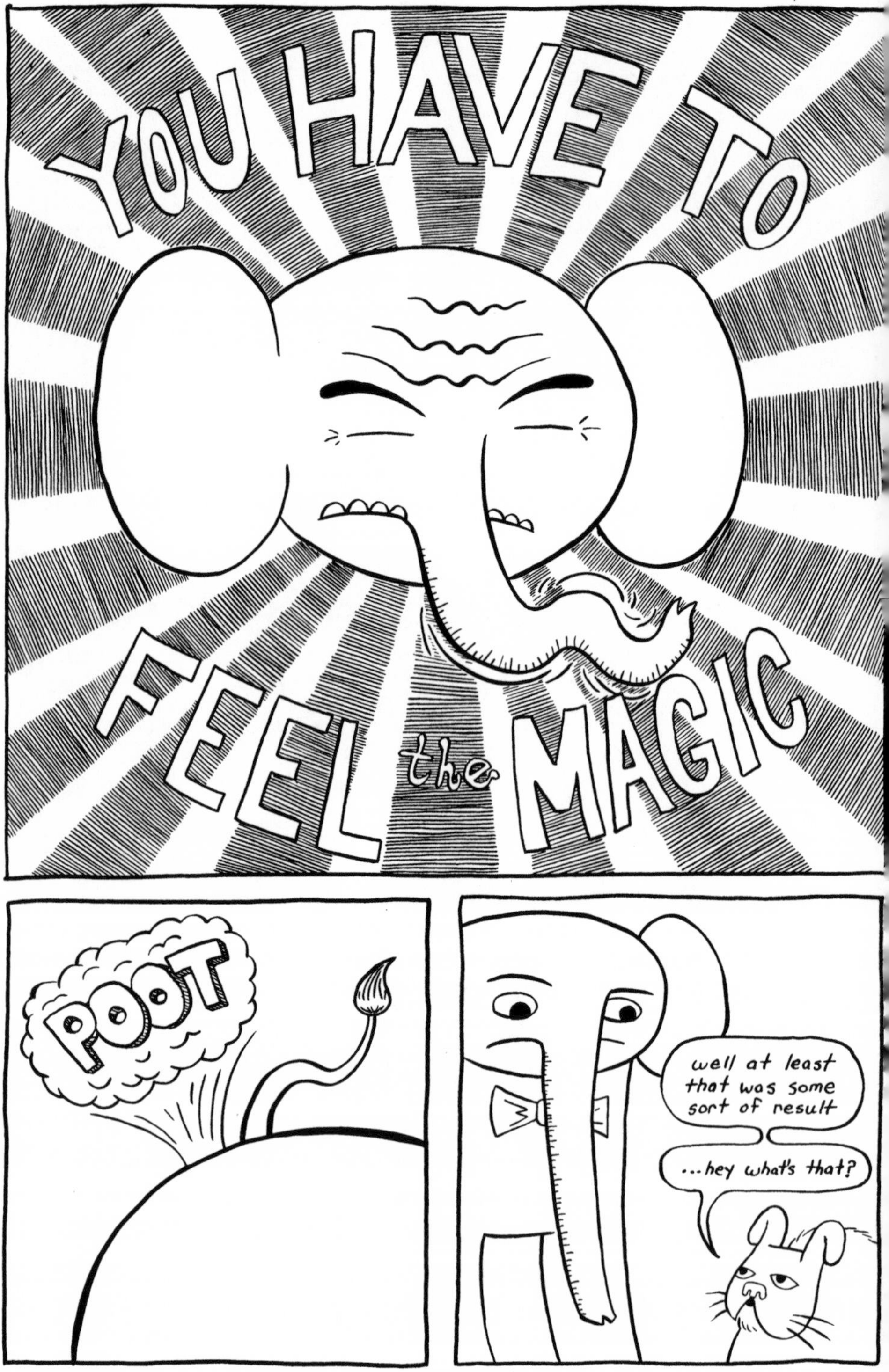
YOU HAVE TO
FEEL the MAGIC
POOT
well at least that was some sort of result
...hey what's that?

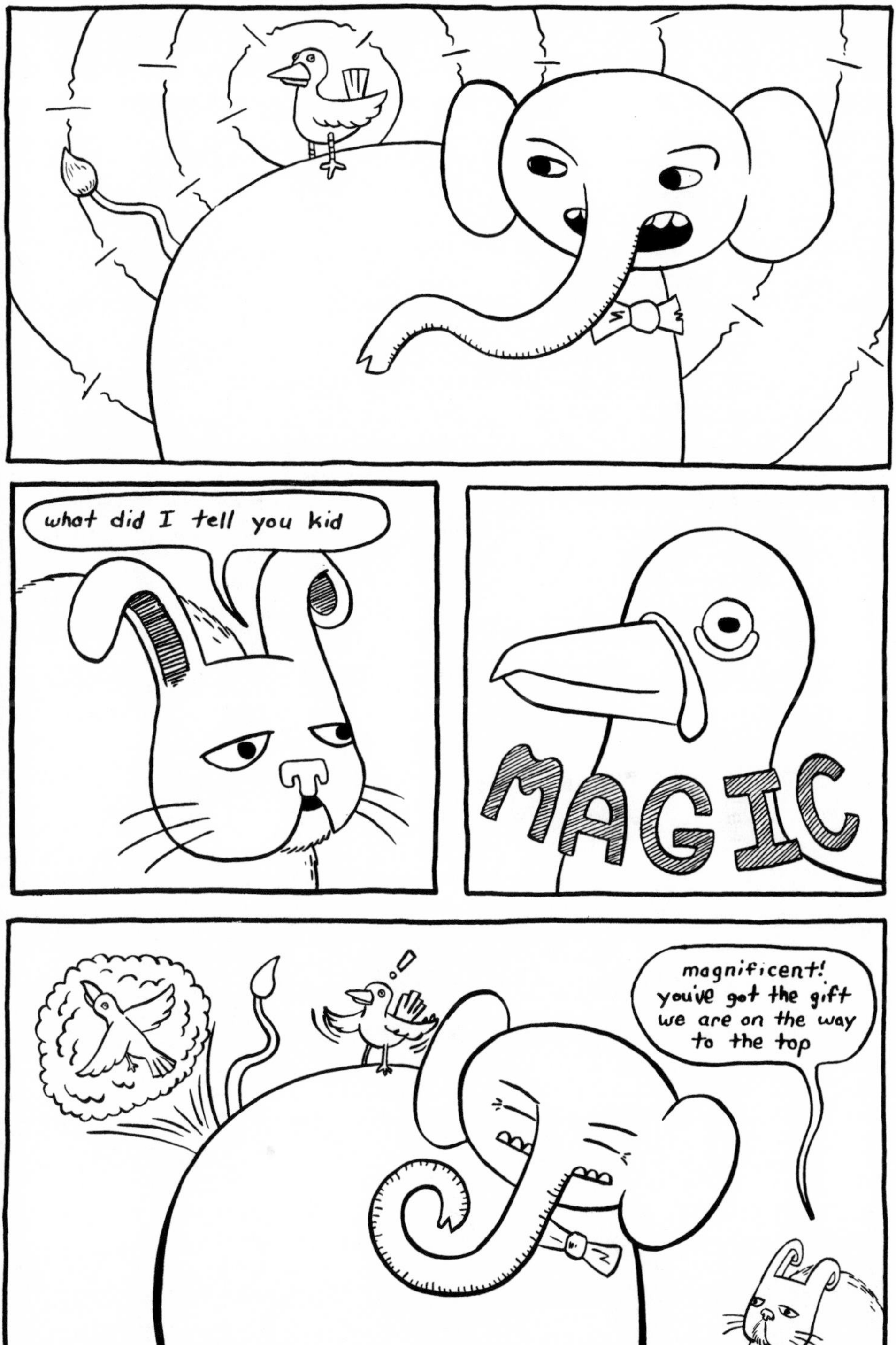
what did I tell you kid
MAGIC
magnificent!
you've got the gift
we are on the way
to the top

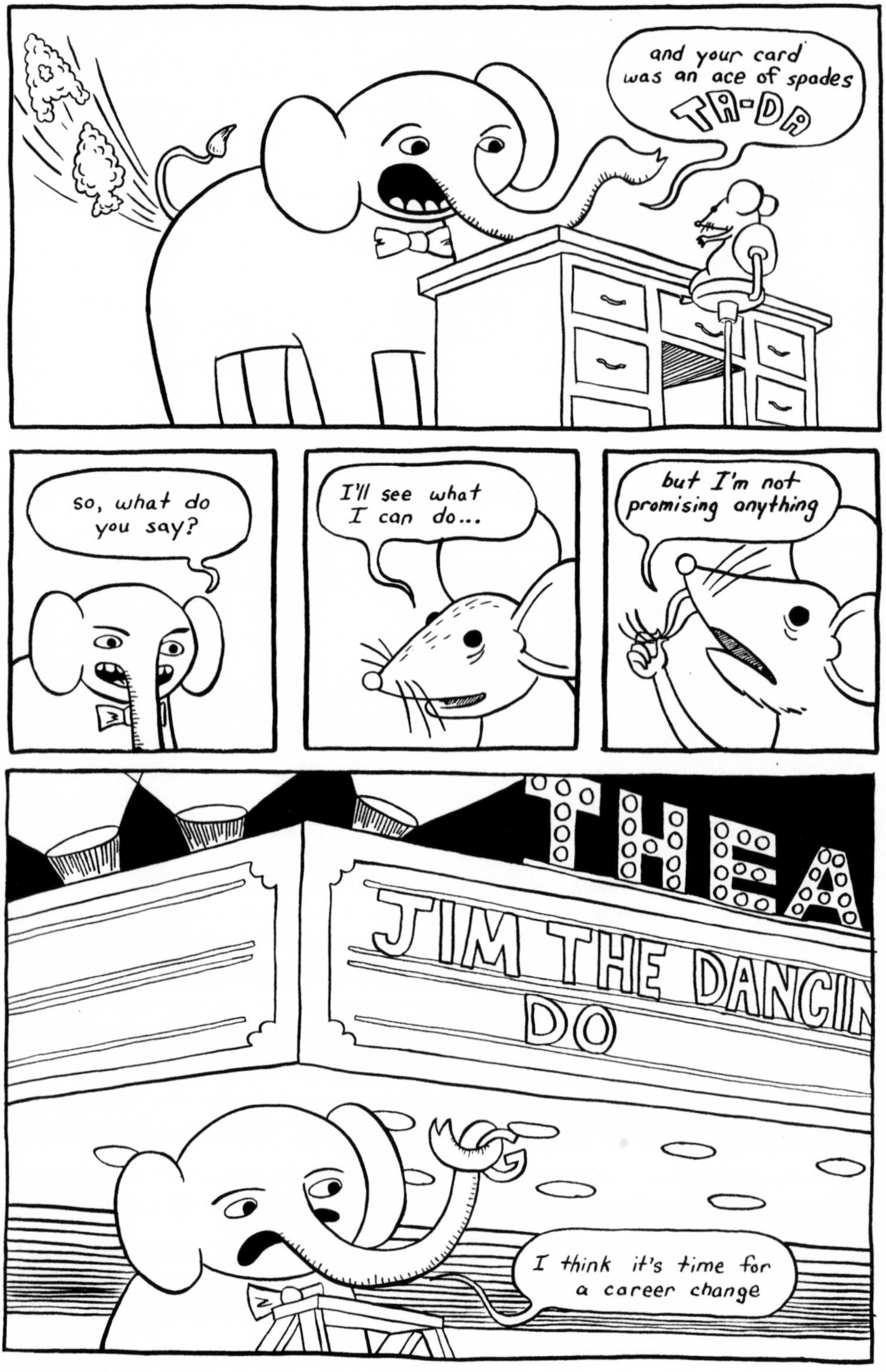

and your card was an ace of spades
TA-DA
so, what do you say?
I'll see what I can do...
but I'm not promising anything
THEA
JIM THE DANCIN
DO
I think it's time for a career change

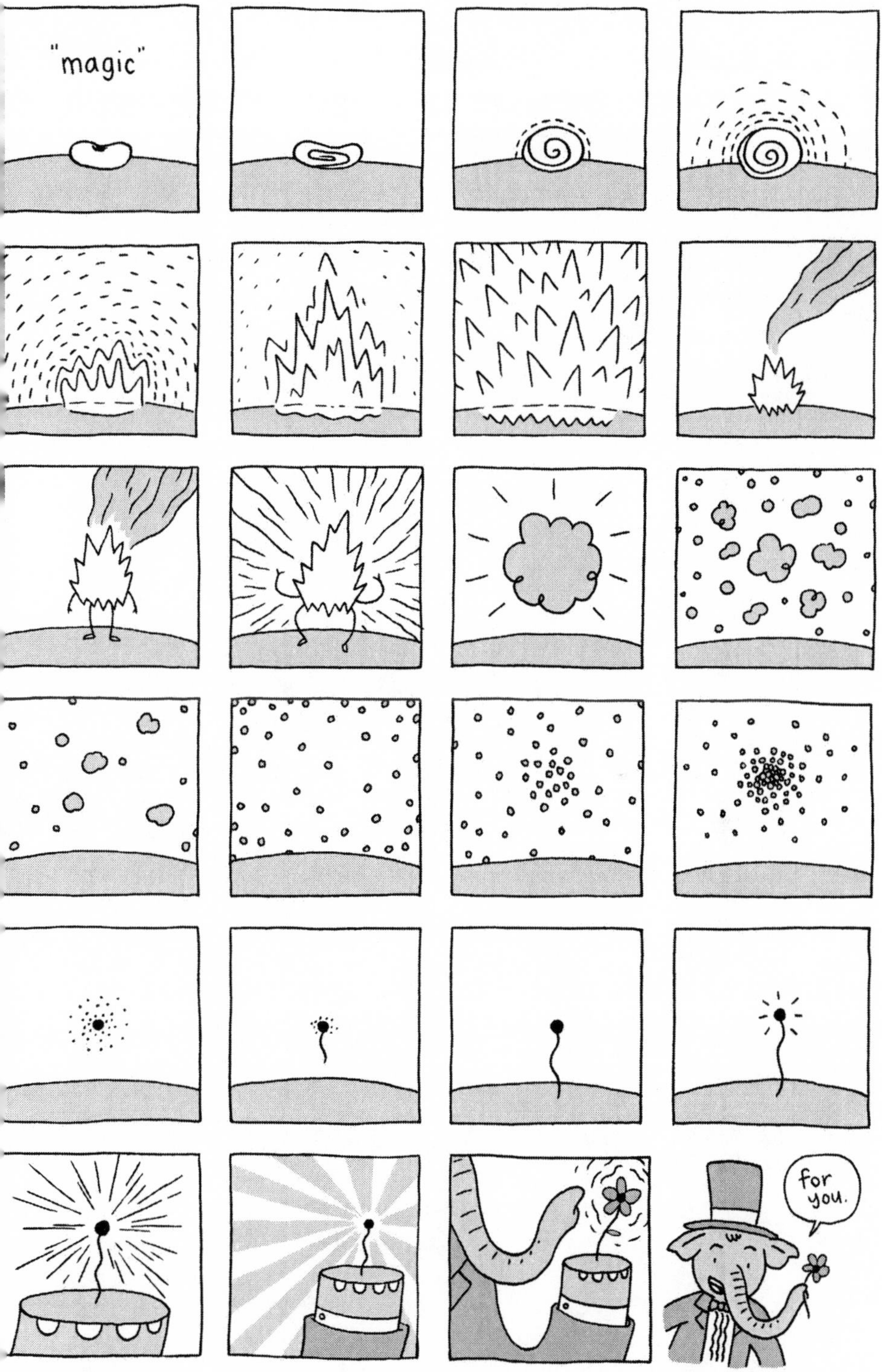
"magic"
for you.

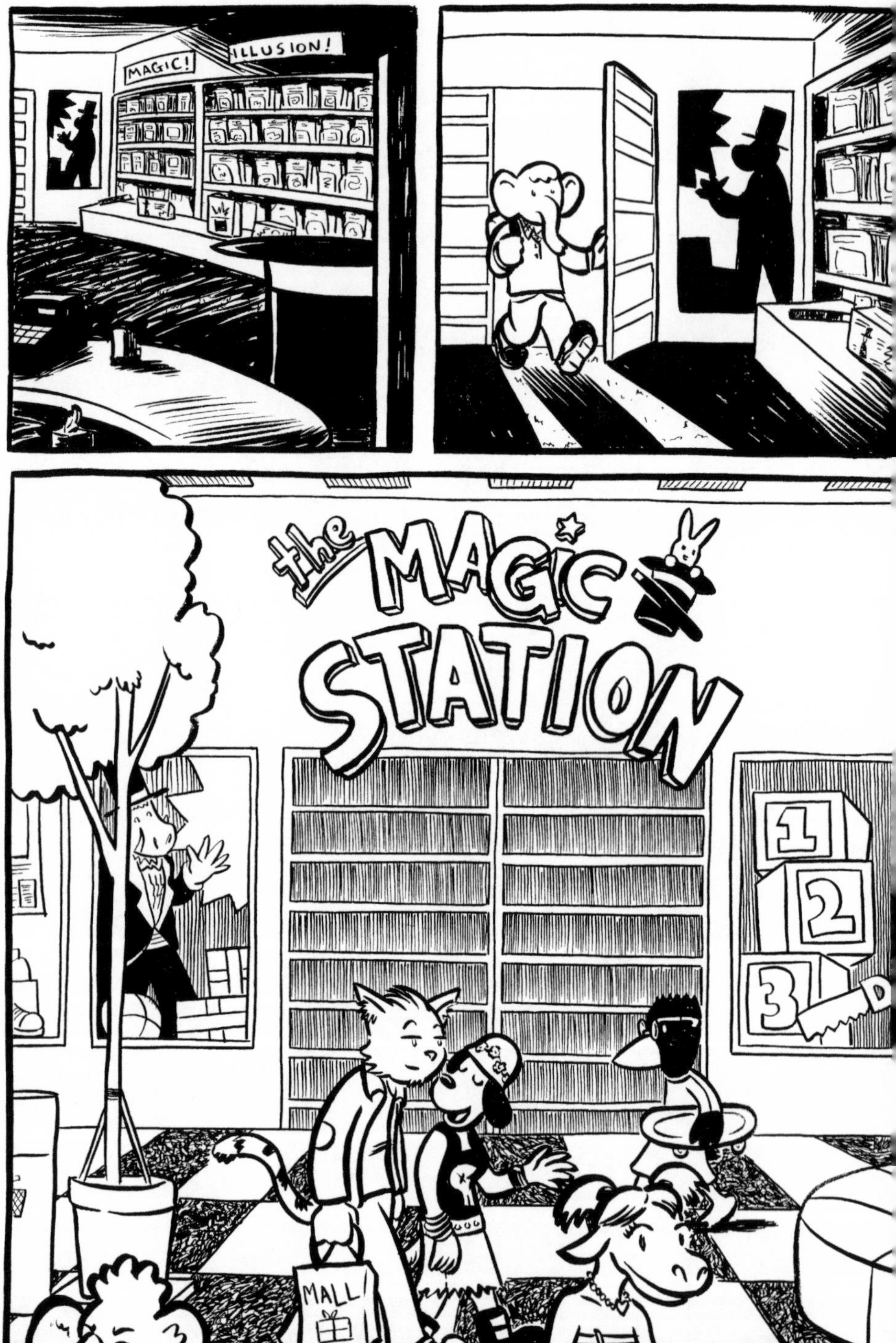
MAGIC!
ILLUSION!
the MAGIC STATION
1
2
3
MALL

by Joey Weiser

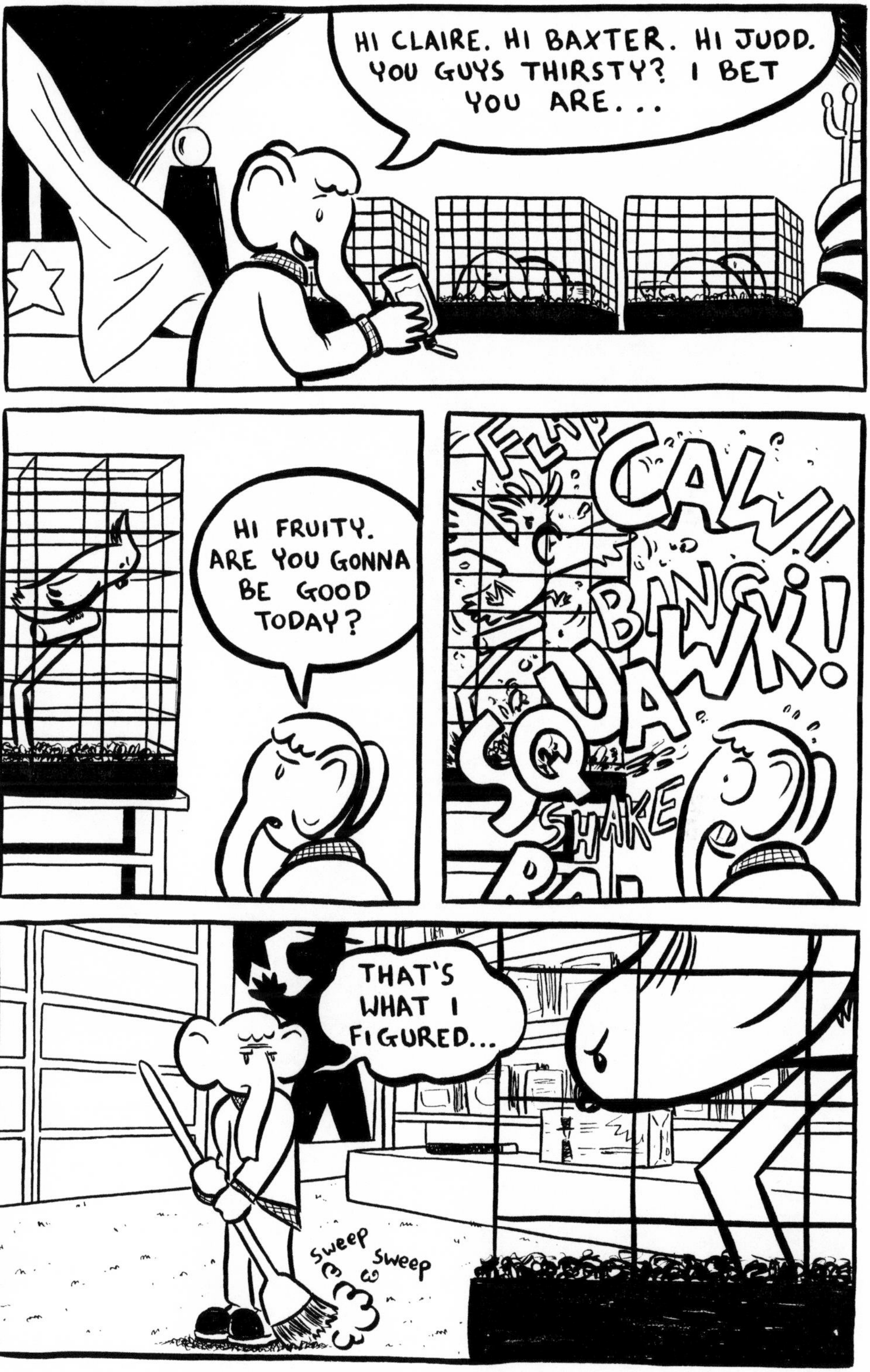

HI CLAIRE. HI BAXTER. HI JUDD. YOU GUYS THIRSTY? I BET YOU ARE...
HI FRUITY. ARE YOU GONNA BE GOOD TODAY?
CAW!
BANG!
SQUAWK!
SHAKE
THAT'S WHAT I FIGURED...
sweep
sweep

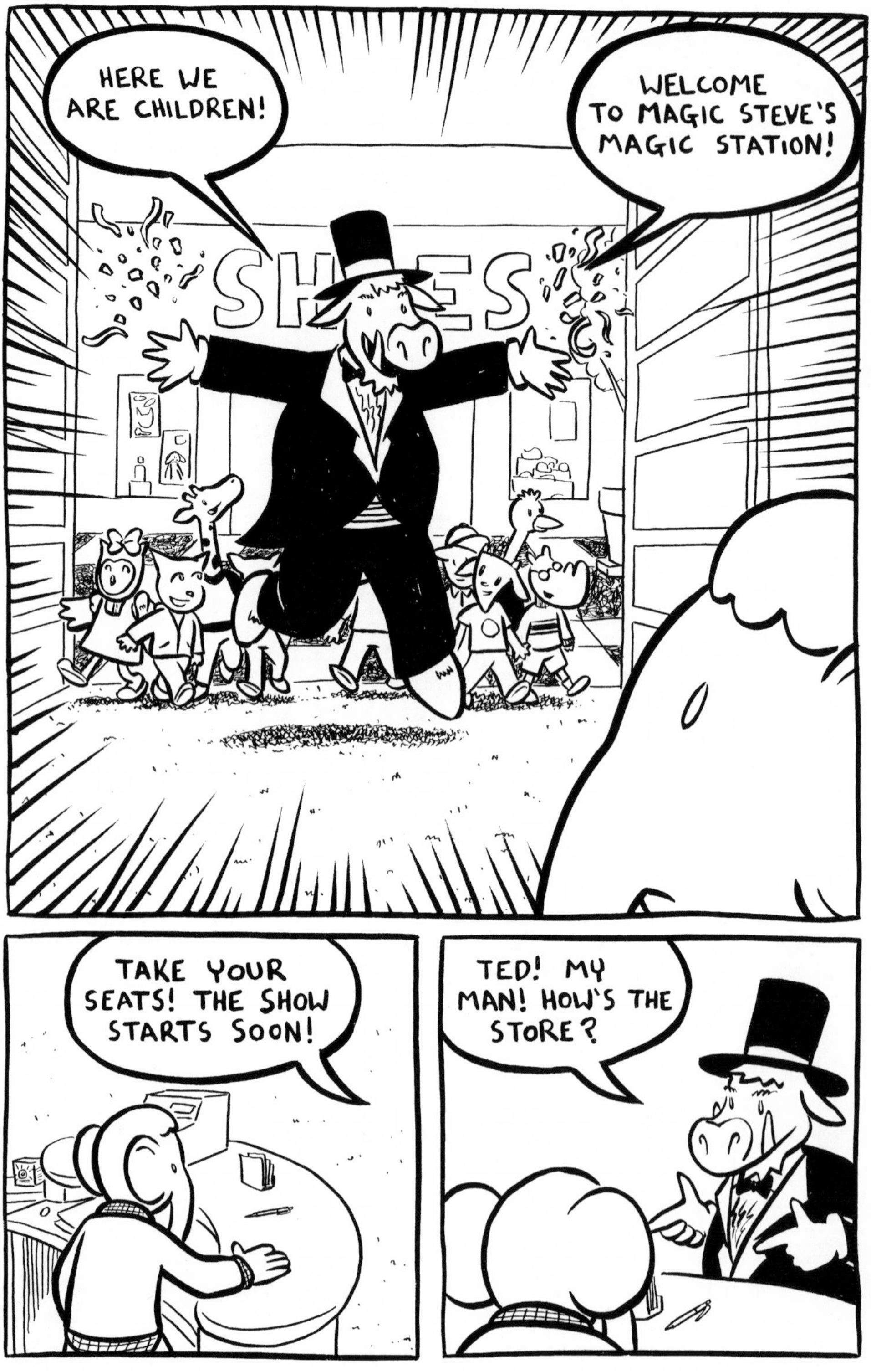
HERE WE ARE CHILDREN!
WELCOME TO MAGIC STEVE'S MAGIC STATION!
SHOES
TAKE YOUR SEATS! THE SHOW STARTS SOON!
TED! MY MAN! HOW'S THE STORE?

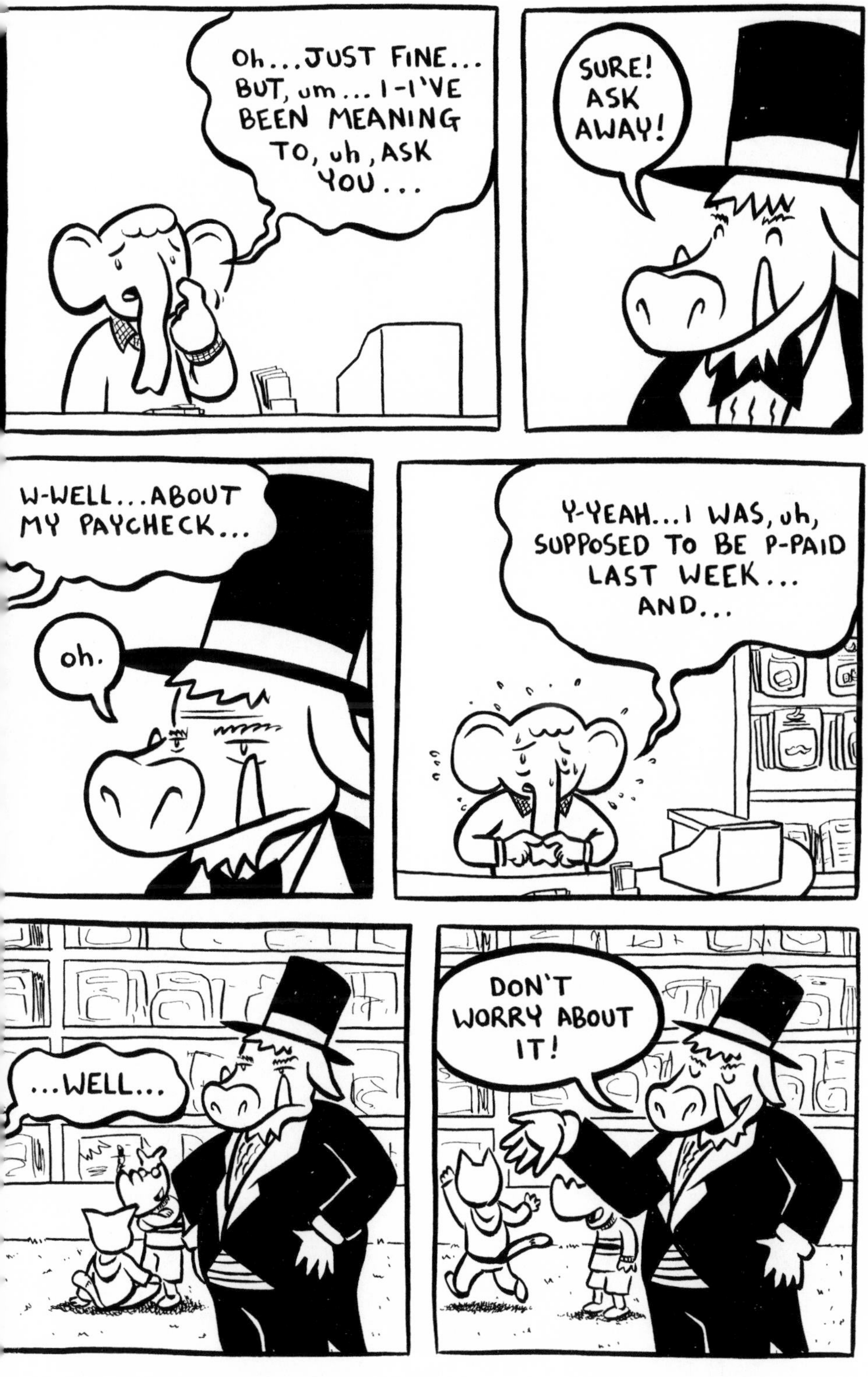
Oh...JUST FINE... BUT, um... I-I'VE BEEN MEANING TO, uh, ASK YOU...
SURE! ASK AWAY!
W-WELL...ABOUT MY PAYCHECK...
oh.
Y-YEAH...I WAS, uh, SUPPOSED TO BE P-PAID LAST WEEK... AND...
...WELL...
DON'T WORRY ABOUT IT!

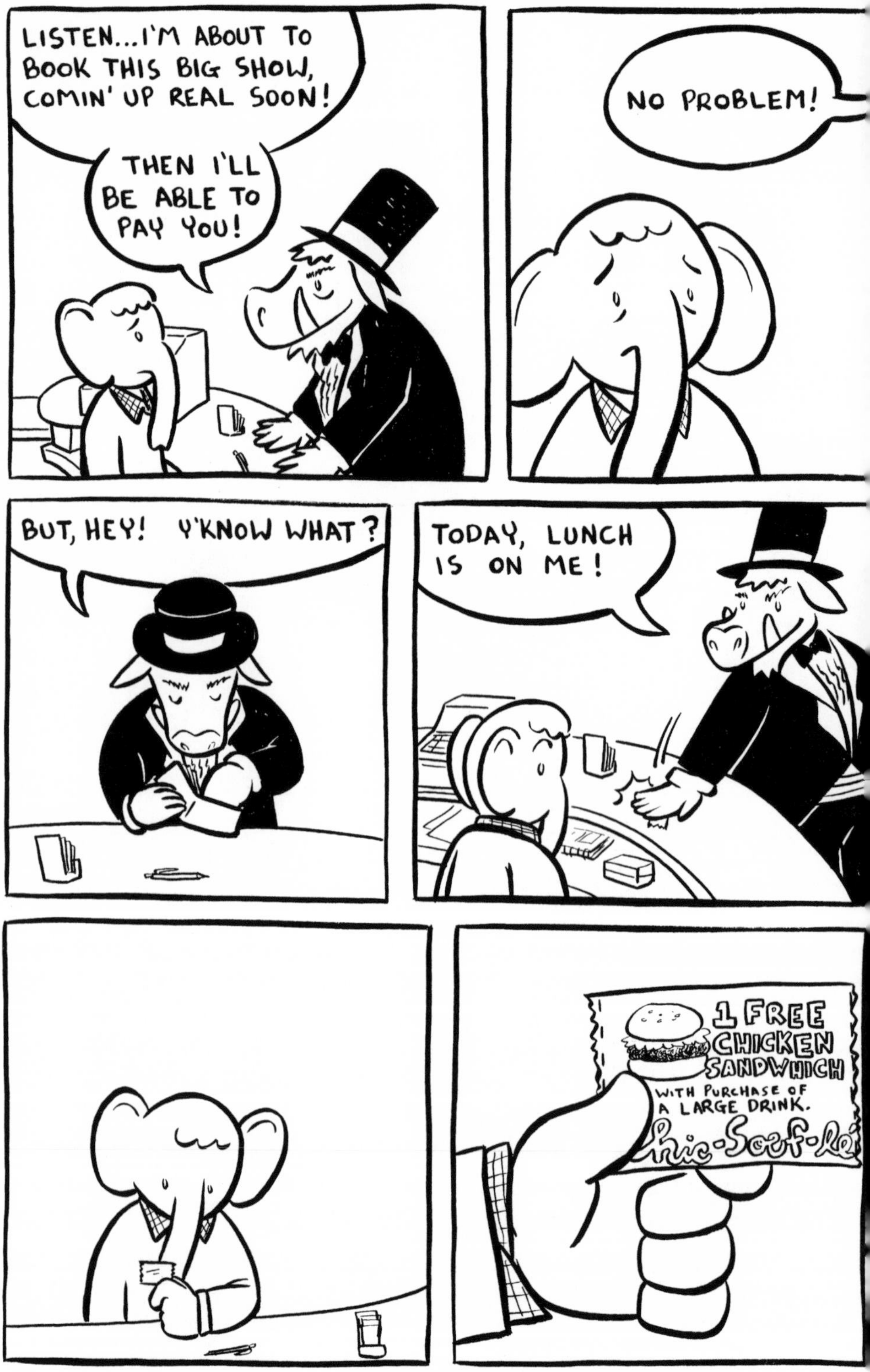
LISTEN...I'M ABOUT TO BOOK THIS BIG SHOW, COMIN' UP REAL SOON!
THEN I'LL BE ABLE TO PAY YOU!
NO PROBLEM!
BUT, HEY! Y'KNOW WHAT?
TODAY, LUNCH IS ON ME!
1 FREE CHICKEN SANDWHICH
WITH PURCHASE OF A LARGE DRINK.
Chic-Sonf-lé

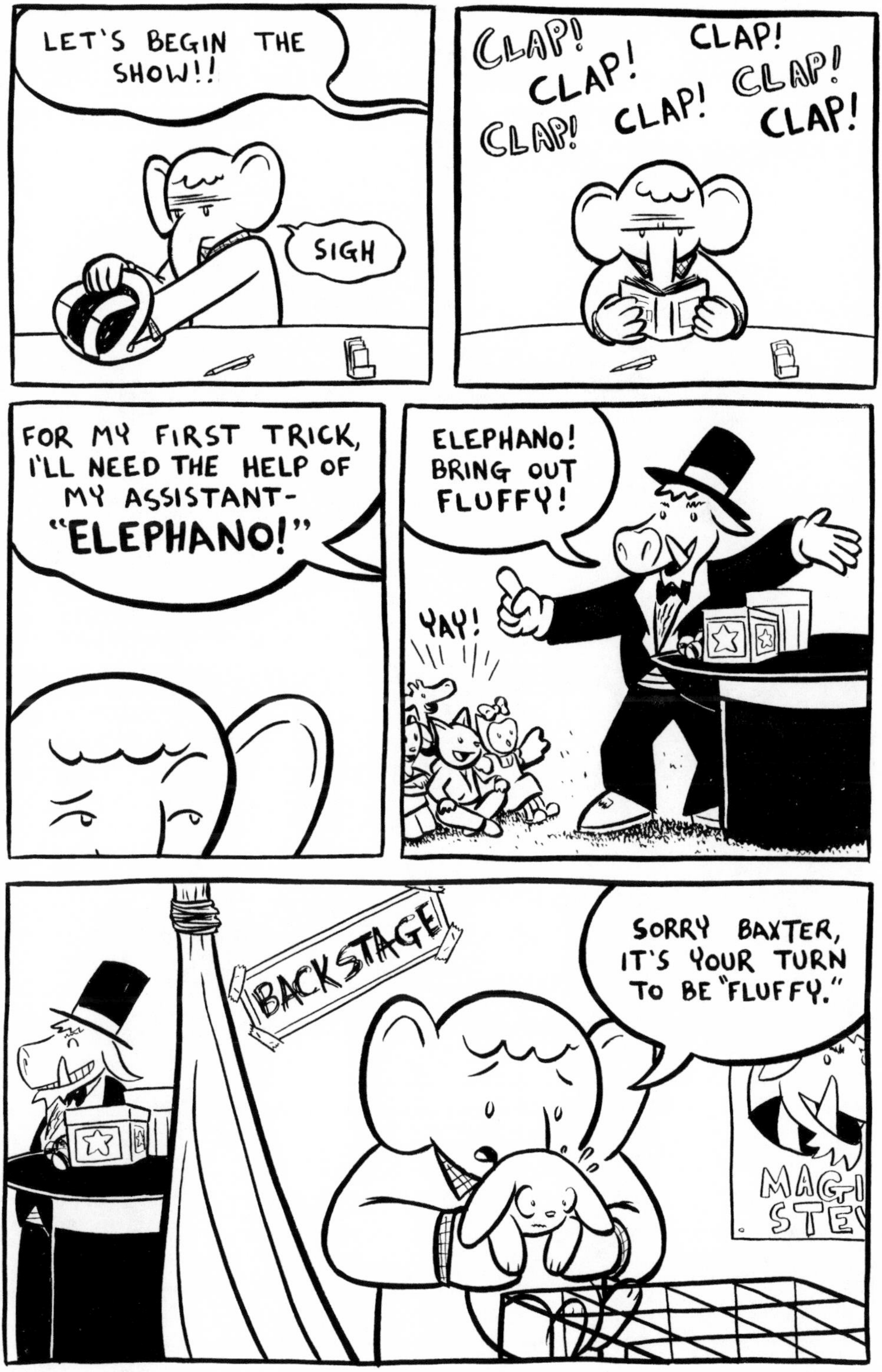
LET'S BEGIN THE SHOW!!
SIGH
CLAP! CLAP! CLAP! CLAP! CLAP! CLAP! CLAP!
FOR MY FIRST TRICK, I'LL NEED THE HELP OF MY ASSISTANT- "ELEPHANO!"
ELEPHANO! BRING OUT FLUFFY!
YAY!
BACKSTAGE
SORRY BAXTER, IT'S YOUR TURN TO BE "FLUFFY."

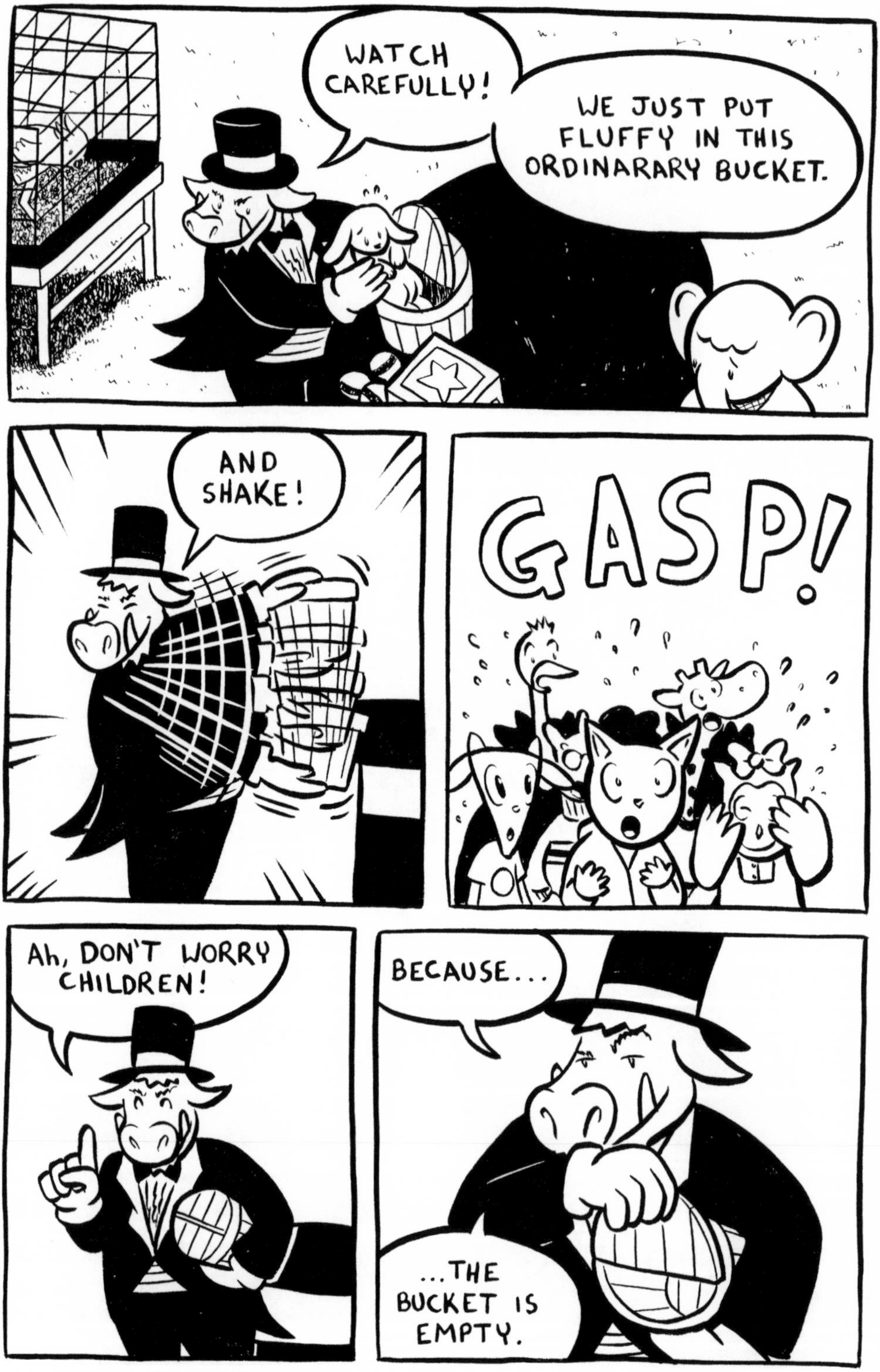
WATCH CAREFULLY!
WE JUST PUT FLUFFY IN THIS ORDINARARY BUCKET.
AND SHAKE!
GASP!
Ah, DON'T WORRY CHILDREN!
BECAUSE...
...THE BUCKET IS EMPTY.

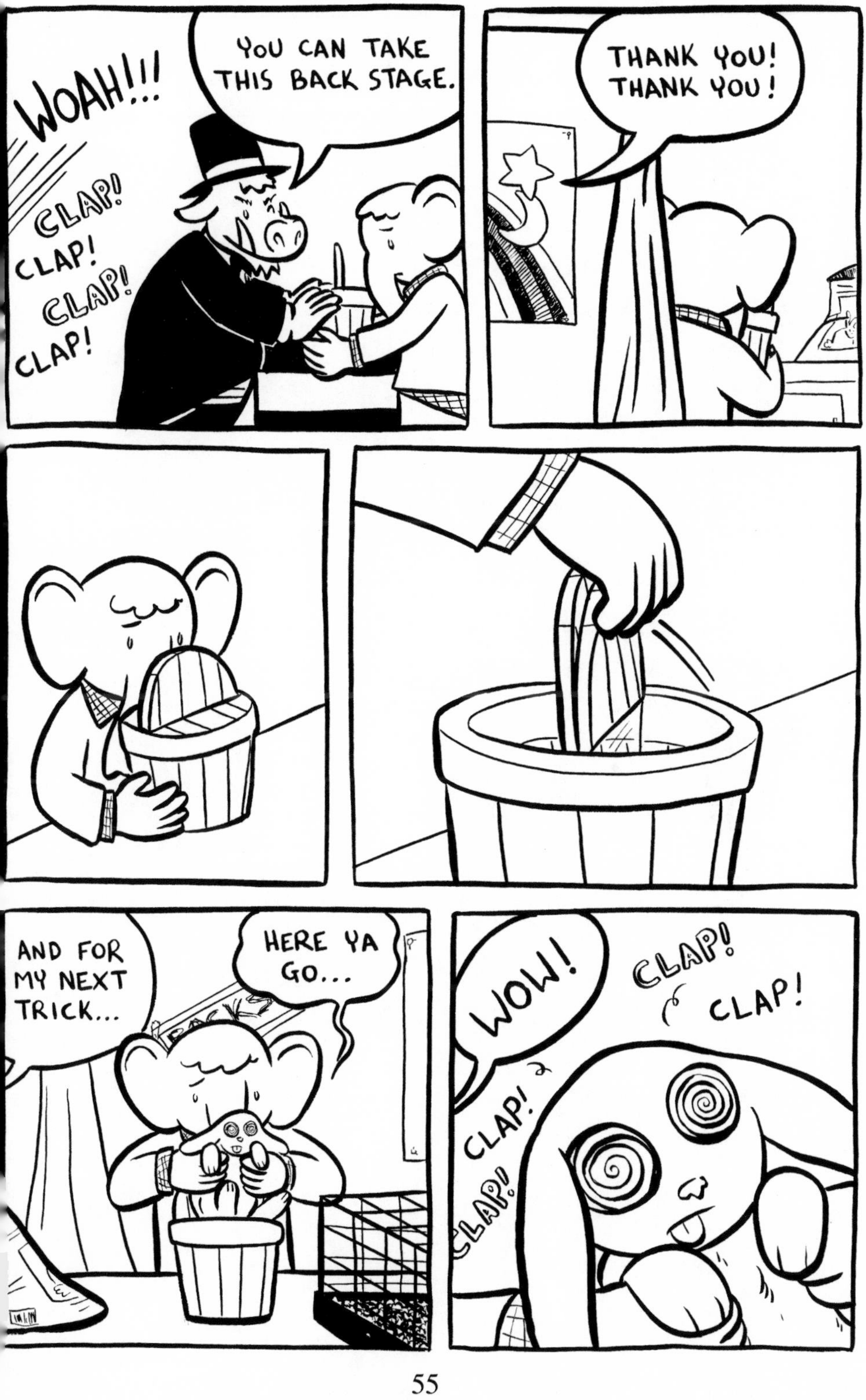
WOAH!!!...
YOU CAN TAKE THIS BACK STAGE.
CLAP!
CLAP!
CLAP!
CLAP!
THANK YOU! THANK YOU!
AND FOR MY NEXT TRICK...
HERE YA GO...
WOW!
CLAP!
CLAP!
CLAP!
CLAP!

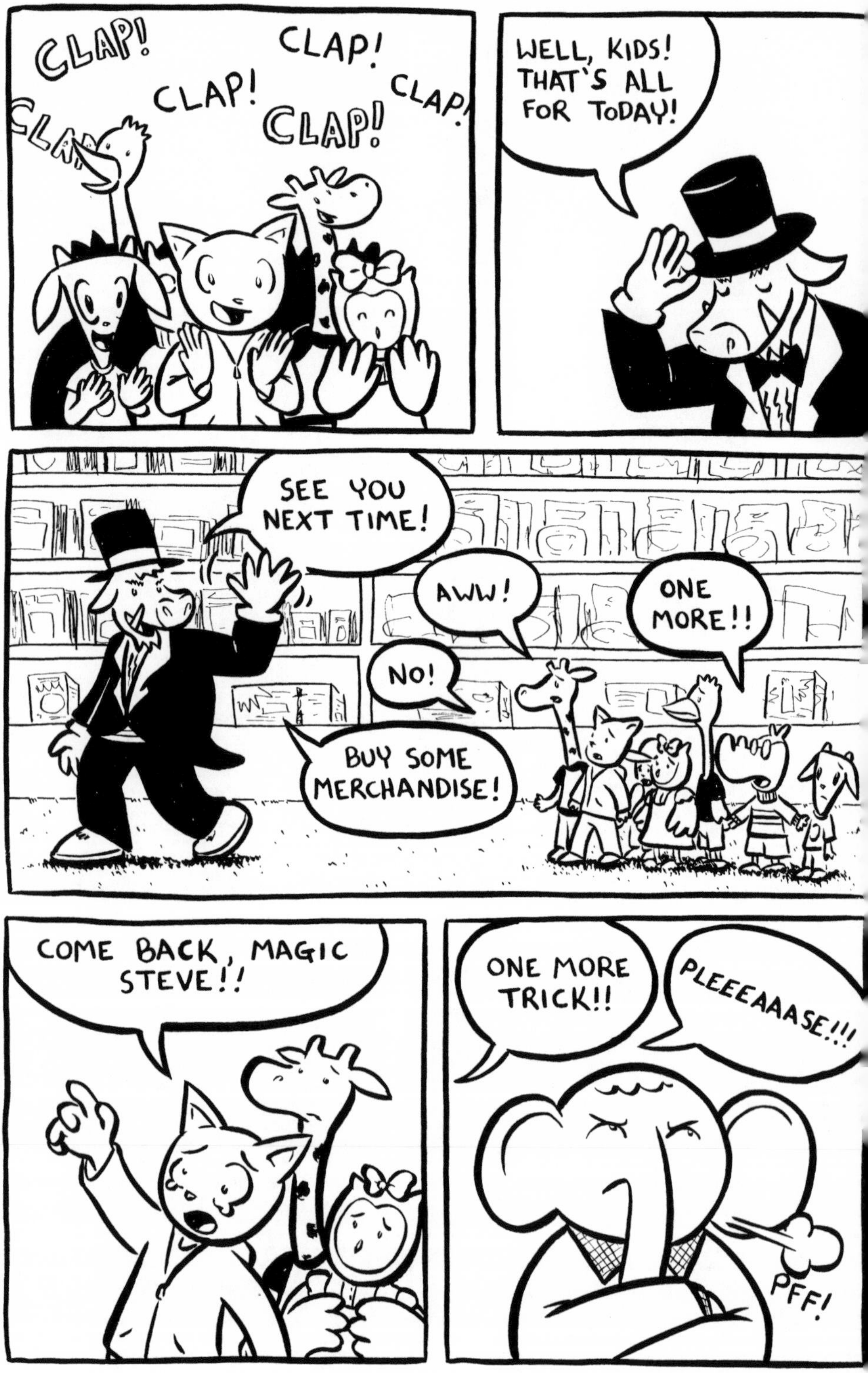
CLAP!
CLAP!
CLAP!
CLAP!
CLAP!
WELL, KIDS! THAT'S ALL FOR TODAY!
SEE YOU NEXT TIME!
AWW!
ONE MORE!!
NO!
BUY SOME MERCHANDISE!
COME BACK, MAGIC STEVE!!
ONE MORE TRICK!!
PLEEEAAAASE!!!
PFF!

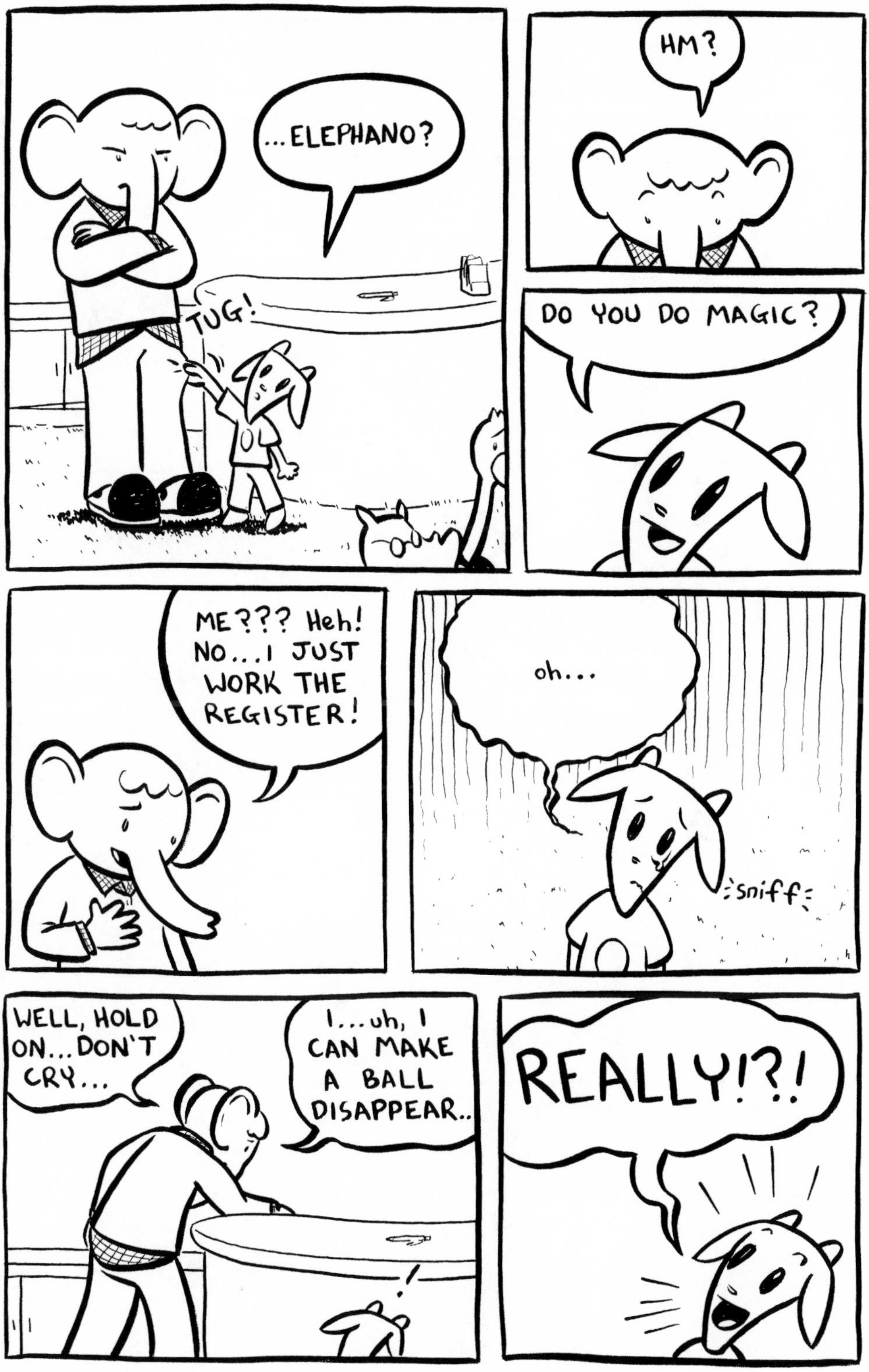
...ELEPHANO?
TUG!
HM?
DO YOU DO MAGIC?
ME??? Heh! NO...I JUST WORK THE REGISTER!
oh...
sniff
WELL, HOLD ON...DON'T CRY...
I...uh, I CAN MAKE A BALL DISAPPEAR..
!
REALLY!?!

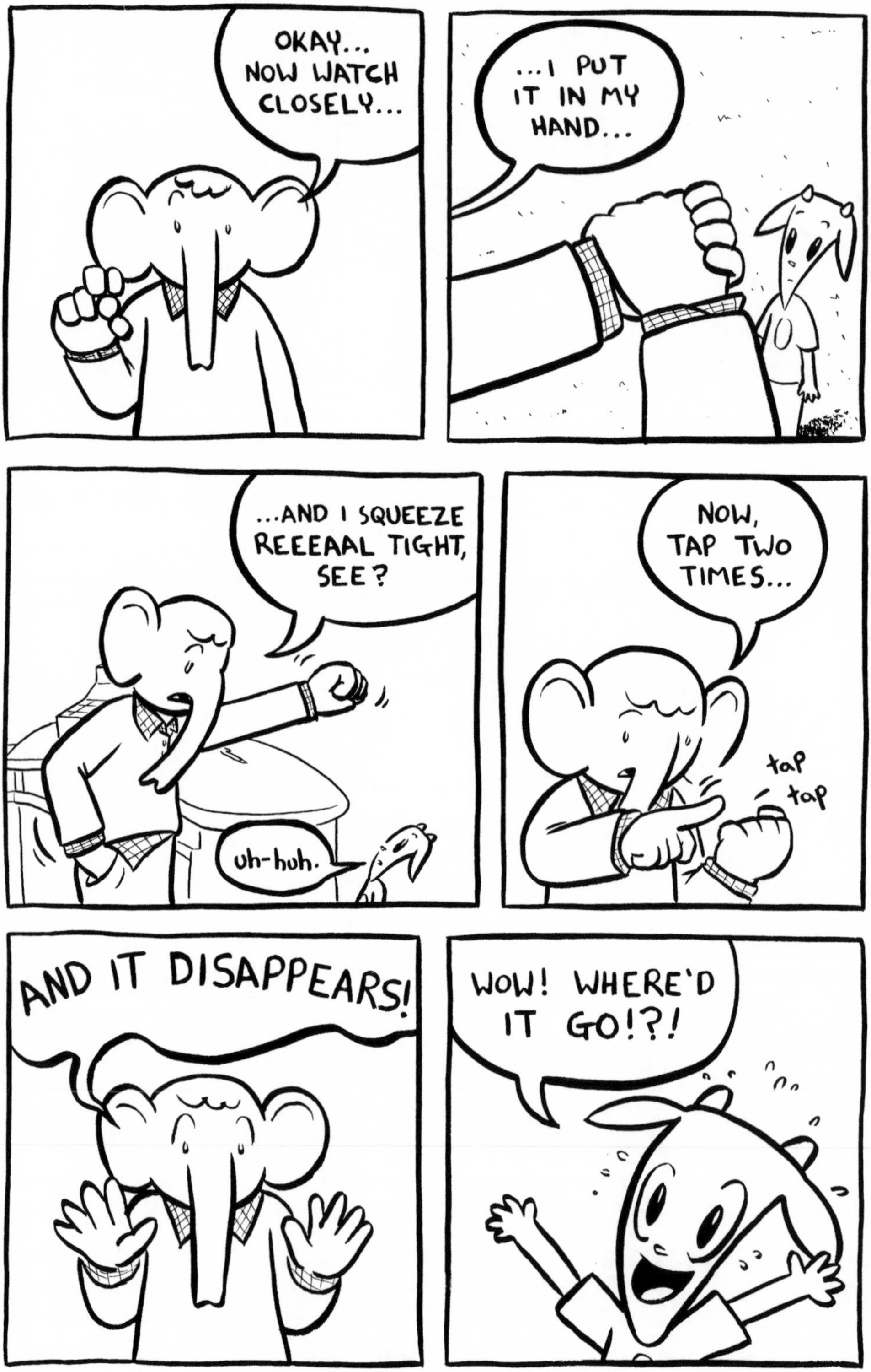
OKAY... NOW WATCH CLOSELY...
...I PUT IT IN MY HAND...
...AND I SQUEEZE REEEAAL TIGHT, SEE?
uh-huh.
NOW, TAP TWO TIMES...
tap tap
AND IT DISAPPEARS!
WOW! WHERE'D IT GO!?!

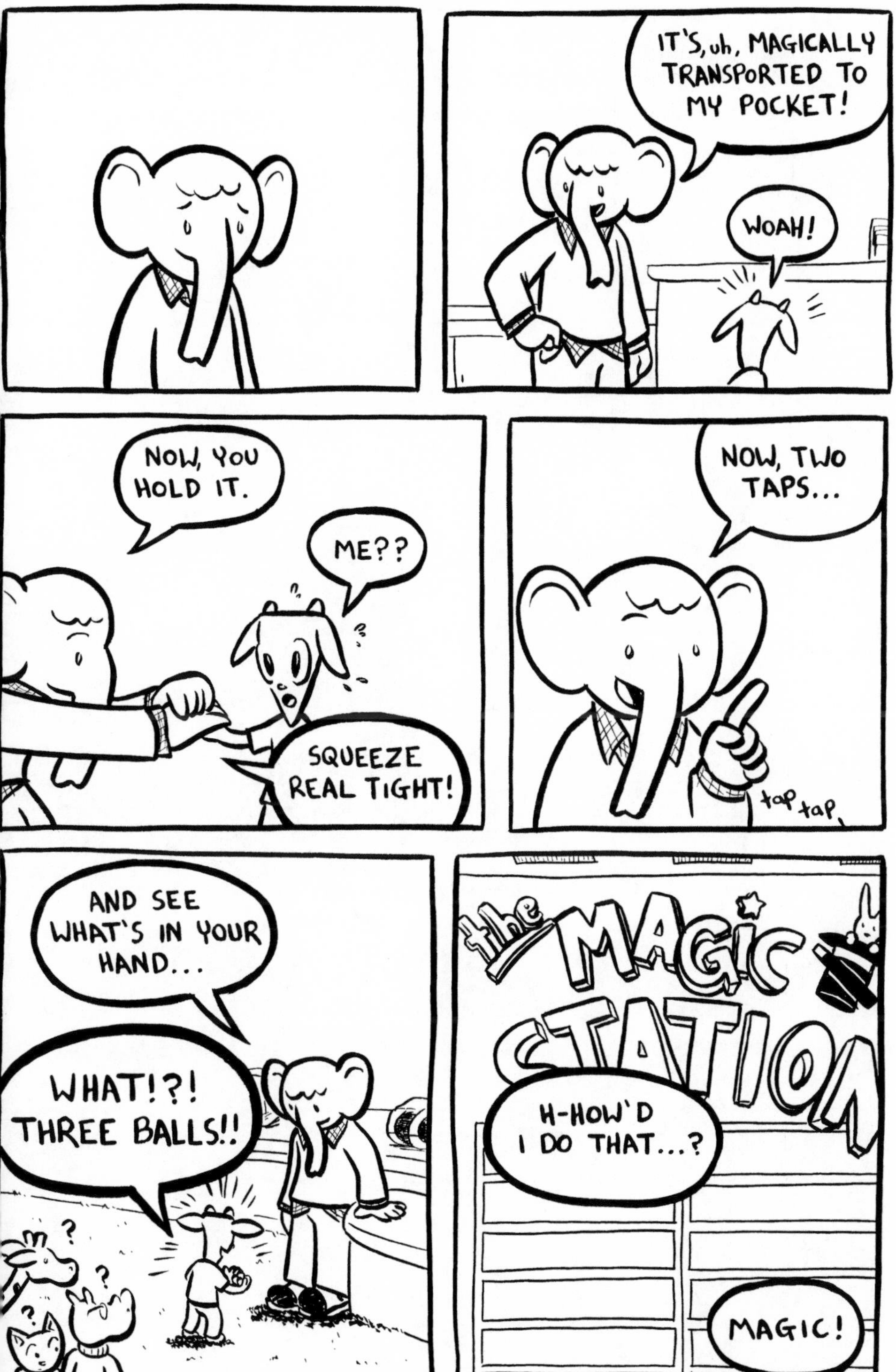
IT'S, uh, MAGICALLY TRANSPORTED TO MY POCKET!
WOAH!
NOW, YOU HOLD IT.
ME??
SQUEEZE REAL TIGHT!
NOW, TWO TAPS...
tap tap
AND SEE WHAT'S IN YOUR HAND...
WHAT!?! THREE BALLS!!
the MAGIC STATION
H-HOW'D I DO THAT...?
MAGIC!

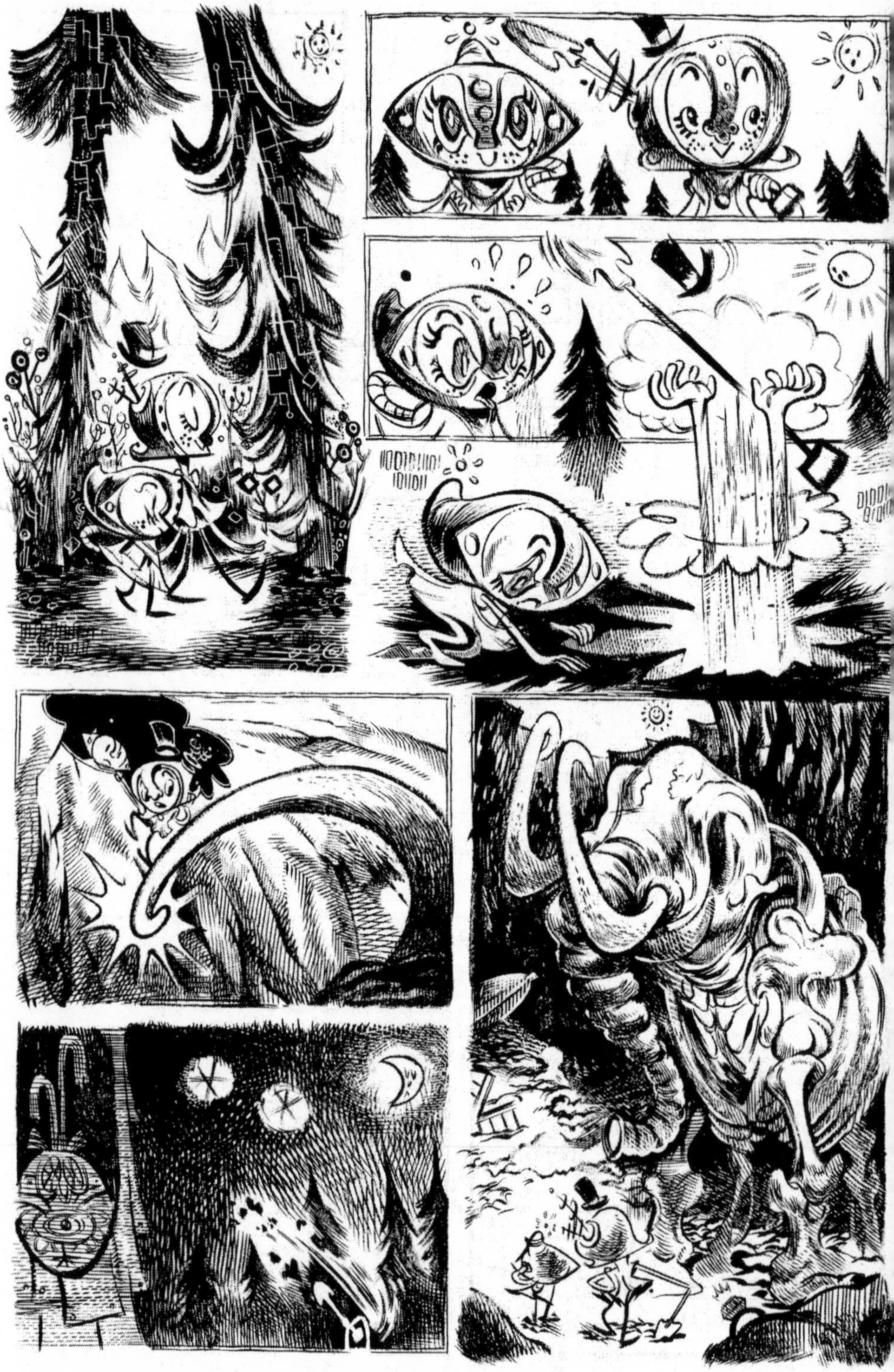

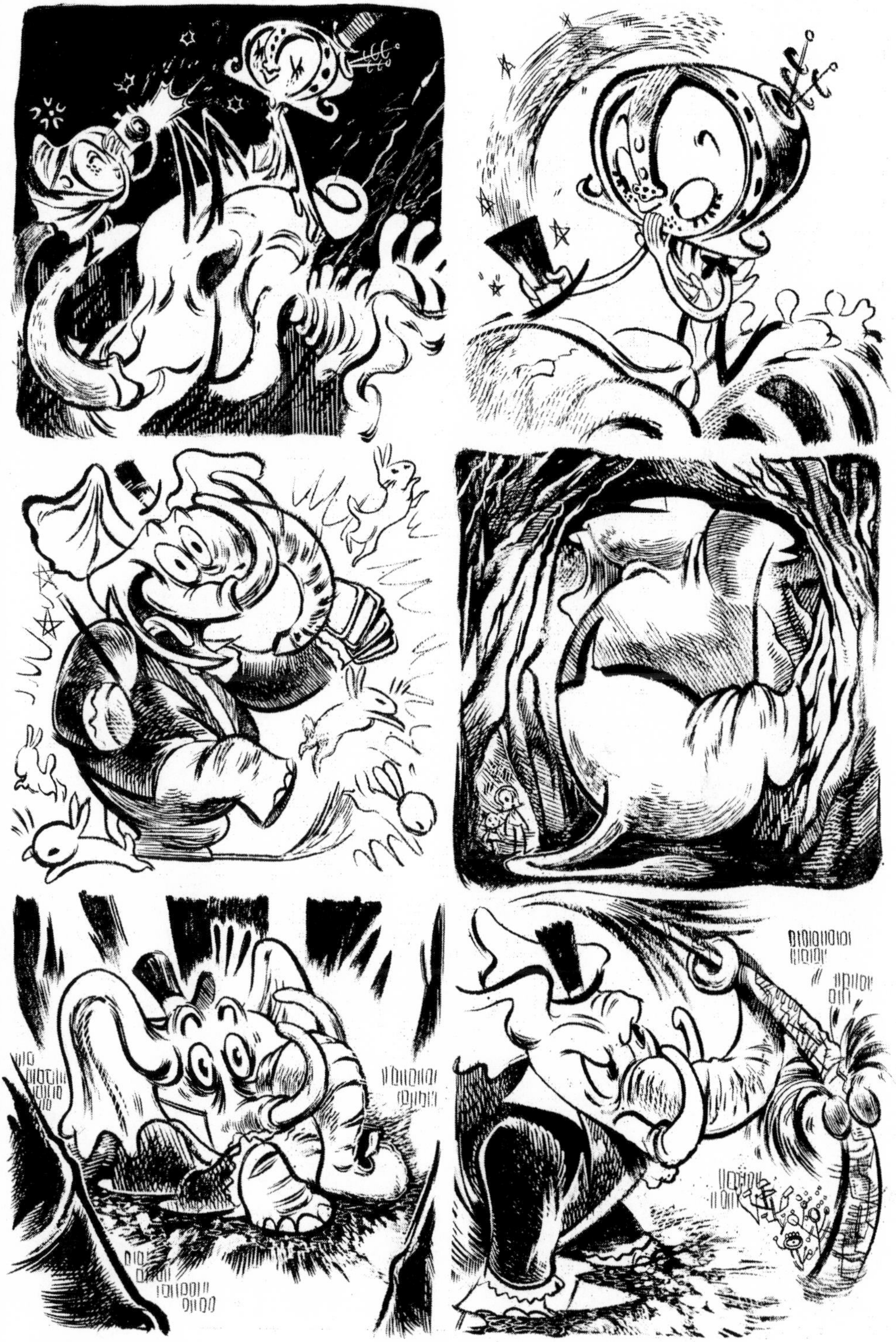

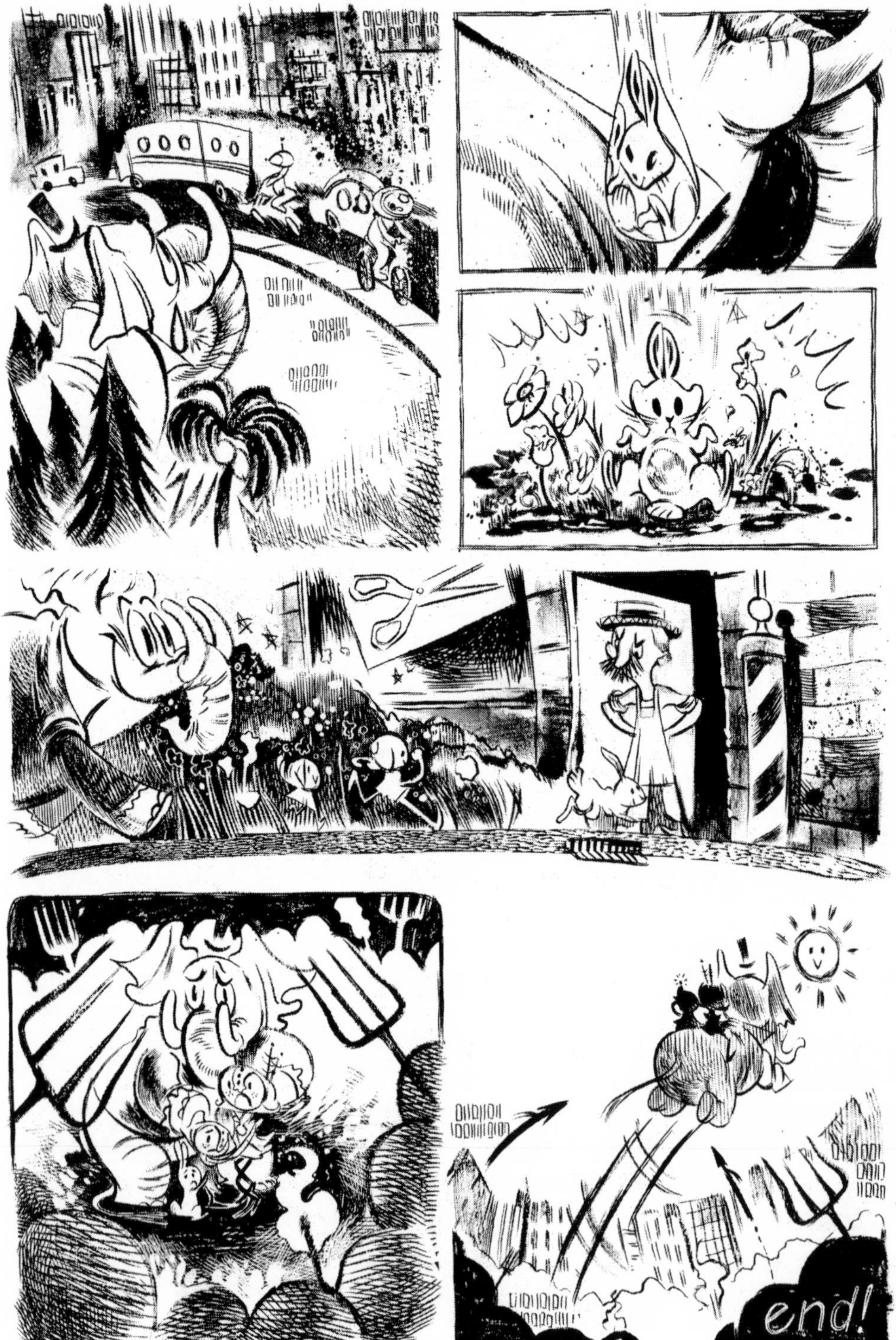
end!

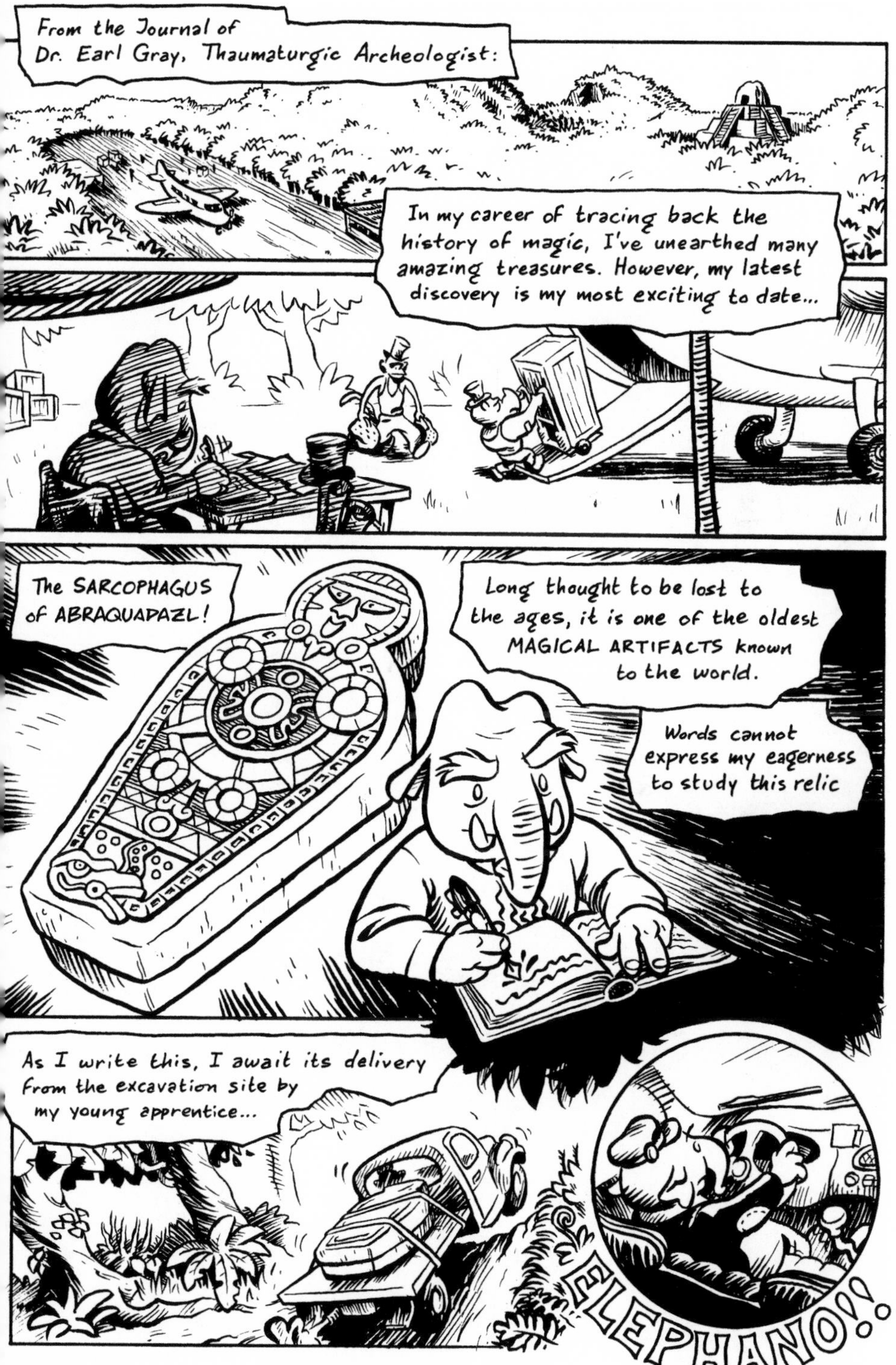
From the Journal of Dr. Earl Gray, Thaumaturgic Archeologist:
In my career of tracing back the history of magic, I've unearthed many amazing treasures. However, my latest discovery is my most exciting to date...
The SARCOPHAGUS of ABRAQUADAZL!
Long thought to be lost to the ages, it is one of the oldest MAGICAL ARTIFACTS known to the world.
Words cannot express my eagerness to study this relic
As I write this, I await its delivery from the excavation site by my young apprentice...
ELEPHANO!!

AW JEEZ...

*SOME KIND OF NEW AGE SYNTHPOP INSTRUMENTAL

HEY! WHAD'YA THINK YOU'RE DOING?!

THWUMP

ZIP

CHOK!

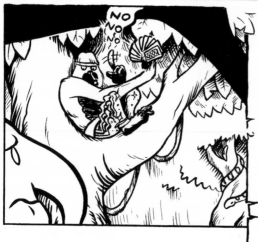

NO NO NO

The allure of the SARCOPHAGUS lies in its MYSTERIOUS PAST. It was the last and possibly greatest invention of ABRAQUADAZL, a prominant magician of the Third Age.

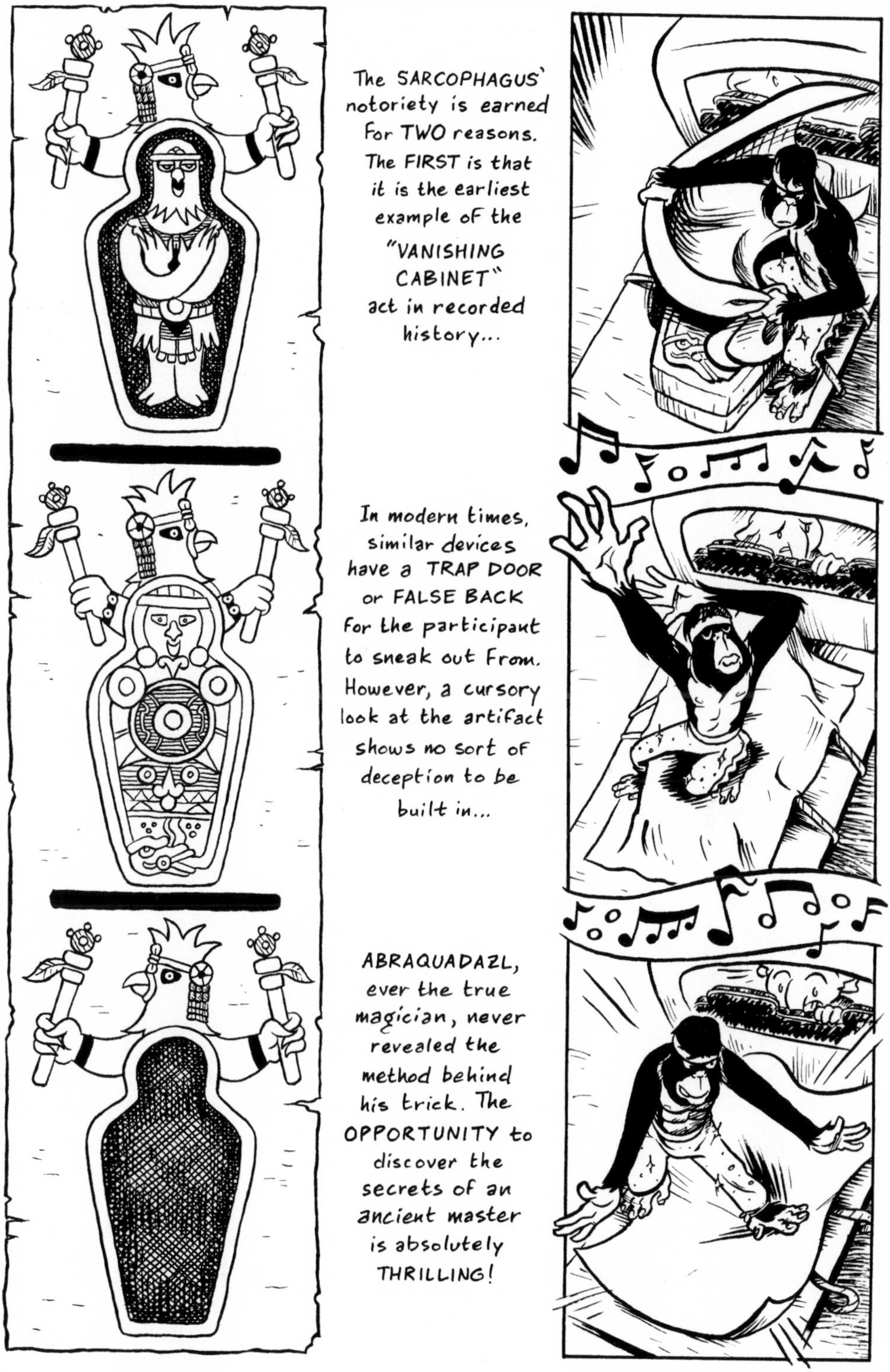
The SARCOPHAGUS' notoriety is earned For TWO reasons. The FIRST is that it is the earliest example of the "VANISHING CABINET" act in recorded history...
In modern times, similar devices have a TRAP DOOR or FALSE BACK For the participant to sneak out From. However, a cursory look at the artifact shows no sort of deception to be built in...
ABRAQUADAZL, ever the true magician, never revealed the method behind his trick. The OPPORTUNITY to discover the secrets of an ancient master is absolutely THRILLING!

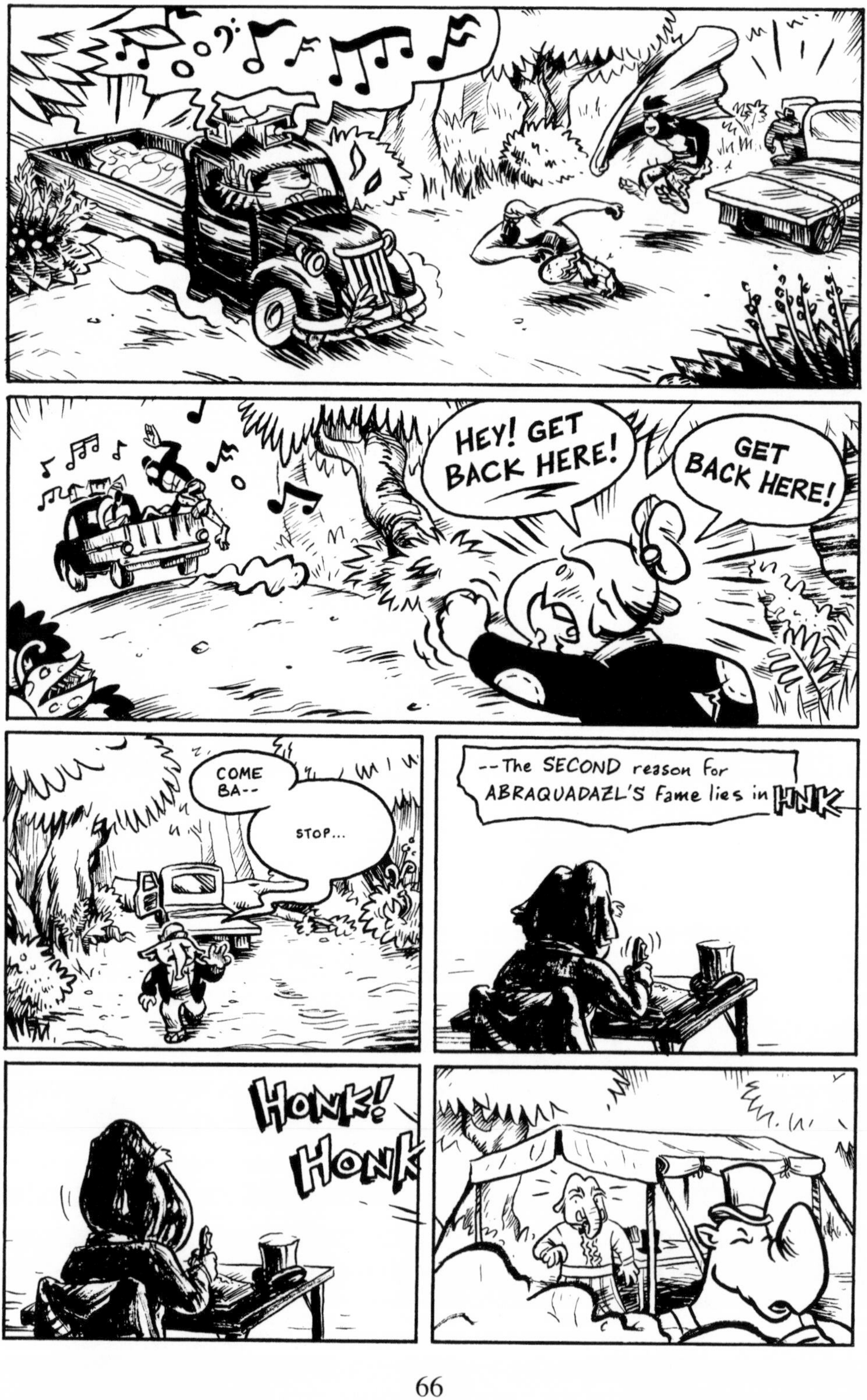
HEY! GET BACK HERE!
GET BACK HERE!
COME BA--
STOP...
--The SECOND reason for ABRAQUADAZL'S fame lies in HNK
HONK!
HONK

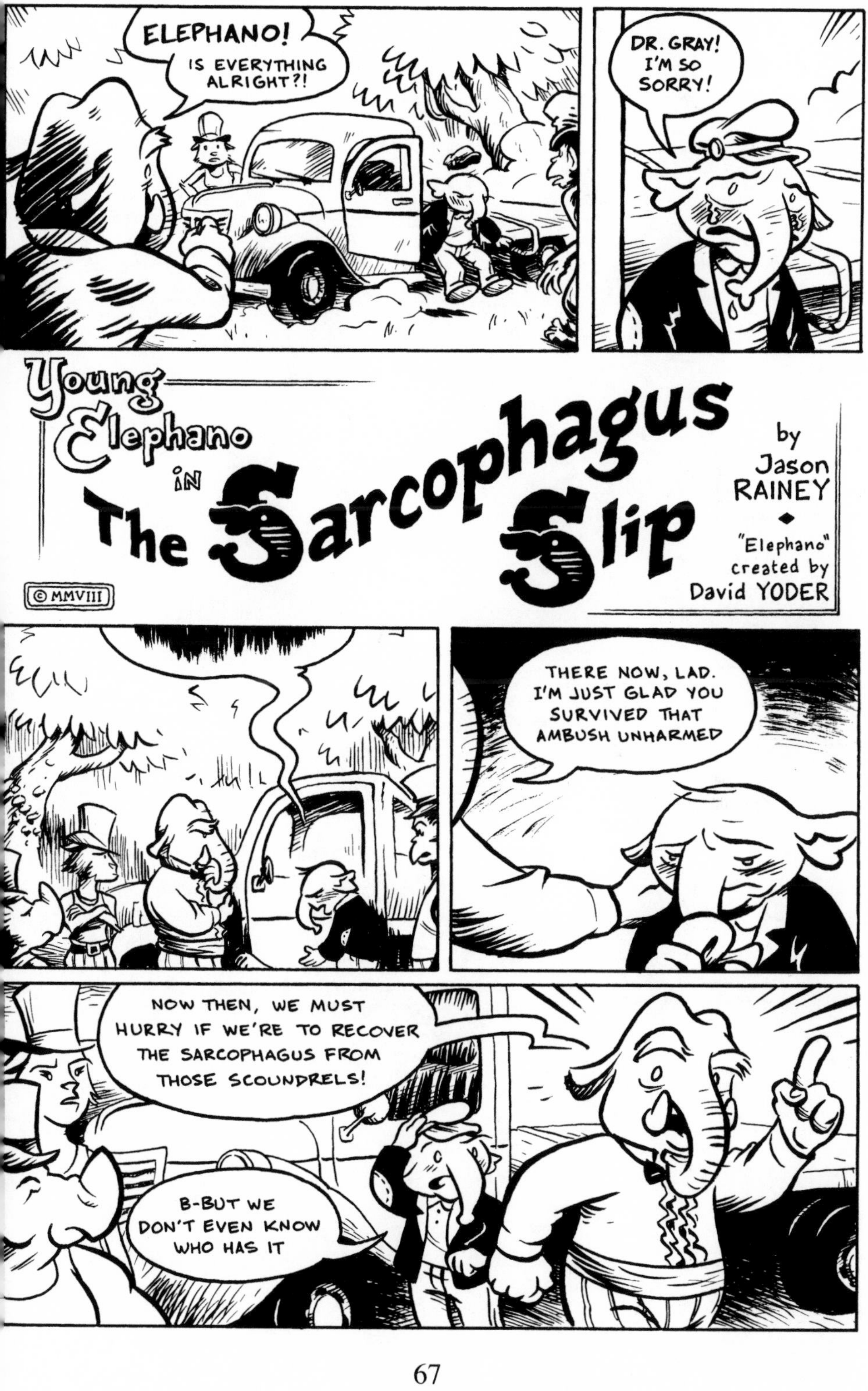
ELEPHANO! IS EVERYTHING ALRIGHT?!
DR. GRAY! I'M SO SORRY!
Young Elephano in The Sarcophagus Slip
by Jason RAINEY
"Elephano" created by David YODER
© MMVIII
THERE NOW, LAD. I'M JUST GLAD YOU SURVIVED THAT AMBUSH UNHARMED
NOW THEN, WE MUST HURRY IF WE'RE TO RECOVER THE SARCOPHAGUS FROM THOSE SCOUNDRELS!
B-BUT WE DON'T EVEN KNOW WHO HAS IT

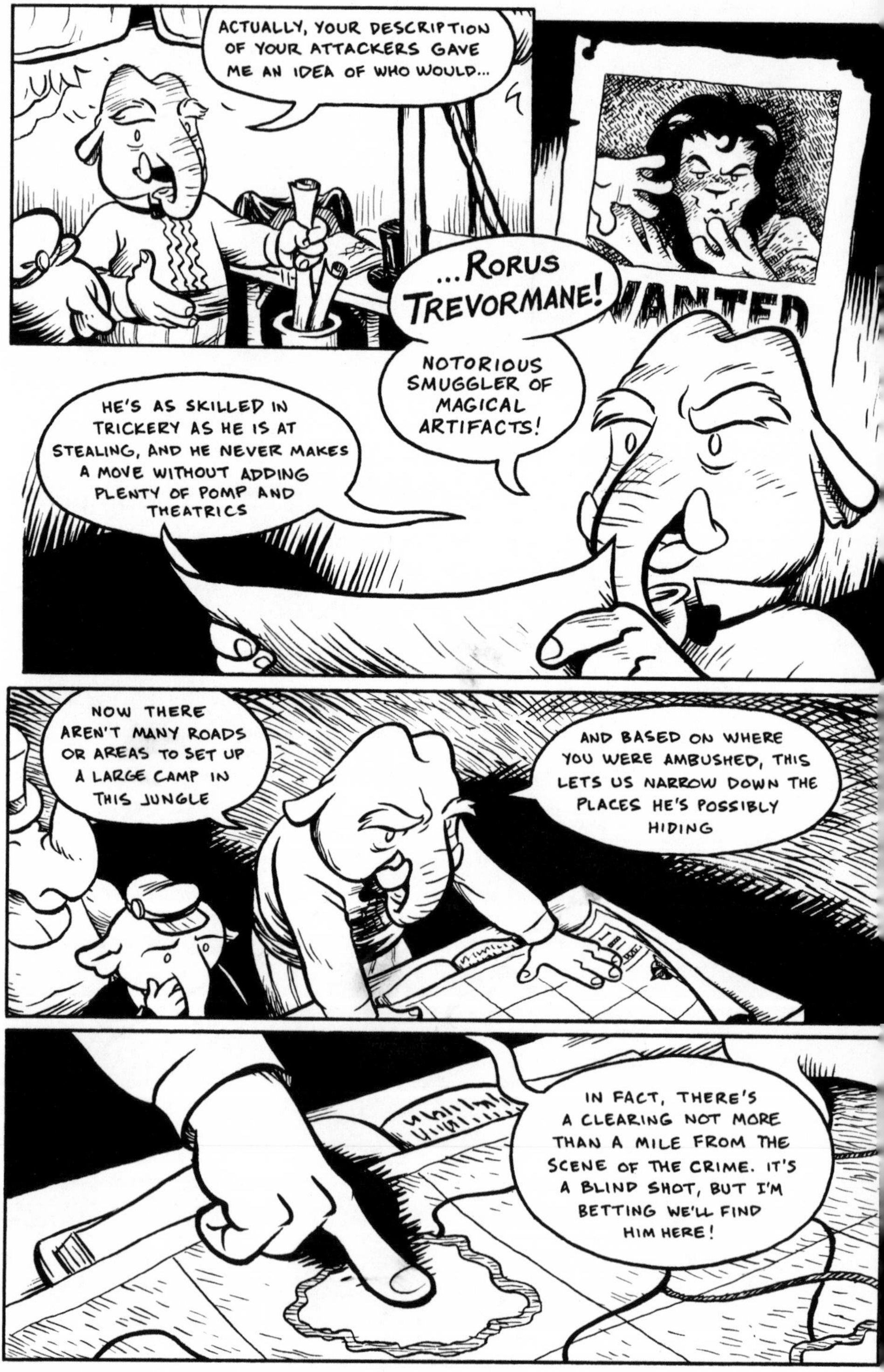
ACTUALLY, YOUR DESCRIPTION OF YOUR ATTACKERS GAVE ME AN IDEA OF WHO WOULD...
...RORUS TREVORMANE!
WANTED
NOTORIOUS SMUGGLER OF MAGICAL ARTIFACTS!
HE'S AS SKILLED IN TRICKERY AS HE IS AT STEALING, AND HE NEVER MAKES A MOVE WITHOUT ADDING PLENTY OF POMP AND THEATRICS
NOW THERE AREN'T MANY ROADS OR AREAS TO SET UP A LARGE CAMP IN THIS JUNGLE
AND BASED ON WHERE YOU WERE AMBUSHED, THIS LETS US NARROW DOWN THE PLACES HE'S POSSIBLY HIDING
IN FACT, THERE'S A CLEARING NOT MORE THAN A MILE FROM THE SCENE OF THE CRIME. IT'S A BLIND SHOT, BUT I'M BETTING WE'LL FIND HIM HERE!

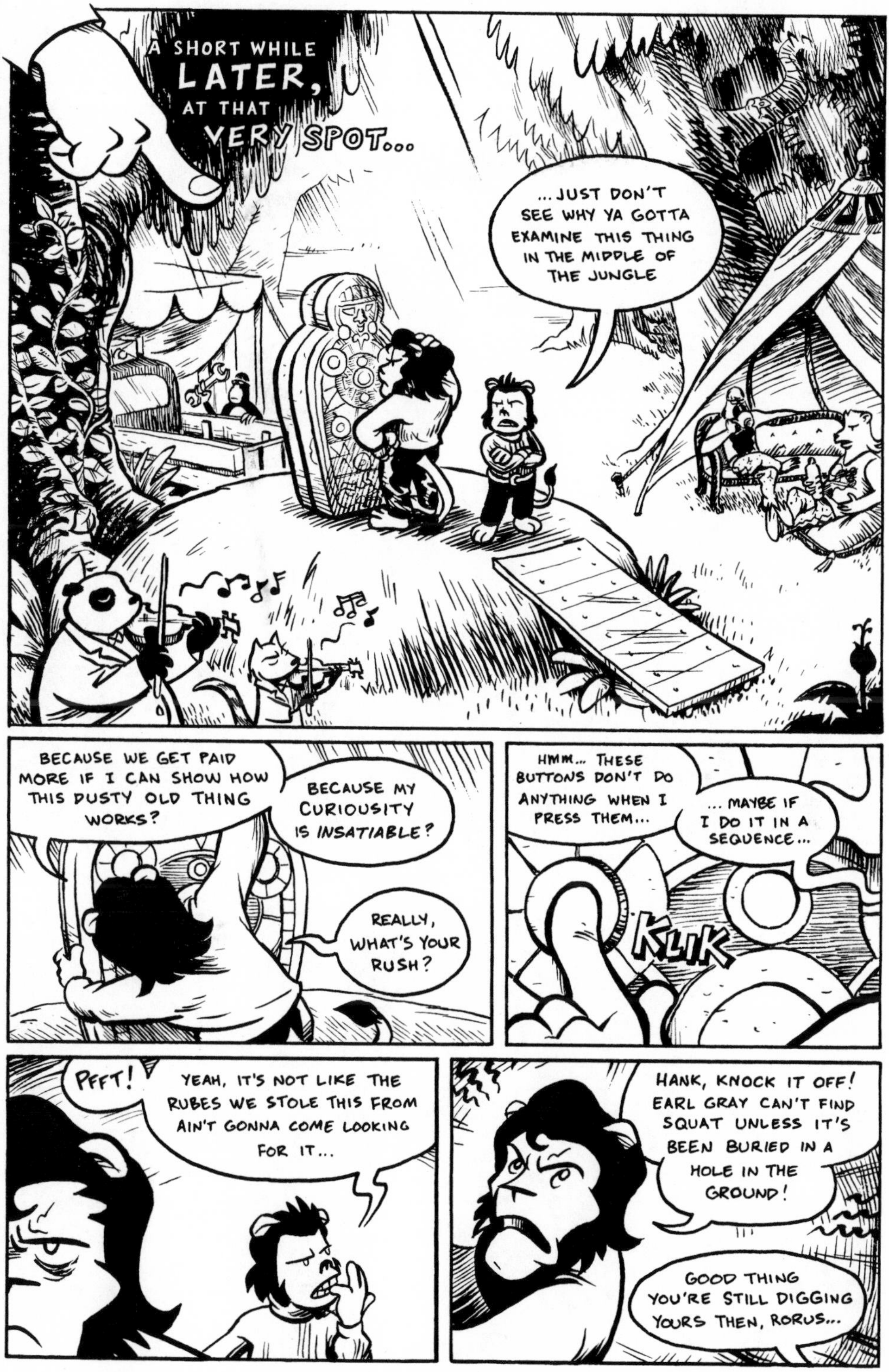
A SHORT WHILE LATER, AT THAT VERY SPOT...
...JUST DON'T SEE WHY YA GOTTA EXAMINE THIS THING IN THE MIDDLE OF THE JUNGLE
BECAUSE WE GET PAID MORE IF I CAN SHOW HOW THIS DUSTY OLD THING WORKS?
BECAUSE MY CURIOUSITY IS INSATIABLE?
REALLY, WHAT'S YOUR RUSH?
HMM... THESE BUTTONS DON'T DO ANYTHING WHEN I PRESS THEM...
...MAYBE IF I DO IT IN A SEQUENCE...
KLIK
PFFT!
YEAH, IT'S NOT LIKE THE RUBES WE STOLE THIS FROM AIN'T GONNA COME LOOKING FOR IT...
HANK, KNOCK IT OFF! EARL GRAY CAN'T FIND SQUAT UNLESS IT'S BEEN BURIED IN A HOLE IN THE GROUND!
GOOD THING YOU'RE STILL DIGGING YOURS THEN, RORUS...

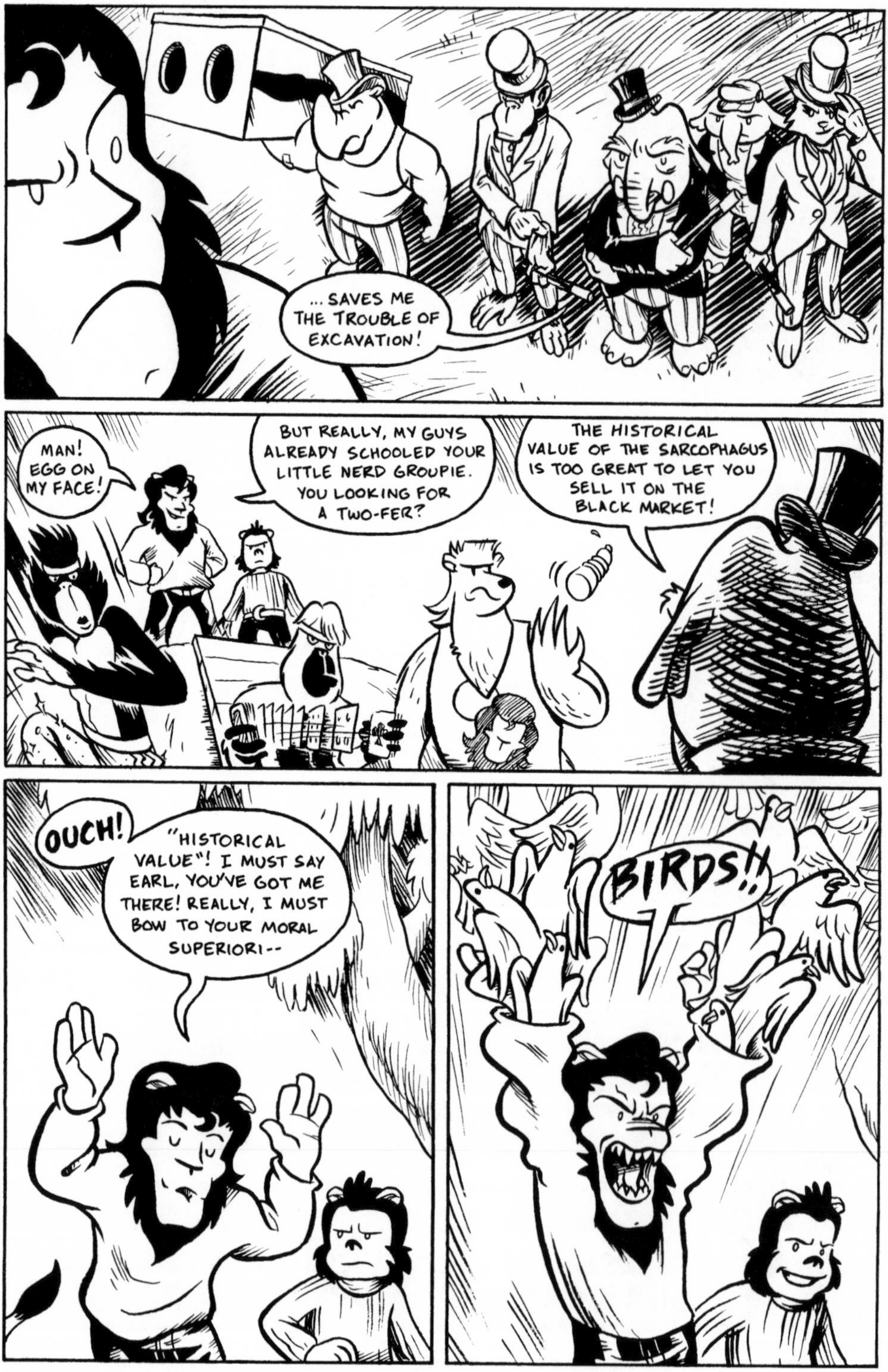

...SAVES ME THE TROUBLE OF EXCAVATION!
MAN! EGG ON MY FACE!
BUT REALLY, MY GUYS ALREADY SCHOOLED YOUR LITTLE NERD GROUPIE. YOU LOOKING FOR A TWO-FER?
THE HISTORICAL VALUE OF THE SARCOPHAGUS IS TOO GREAT TO LET YOU SELL IT ON THE BLACK MARKET!
OUCH!
"HISTORICAL VALUE"! I MUST SAY EARL, YOU'VE GOT ME THERE! REALLY, I MUST BOW TO YOUR MORAL SUPERIORI--
BIRDS!!

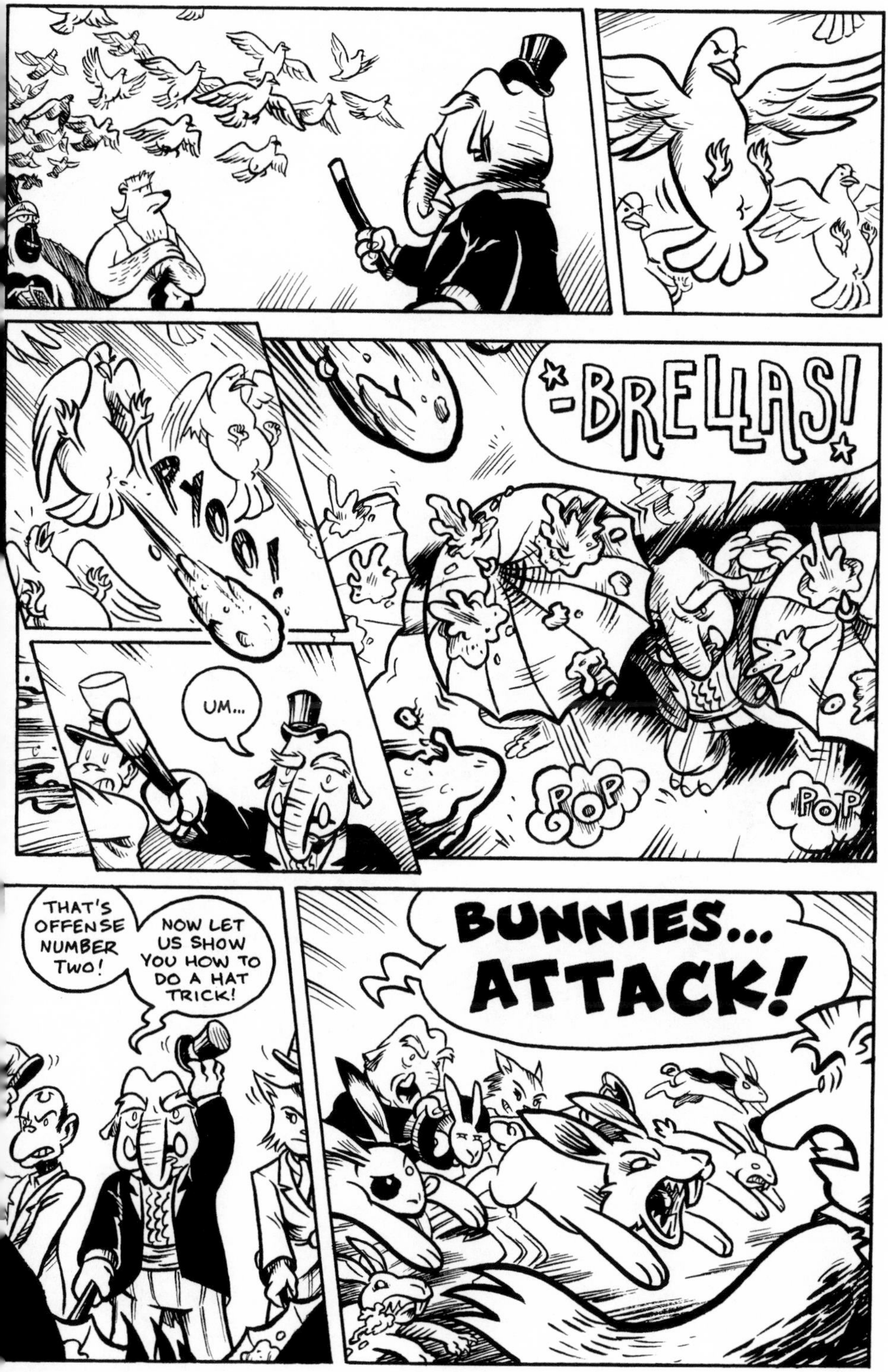
PYOO!
-BRELLAS!
UM...
POP
POP
THAT'S OFFENSE NUMBER TWO!
NOW LET US SHOW YOU HOW TO DO A HAT TRICK!
BUNNIES... ATTACK!

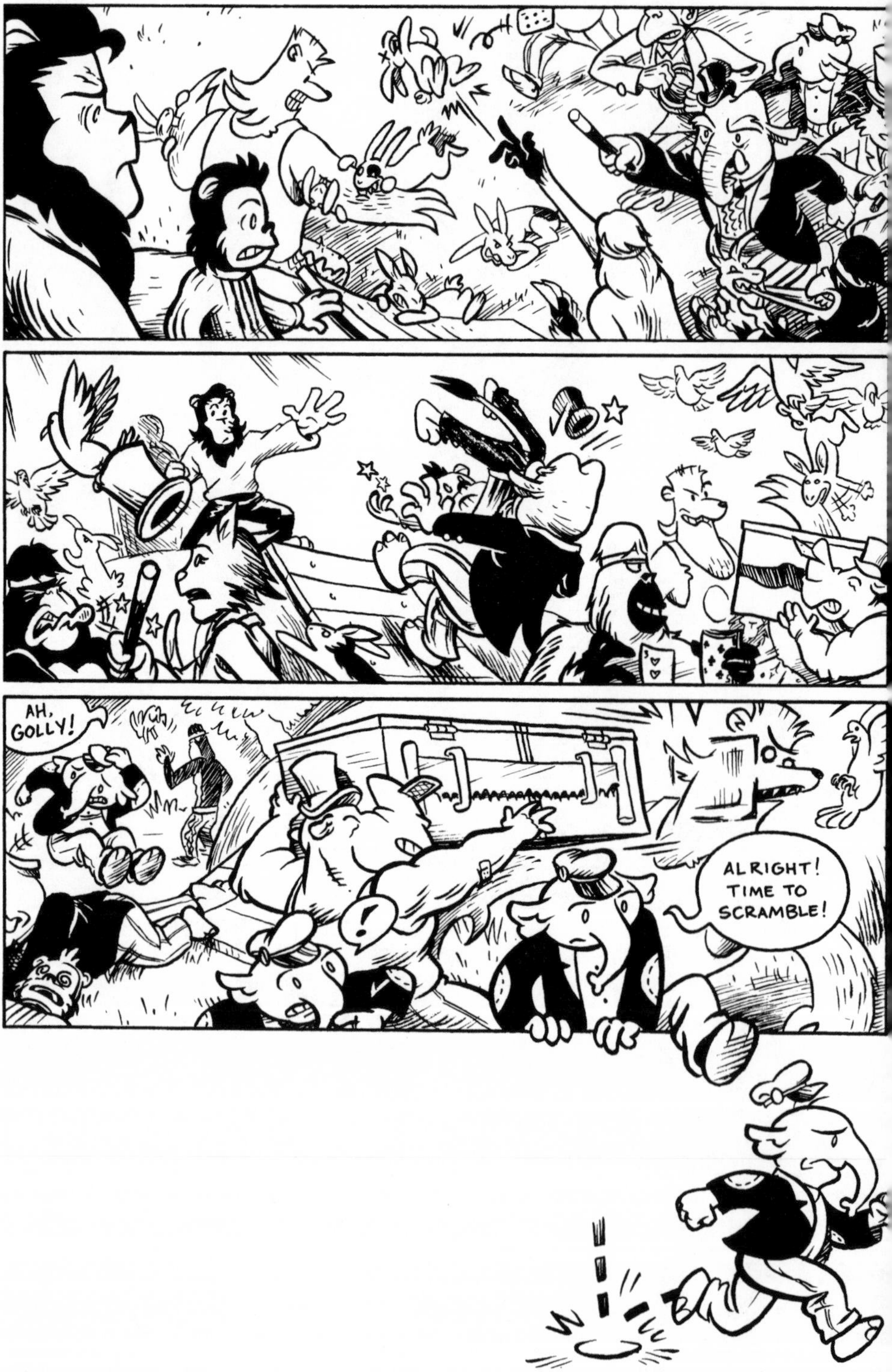
AH, GOLLY!
ALRIGHT! TIME TO SCRAMBLE!

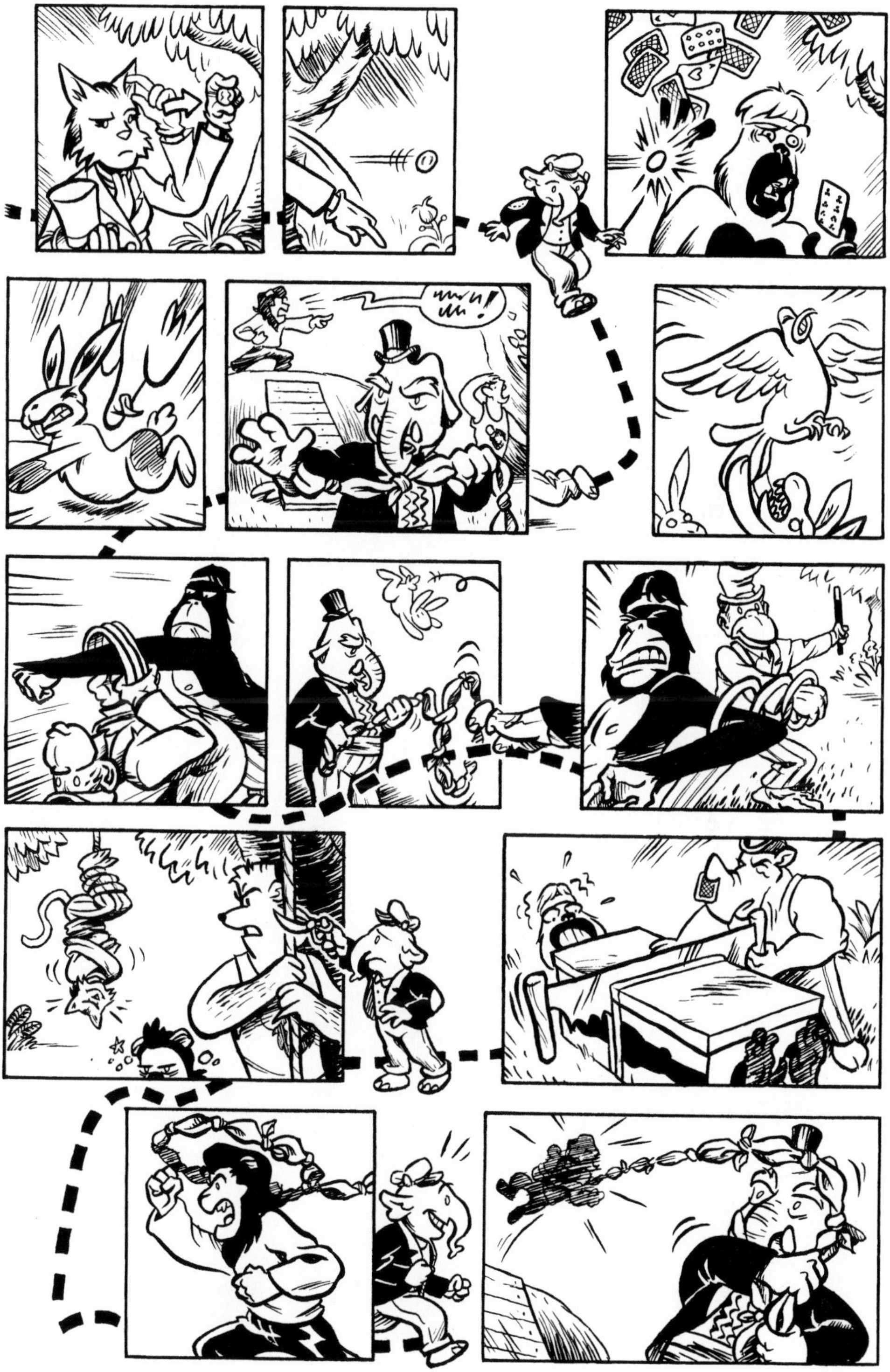

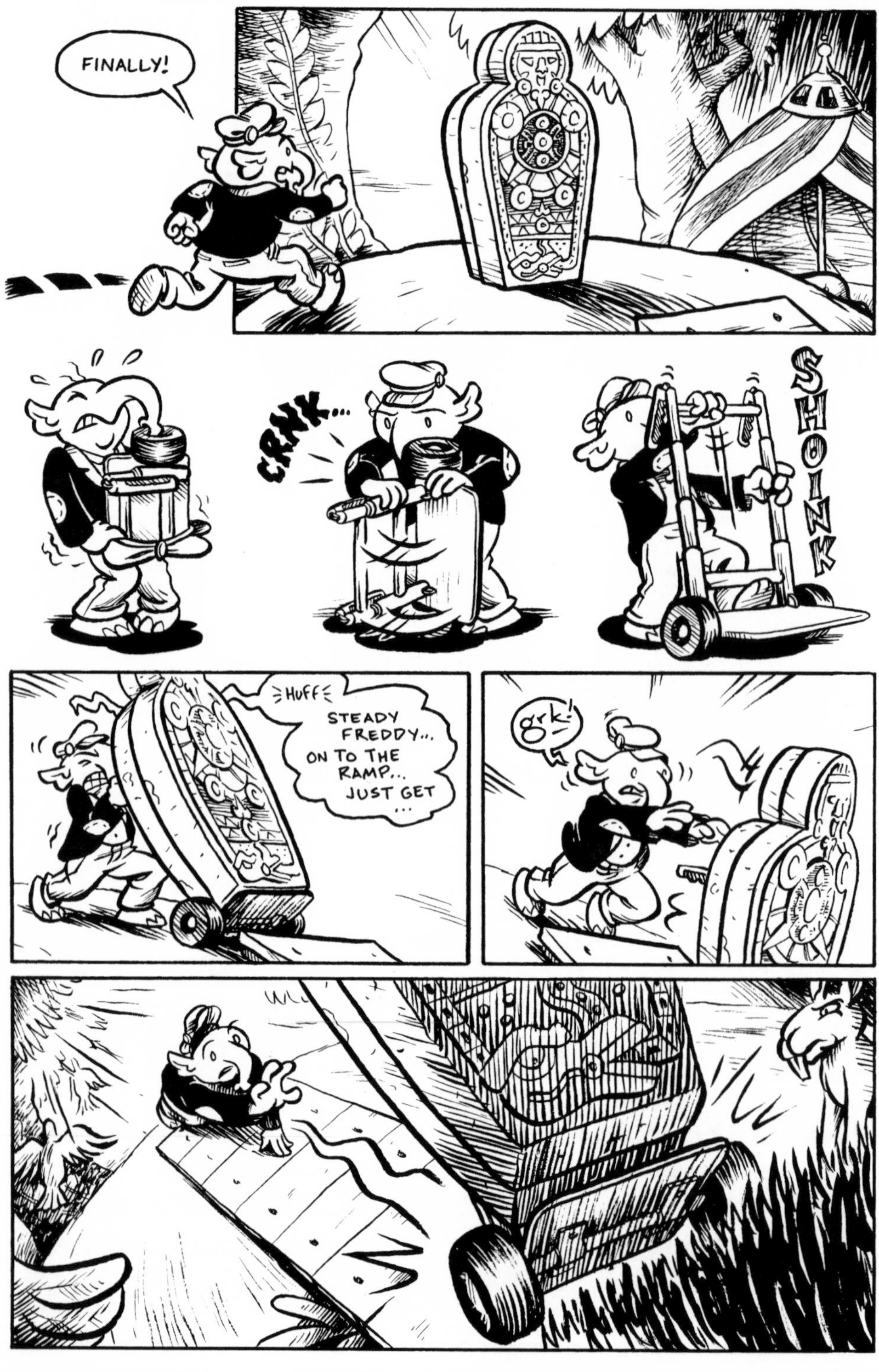
FINALLY!
CRNK...
SHOINK
HUFF
STEADY FREDDY... ON TO THE RAMP... JUST GET ...
grk!

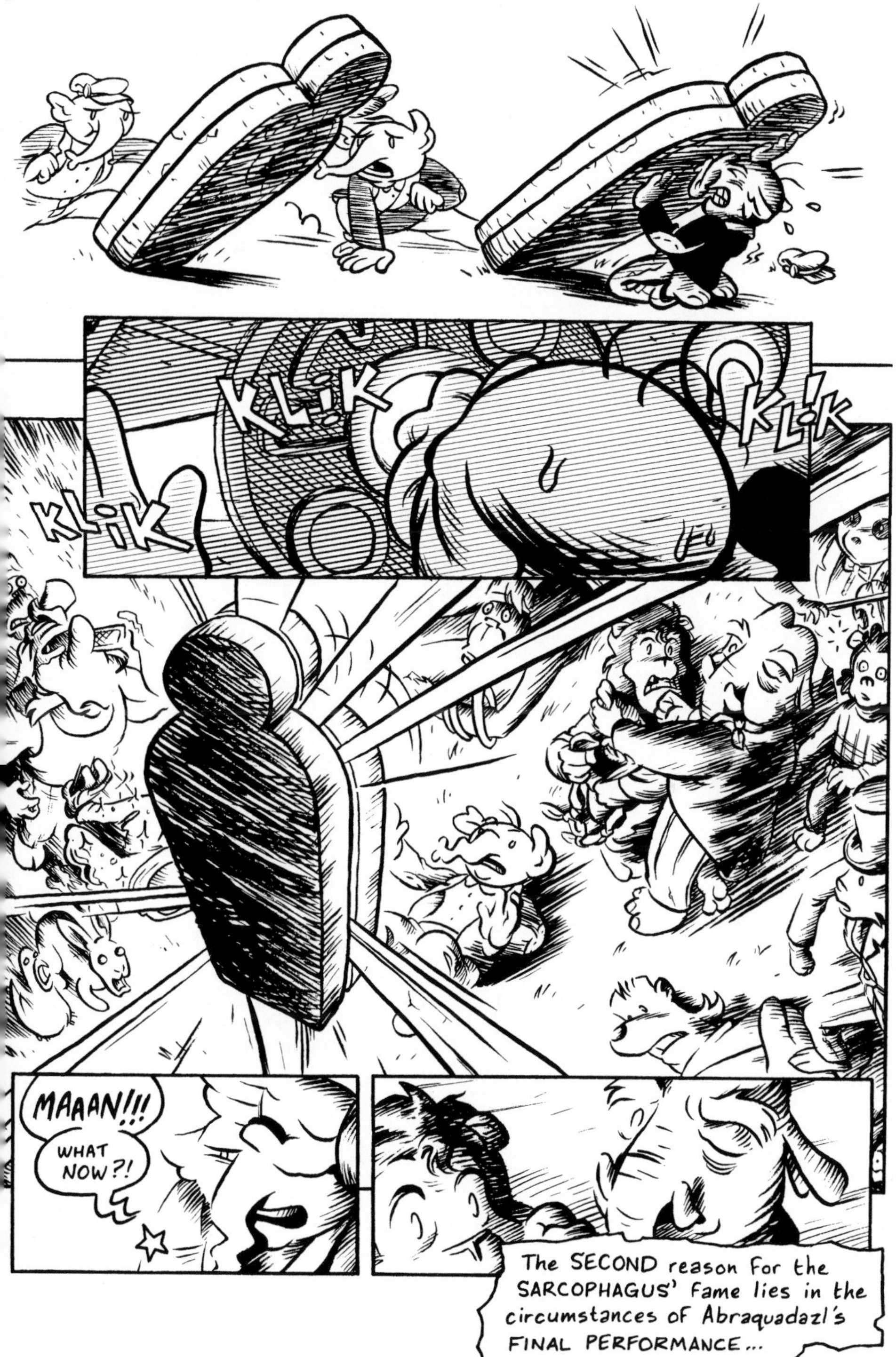
KLIK
KLIK
KLIK
MAAAN!!!
WHAT NOW?!
The SECOND reason for the SARCOPHAGUS' fame lies in the circumstances of Abraquadazl's FINAL PERFORMANCE...

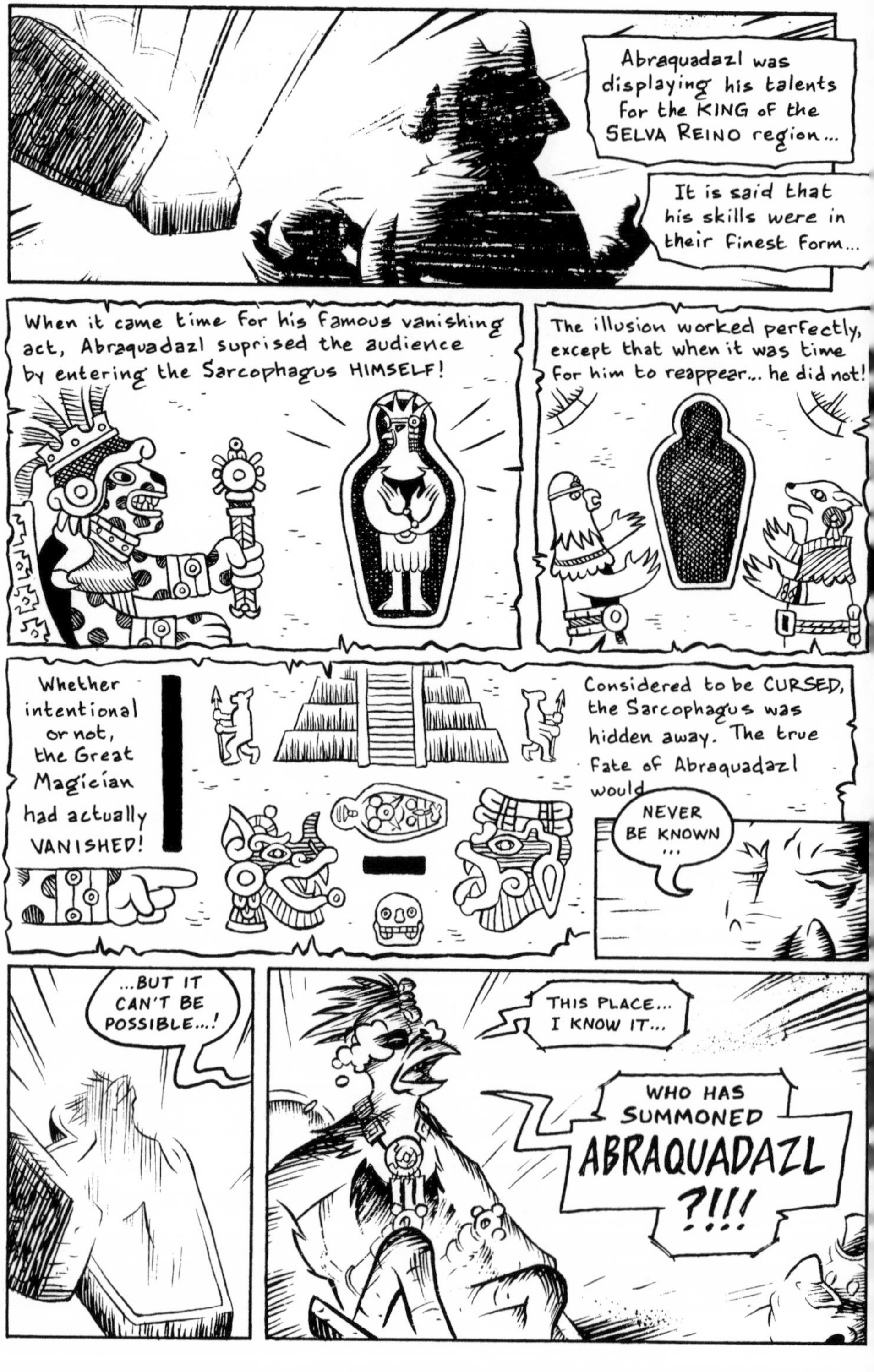
Abraquadazl was displaying his talents for the KING of the SELVA REINO region...
It is said that his skills were in their finest form...
When it came time for his famous vanishing act, Abraquadazl suprised the audience by entering the Sarcophagus HIMSELF!
The illusion worked perfectly, except that when it was time for him to reappear... he did not!
Whether intentional or not, the Great Magician had actually VANISHED!
Considered to be CURSED, the Sarcophagus was hidden away. The true fate of Abraquadazl would
NEVER BE KNOWN ...
...BUT IT CAN'T BE POSSIBLE...!
THIS PLACE... I KNOW IT...
WHO HAS SUMMONED ABRAQUADAZL ?!!!

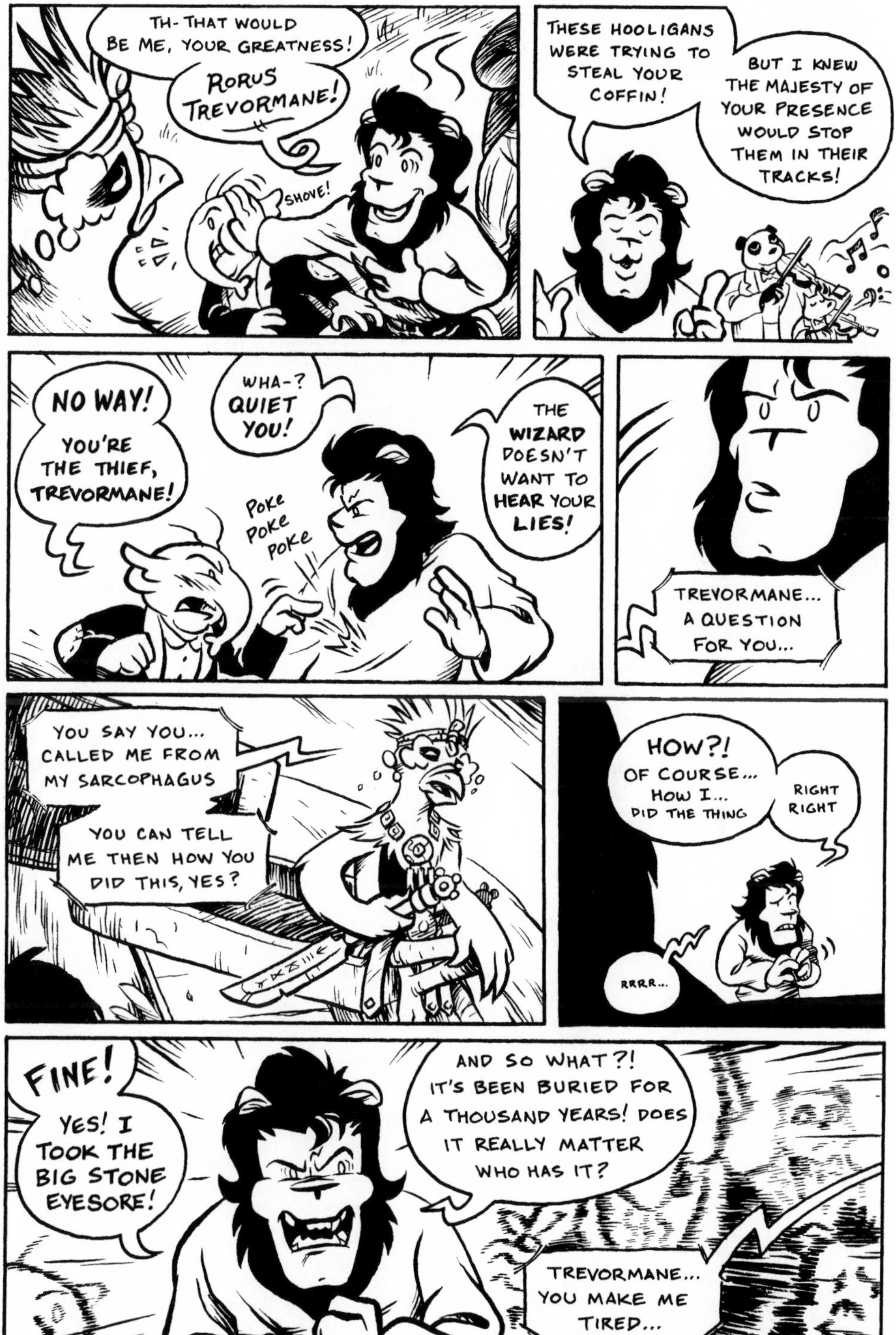
TH- THAT WOULD BE ME, YOUR GREATNESS!
RORUS TREVORMANE!
SHOVE!
THESE HOOLIGANS WERE TRYING TO STEAL YOUR COFFIN!
BUT I KNEW THE MAJESTY OF YOUR PRESENCE WOULD STOP THEM IN THEIR TRACKS!
NO WAY!
YOU'RE THE THIEF, TREVORMANE!
WHA-? QUIET YOU!
POKE POKE POKE
THE WIZARD DOESN'T WANT TO HEAR YOUR LIES!
TREVORMANE... A QUESTION FOR YOU...
YOU SAY YOU... CALLED ME FROM MY SARCOPHAGUS
YOU CAN TELL ME THEN HOW YOU DID THIS, YES?
HOW?!
OF COURSE... HOW I... DID THE THING
RIGHT RIGHT
RRRR...
FINE!
YES! I TOOK THE BIG STONE EYESORE!
AND SO WHAT?! IT'S BEEN BURIED FOR A THOUSAND YEARS! DOES IT REALLY MATTER WHO HAS IT?
TREVORMANE... YOU MAKE ME TIRED...

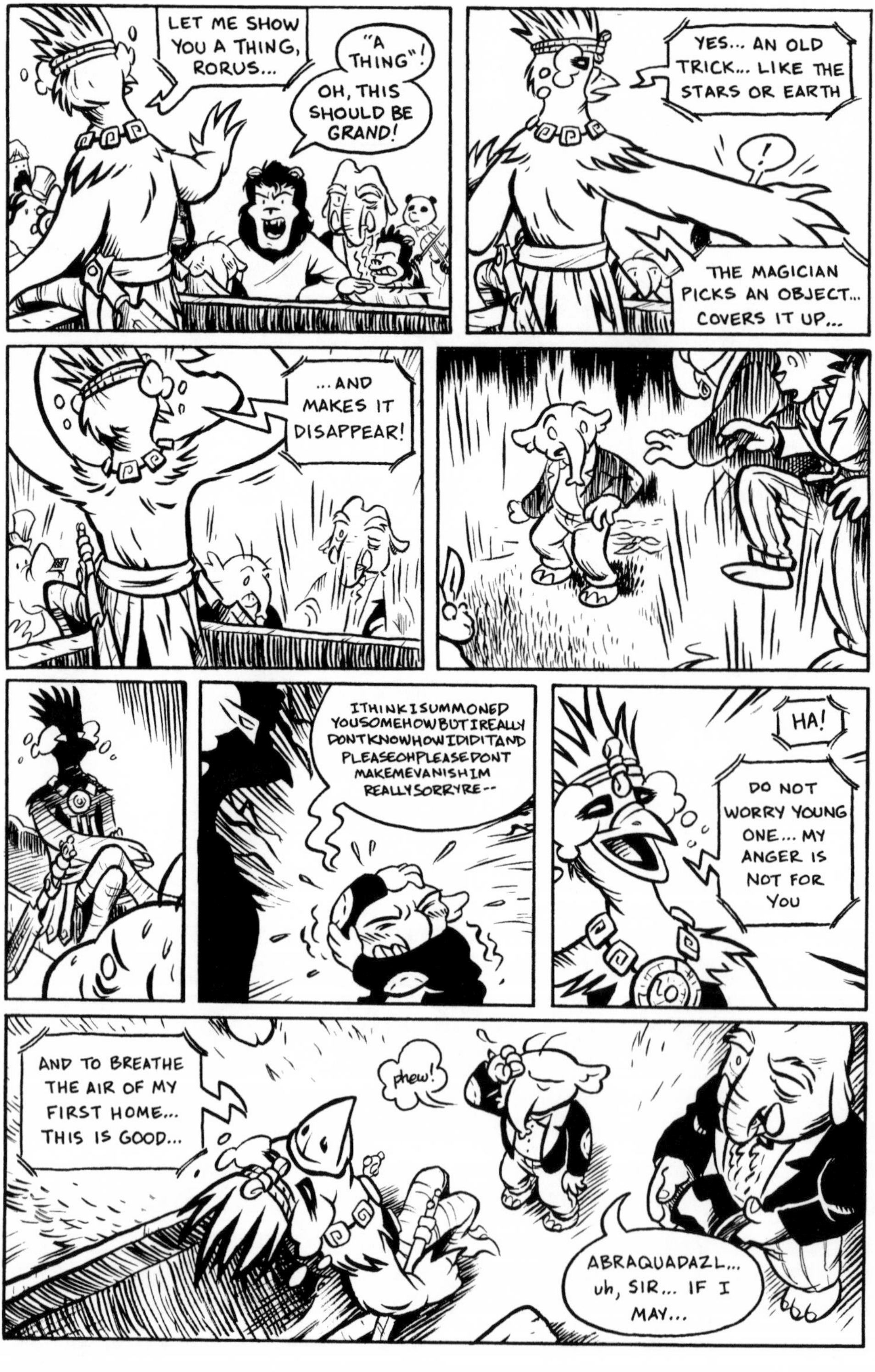

LET ME SHOW YOU A THING, RORUS...
"A THING"!
OH, THIS SHOULD BE GRAND!
YES... AN OLD TRICK... LIKE THE STARS OR EARTH
!
THE MAGICIAN PICKS AN OBJECT... COVERS IT UP...
...AND MAKES IT DISAPPEAR!
ITHINKISUMMONED YOUSOMEHOWBUTIREALLY DONTKNOWHOWIDIDITAND PLEASEOHPLEASEDONT MAKEMEVANISHIM REALLYSORRYRE--
HA!
DO NOT WORRY YOUNG ONE... MY ANGER IS NOT FOR YOU
AND TO BREATHE THE AIR OF MY FIRST HOME... THIS IS GOOD...
phew!
ABRAQUADAZL... uh, SIR... IF I MAY...

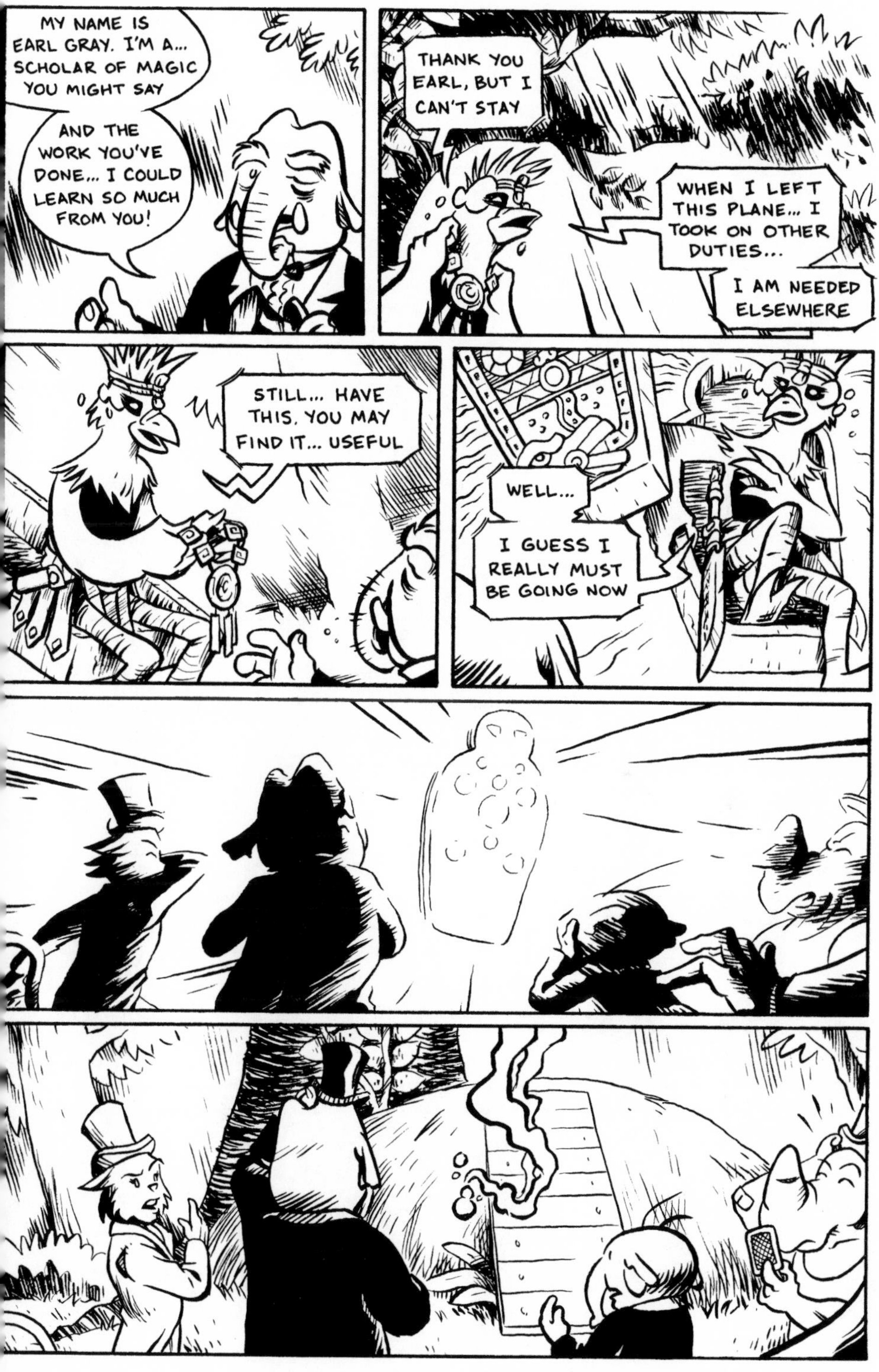
MY NAME IS EARL GRAY. I'M A... SCHOLAR OF MAGIC YOU MIGHT SAY
AND THE WORK YOU'VE DONE... I COULD LEARN SO MUCH FROM YOU!
THANK YOU EARL, BUT I CAN'T STAY
WHEN I LEFT THIS PLANE... I TOOK ON OTHER DUTIES...
I AM NEEDED ELSEWHERE
STILL... HAVE THIS. YOU MAY FIND IT... USEFUL
WELL...
I GUESS I REALLY MUST BE GOING NOW

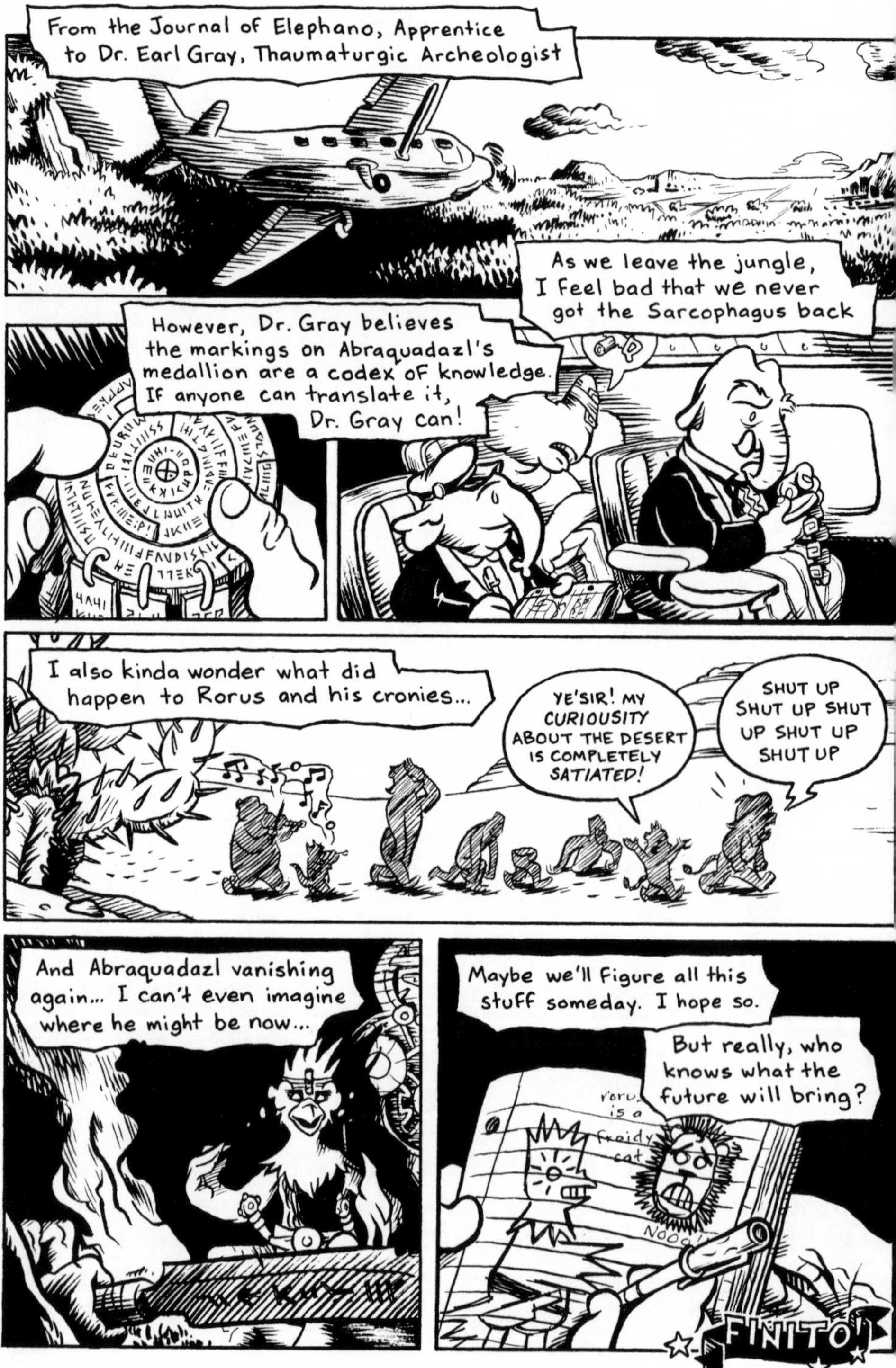
From the Journal of Elephano, Apprentice to Dr. Earl Gray, Thaumaturgic Archeologist
As we leave the jungle, I feel bad that we never got the Sarcophagus back
However, Dr. Gray believes the markings on Abraquadazl's medallion are a codex of knowledge. If anyone can translate it, Dr. Gray can!
I also kinda wonder what did happen to Rorus and his cronies...
YE'SIR! MY CURIOUSITY ABOUT THE DESERT IS COMPLETELY SATIATED!
SHUT UP SHUT UP SHUT UP SHUT UP SHUT UP
And Abraquadazl vanishing again... I can't even imagine where he might be now...
Maybe we'll figure all this stuff someday. I hope so.
But really, who knows what the future will bring?
FINITO!

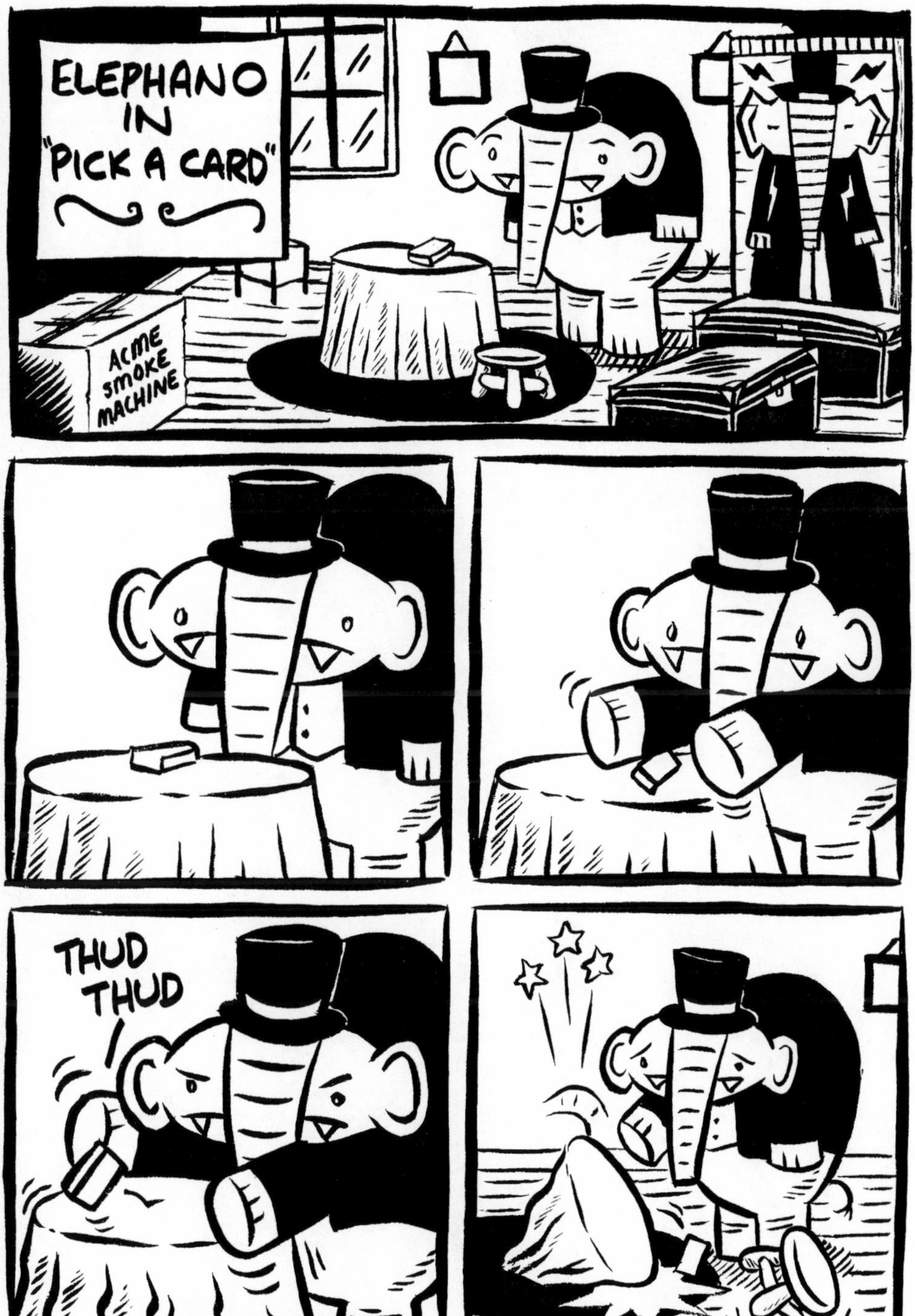
ELEPHANO
IN
"PICK A CARD"
ACME
SMOKE
MACHINE
THUD
THUD

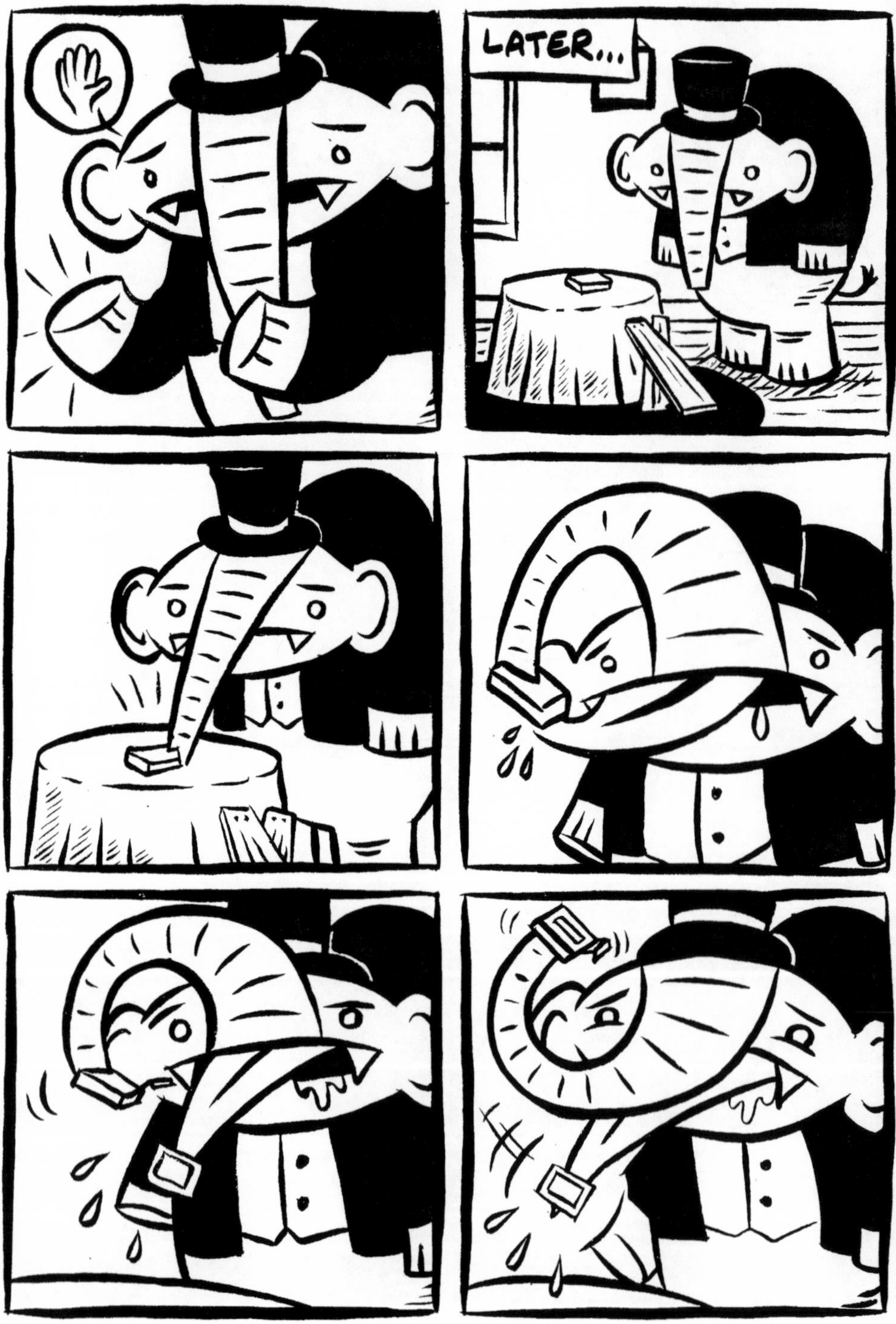
LATER...

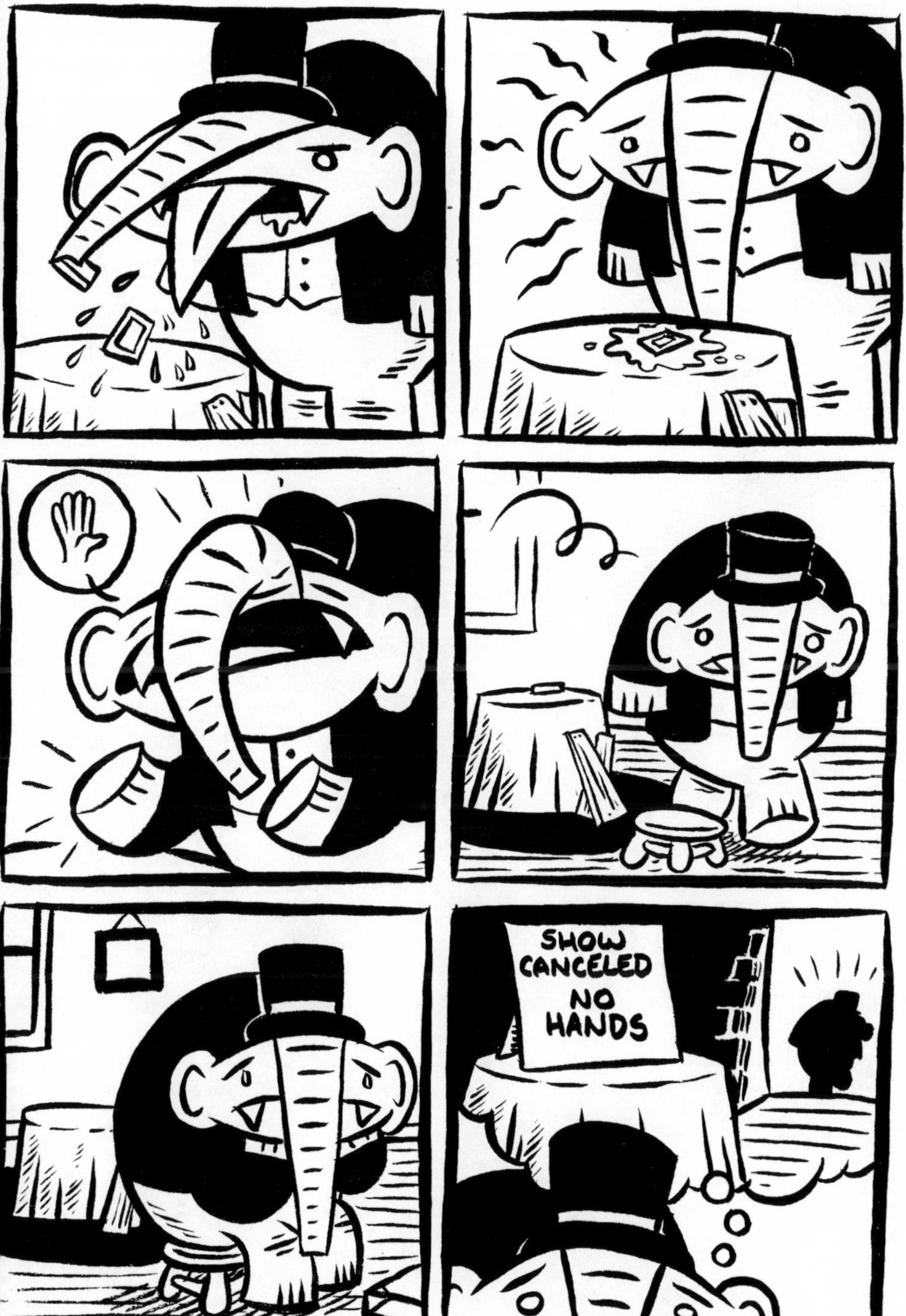
SHOW
CANCELED
NO
HANDS

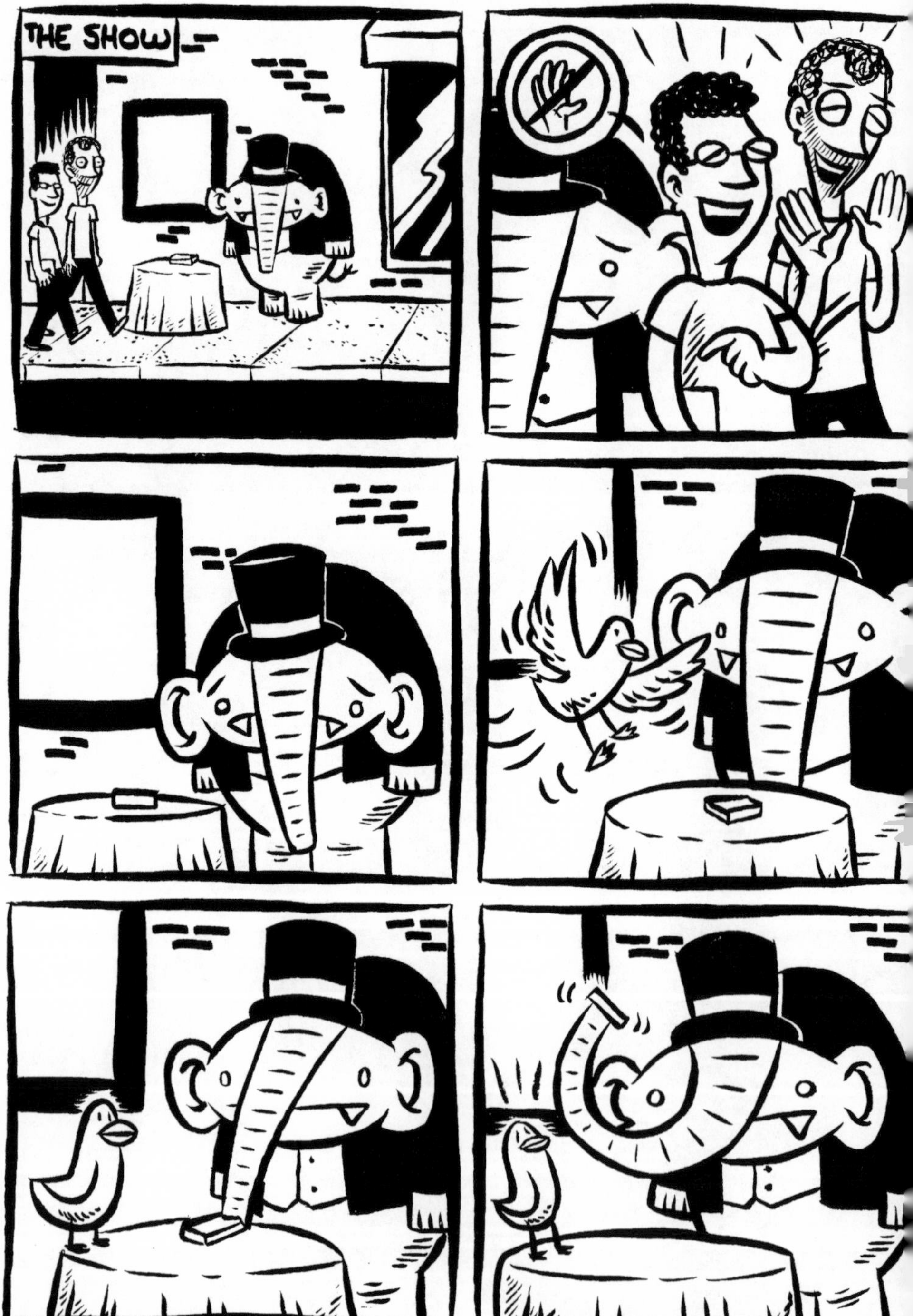
THE SHOW

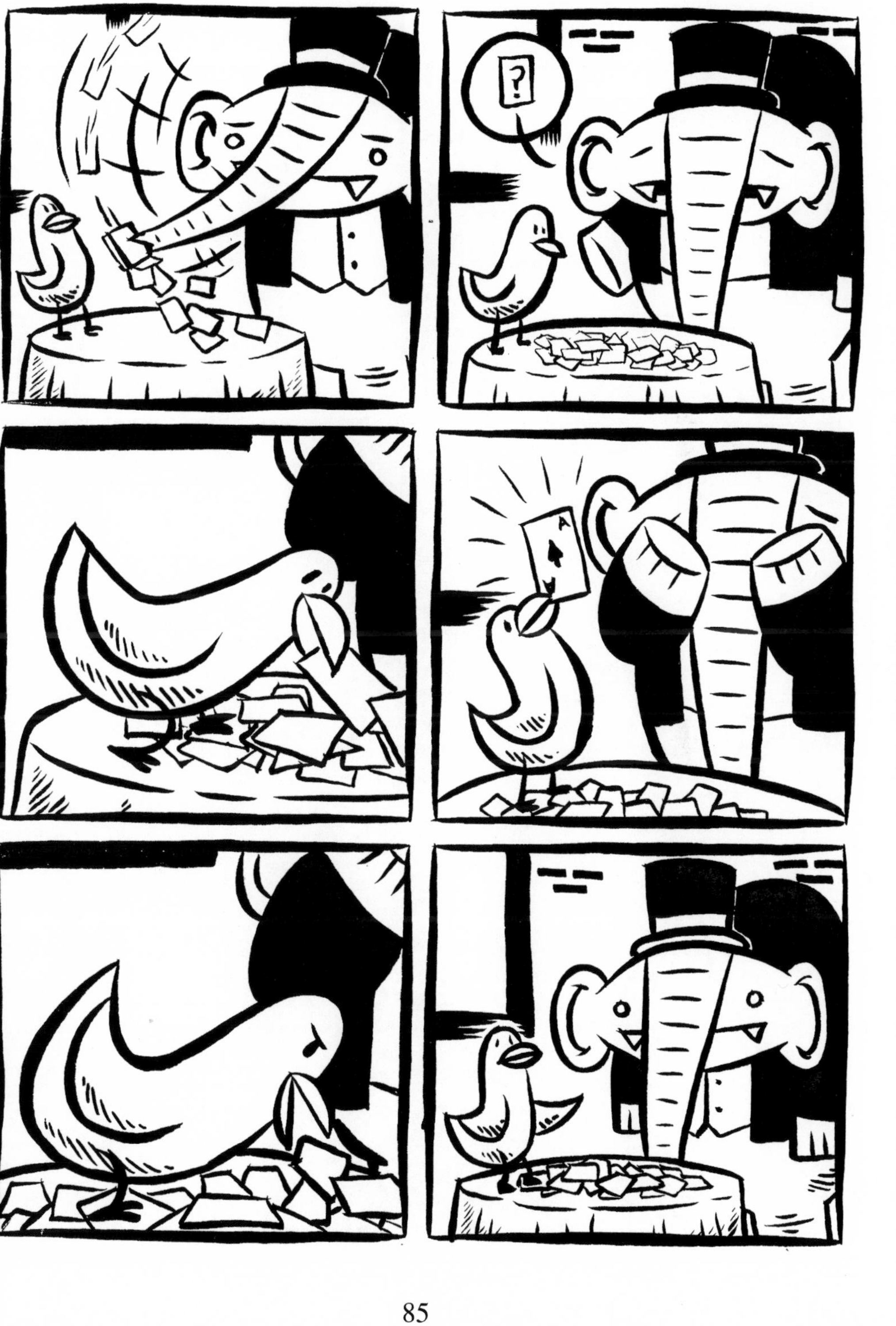
?

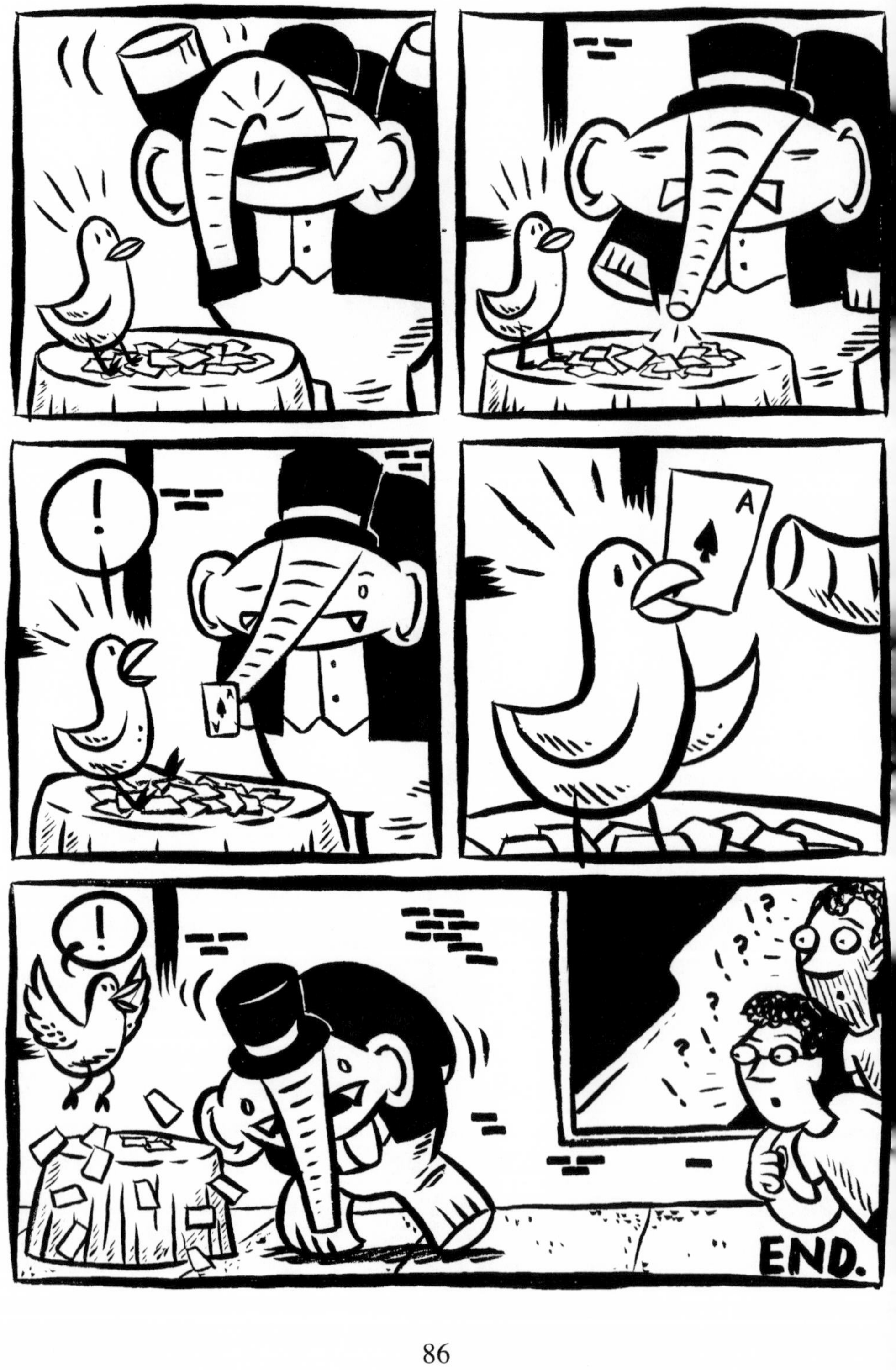
!
!
?
END.

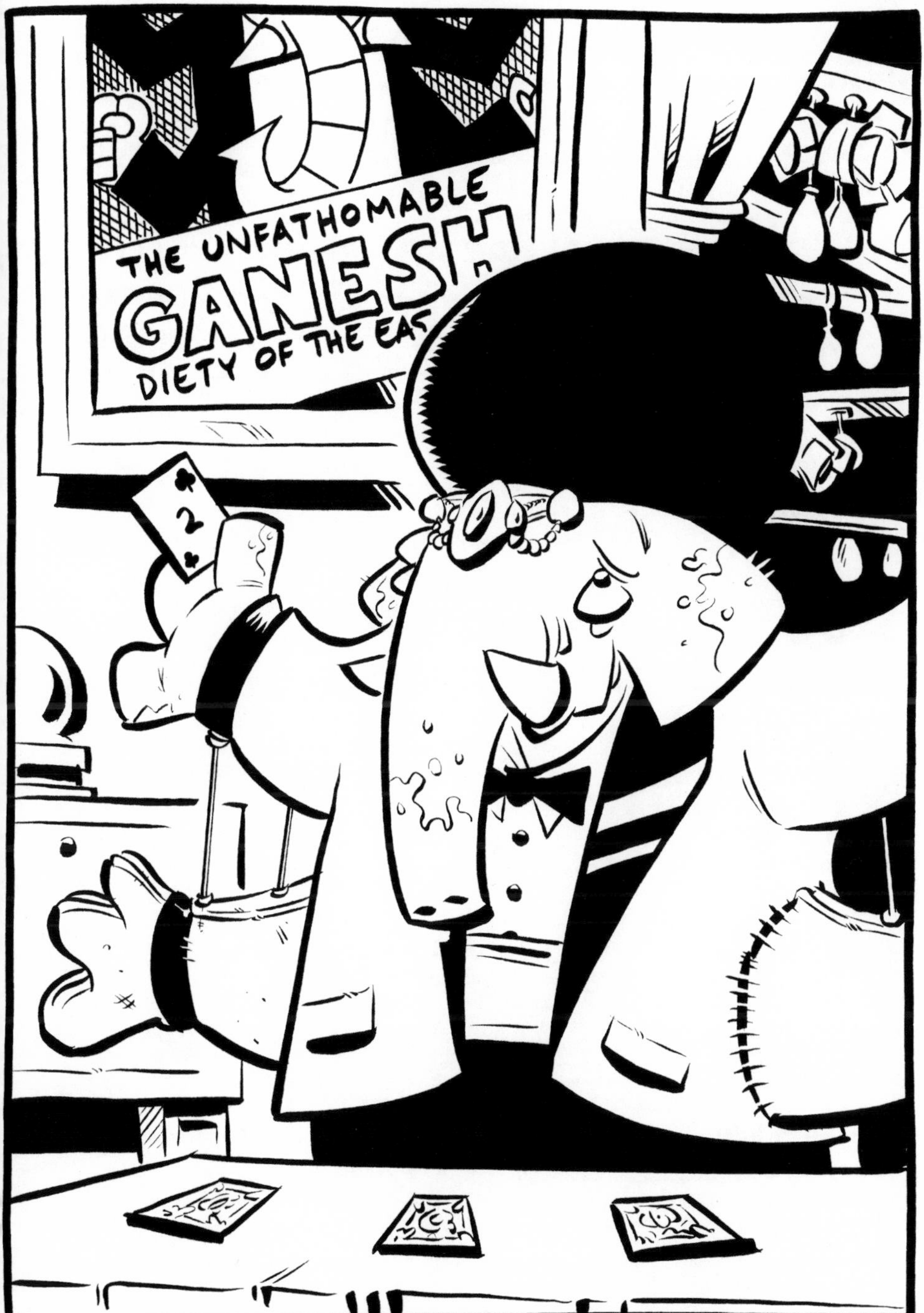
THE UNFATHOMABLE
GANESH
DIETY OF THE EAS

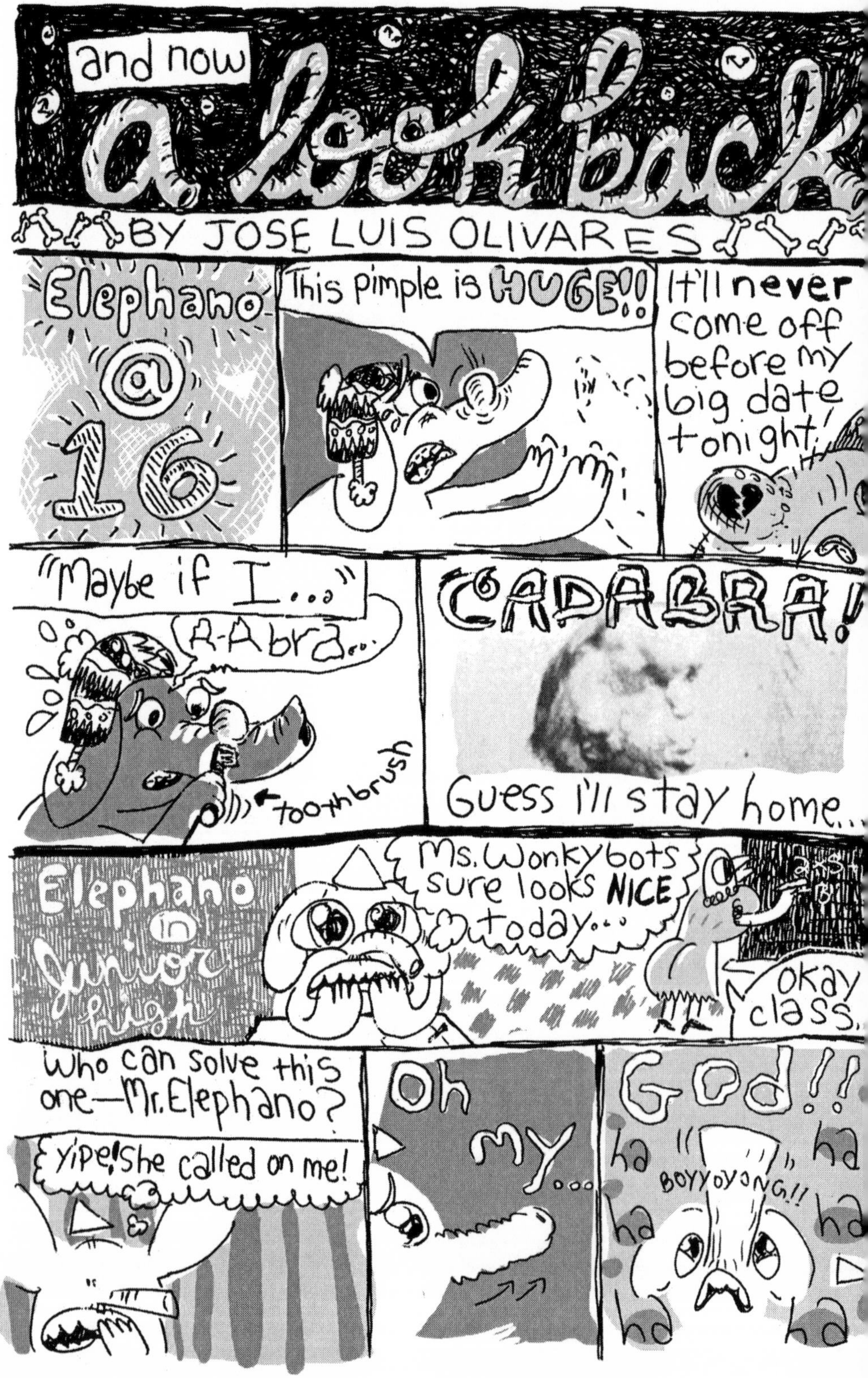
and now
a look back
BY JOSE LUIS OLIVARES
Elephano @ 16
This pimple is HUGE!!
It'll never come off before my big date tonight.
"Maybe if I..."
A-Abra...
toothbrush
CADABRA!
Guess I'll stay home...
Elephano in junior high
Ms. Wonkybots sure looks NICE today...
okay class.
Who can solve this one—Mr. Elephano?
Yipe! She called on me!
Oh my...
God!!
ha ha ha ha ha ha
BOYYOYONG!!

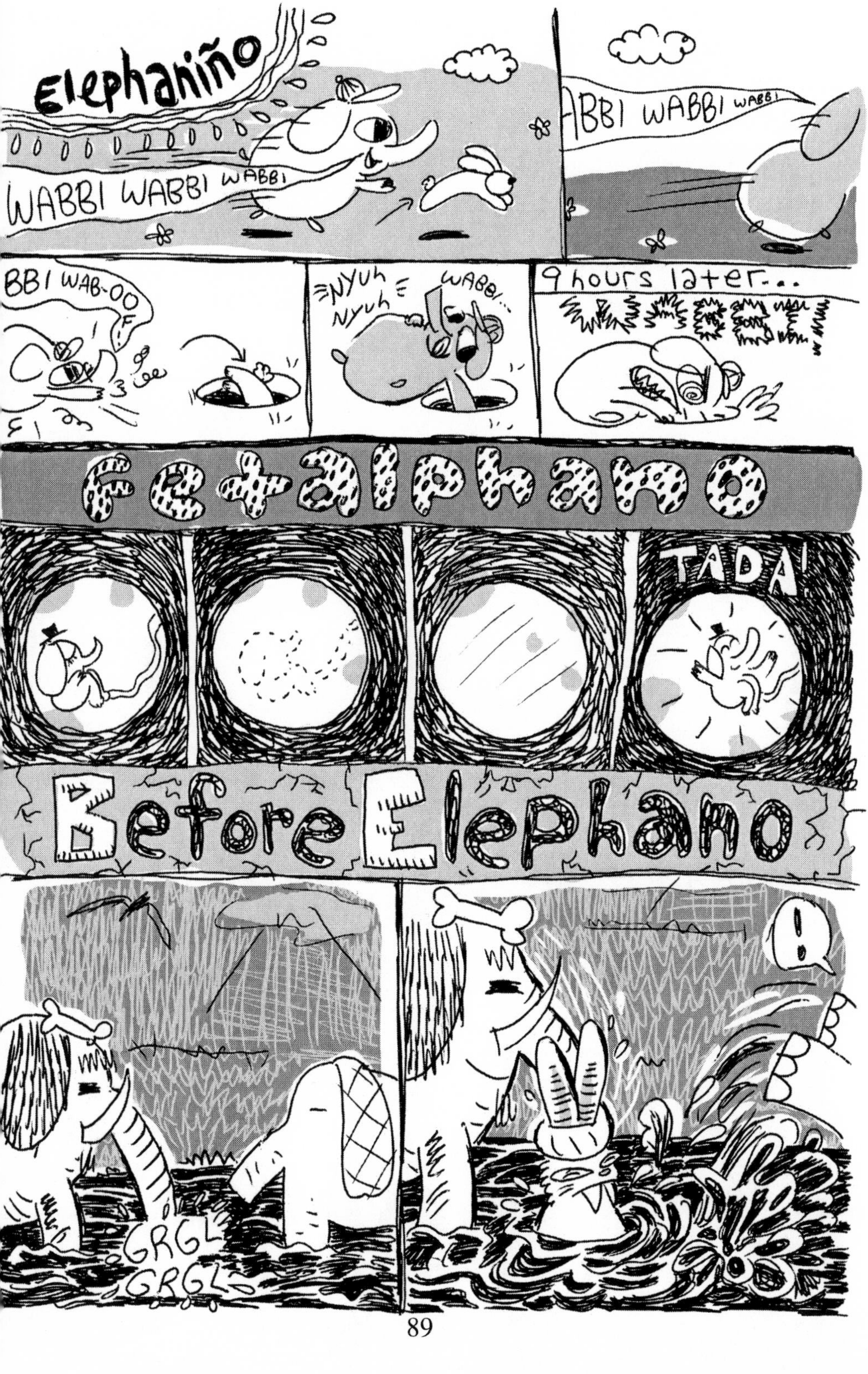
Elephaniño
WABBI WABBI WABBI
WABBI WABBI WABBI
BBI WAB-OOF
NYUH NYUH
WABBI...
9 hours later...
Fetalphano
TADA!
Before Elephano
!
GRGL GRGL

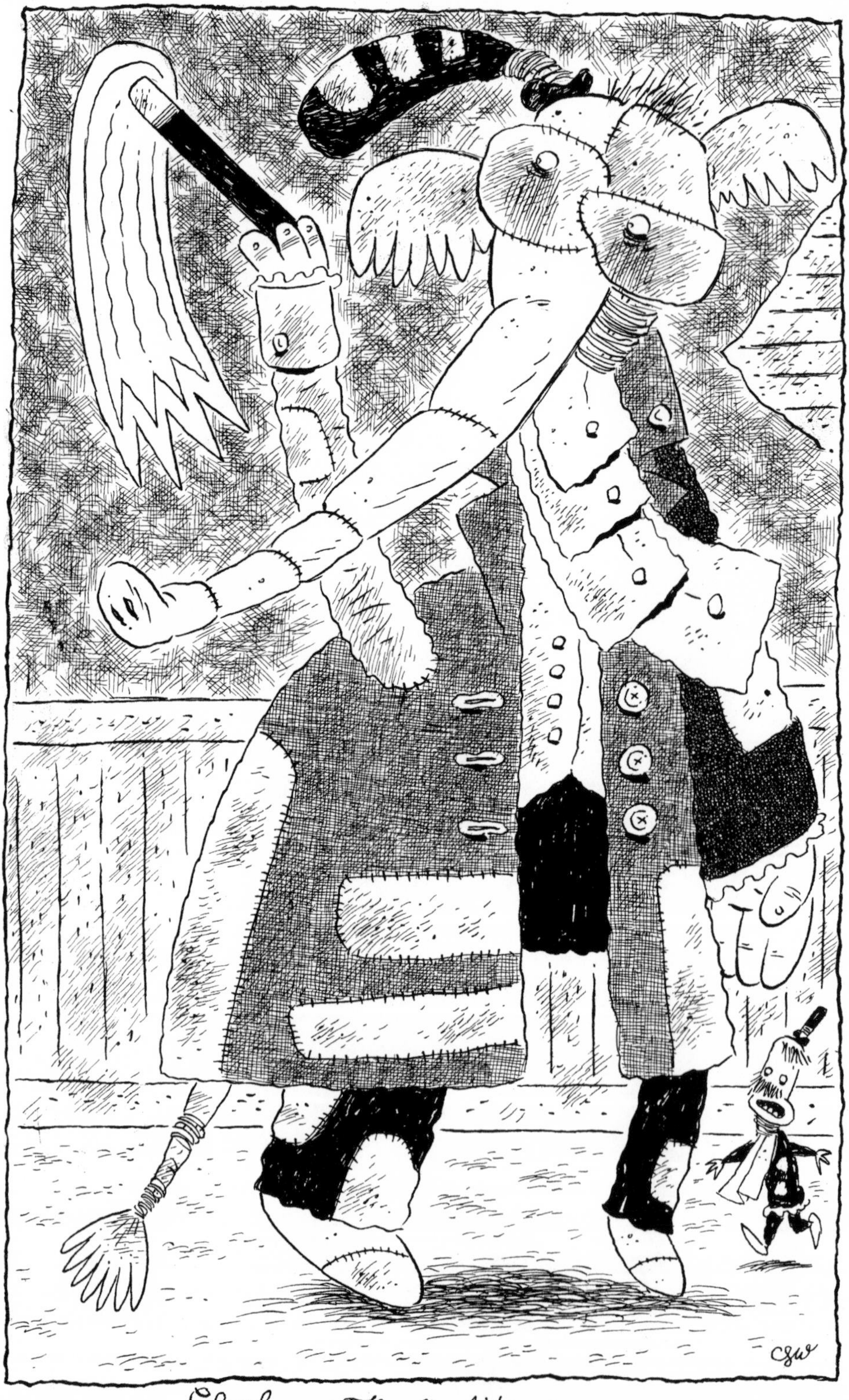
CGW

Elephano The Ambitious

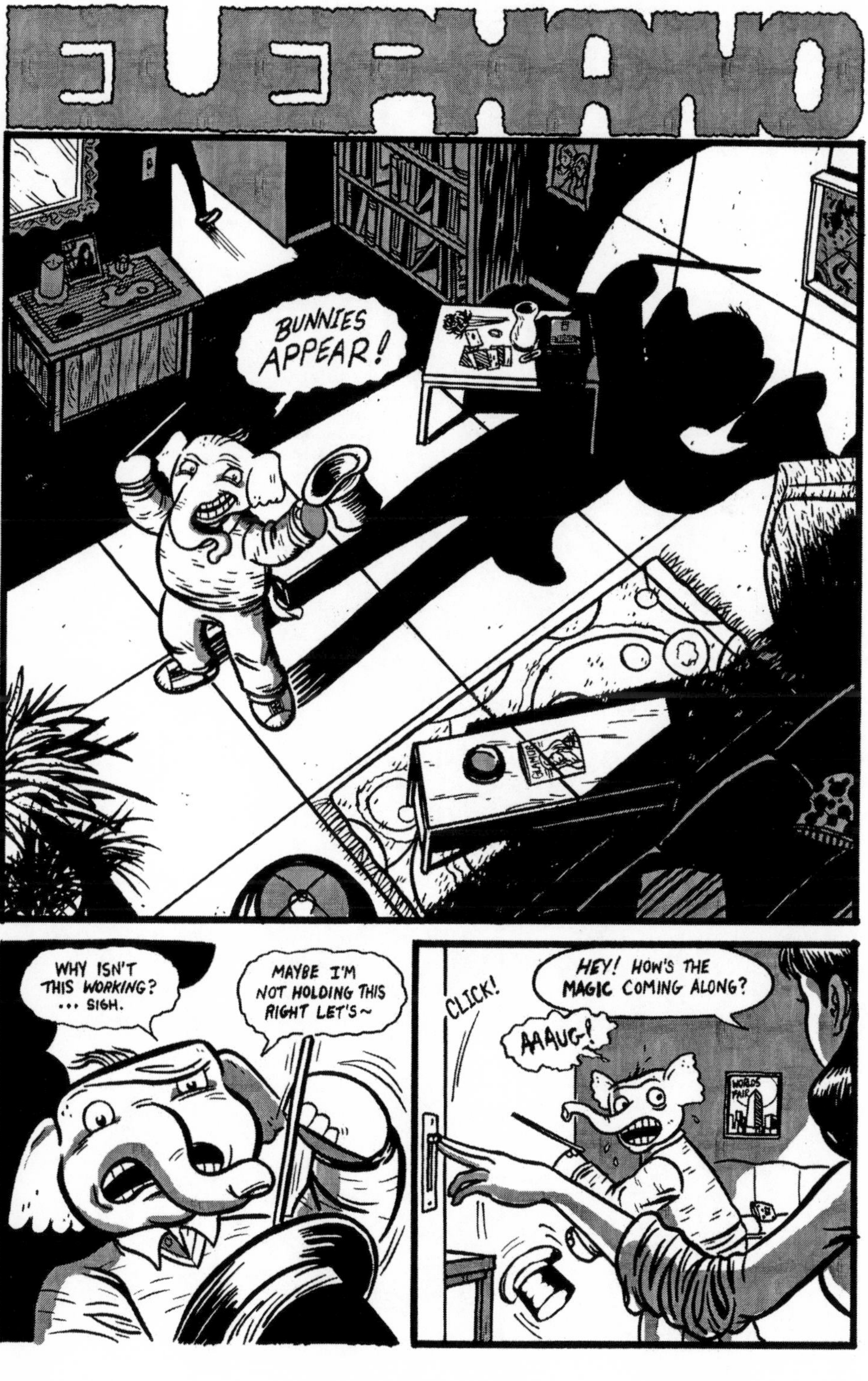
BUNNIES APPEAR!
WHY ISN'T THIS WORKING? ... SIGH.
MAYBE I'M NOT HOLDING THIS RIGHT LET'S~
CLICK!
HEY! HOW'S THE MAGIC COMING ALONG?
AAAUG!
WORLDS FAIR

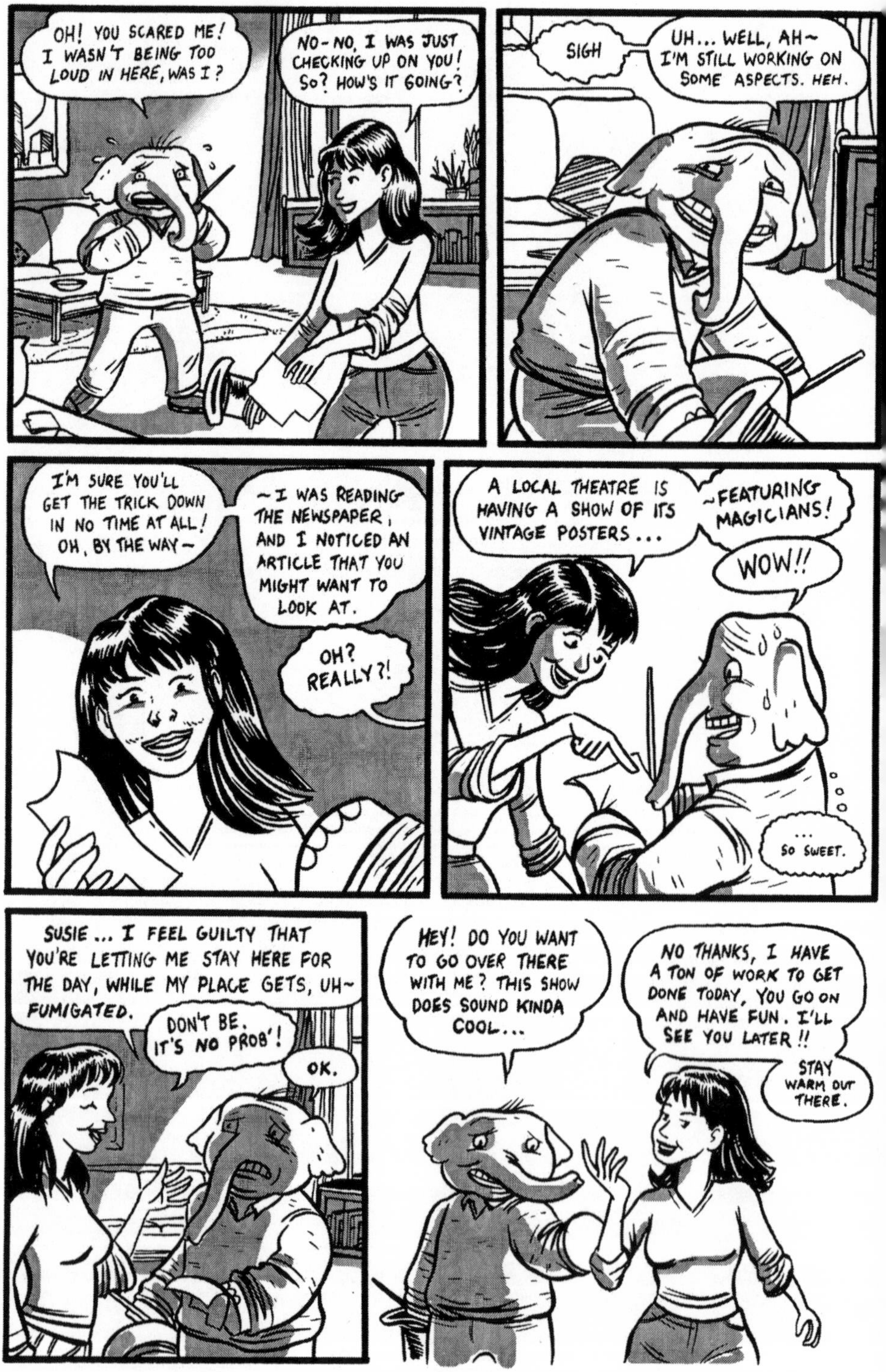
OH! YOU SCARED ME! I WASN'T BEING TOO LOUD IN HERE, WAS I?
NO-NO, I WAS JUST CHECKING UP ON YOU! SO? HOW'S IT GOING?
SIGH
UH... WELL, AH~ I'M STILL WORKING ON SOME ASPECTS. HEH.
I'M SURE YOU'LL GET THE TRICK DOWN IN NO TIME AT ALL! OH, BY THE WAY~
~I WAS READING THE NEWSPAPER, AND I NOTICED AN ARTICLE THAT YOU MIGHT WANT TO LOOK AT.
OH? REALLY?!
A LOCAL THEATRE IS HAVING A SHOW OF ITS VINTAGE POSTERS...
~FEATURING MAGICIANS!
WOW!!
... SO SWEET.
SUSIE... I FEEL GUILTY THAT YOU'RE LETTING ME STAY HERE FOR THE DAY, WHILE MY PLACE GETS, UH~ FUMIGATED.
DON'T BE. IT'S NO PROB'!
OK.
HEY! DO YOU WANT TO GO OVER THERE WITH ME? THIS SHOW DOES SOUND KINDA COOL...
NO THANKS, I HAVE A TON OF WORK TO GET DONE TODAY. YOU GO ON AND HAVE FUN. I'LL SEE YOU LATER!!
STAY WARM OUT THERE.

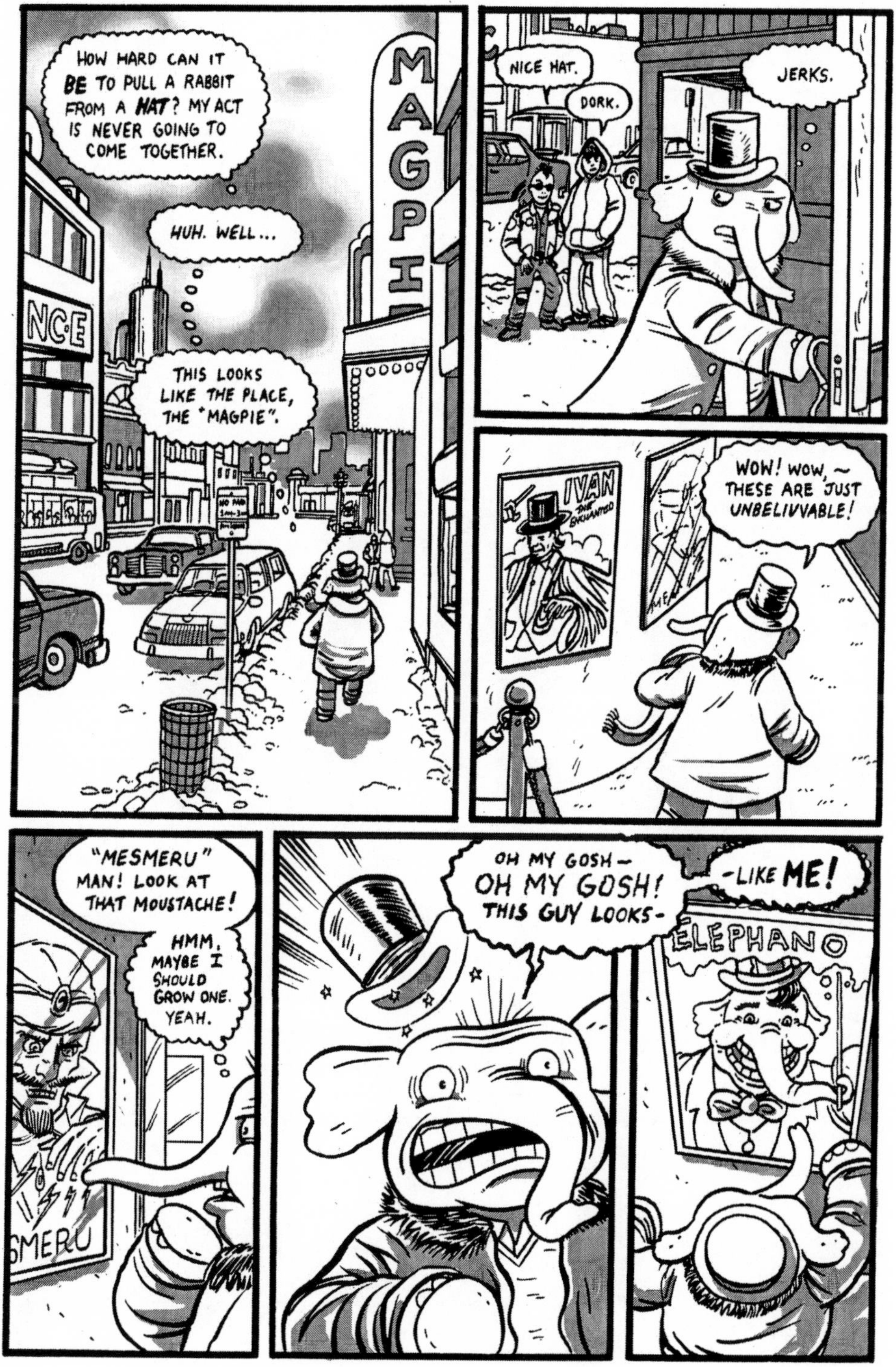
HOW HARD CAN IT BE TO PULL A RABBIT FROM A HAT? MY ACT IS NEVER GOING TO COME TOGETHER.
HUH. WELL...
THIS LOOKS LIKE THE PLACE, THE "MAGPIE".
MAGPIE
NCE
NICE HAT.
DORK.
JERKS.
IVAN THE ENCHANTED
WOW! WOW, ~ THESE ARE JUST UNBELIVVABLE!
"MESMERU" MAN! LOOK AT THAT MOUSTACHE!
HMM, MAYBE I SHOULD GROW ONE. YEAH.
SMERU
OH MY GOSH — OH MY GOSH! THIS GUY LOOKS-
-LIKE ME!
ELEPHANO

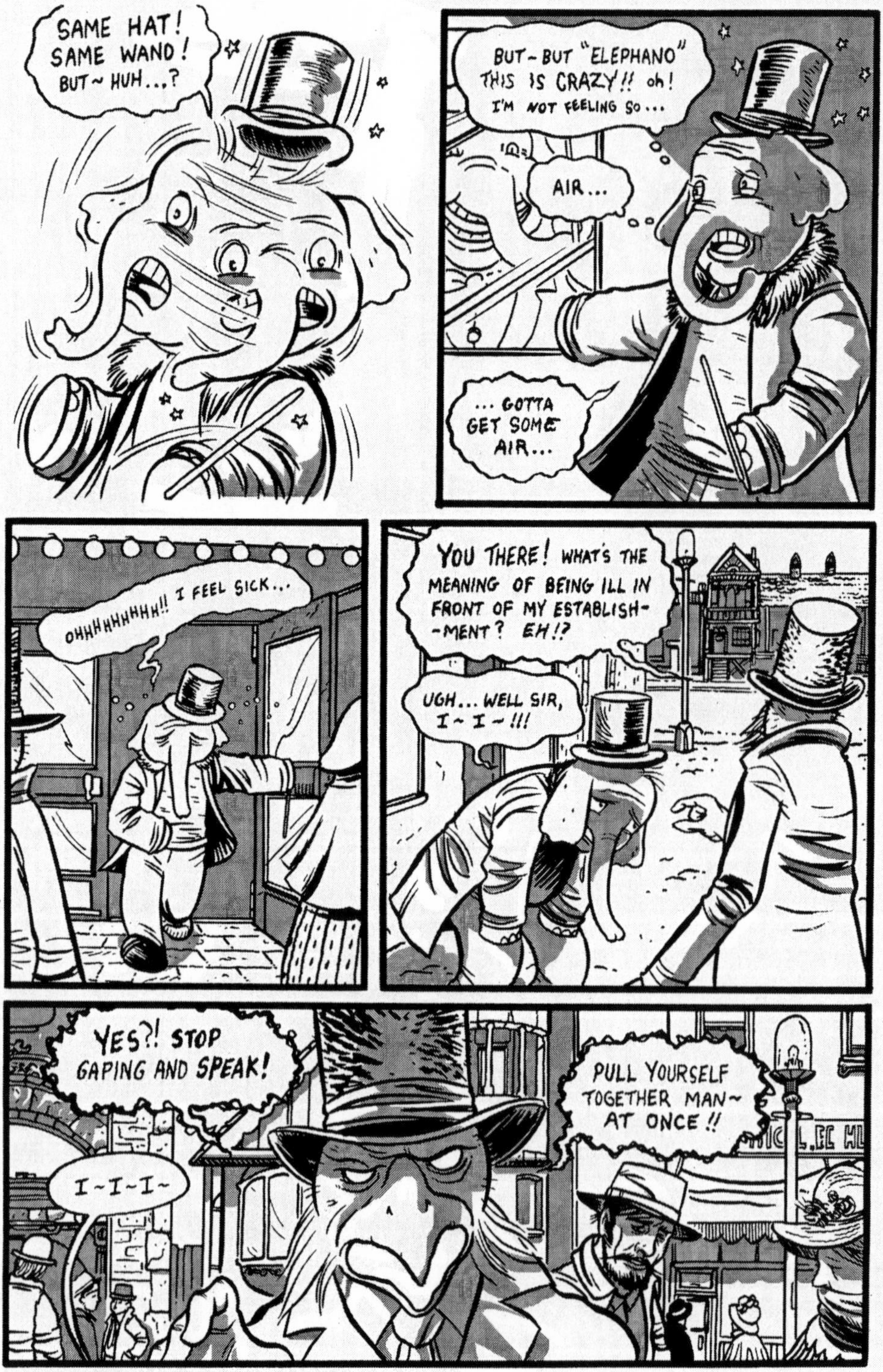
SAME HAT! SAME WAND! BUT~ HUH...?
BUT-BUT "ELEPHANO" THIS IS CRAZY!! oh! I'M NOT FEELING SO...
AIR...
... GOTTA GET SOME AIR...
OHHHHHHHHH!! I FEEL SICK...
YOU THERE! WHAT'S THE MEANING OF BEING ILL IN FRONT OF MY ESTABLISH--MENT? EH!?
UGH... WELL SIR, I~I~!!!
YES?! STOP GAPING AND SPEAK!
I~I~I~
PULL YOURSELF TOGETHER MAN~ AT ONCE!!

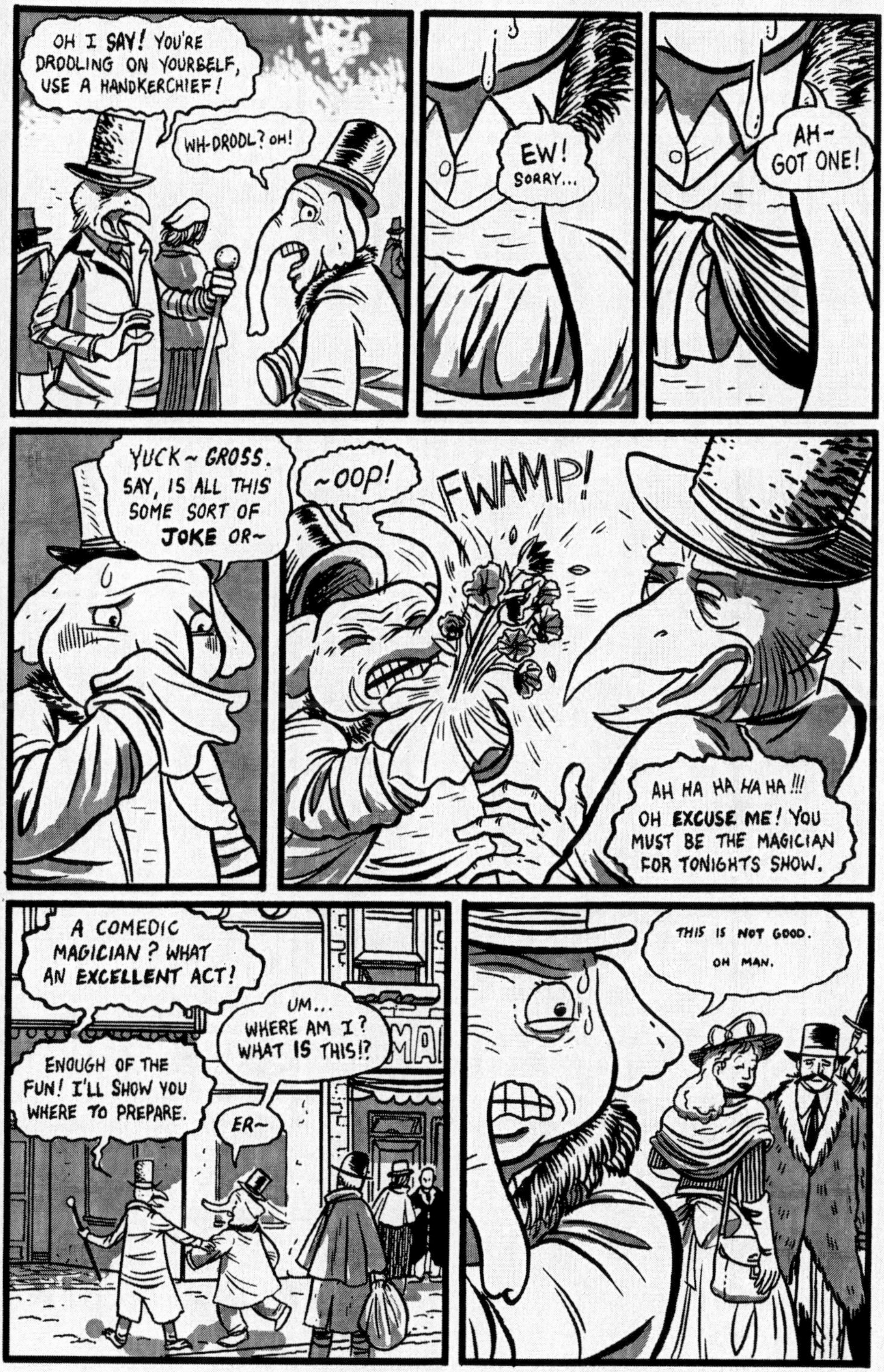
OH I SAY! YOU'RE DROOLING ON YOURSELF, USE A HANDKERCHIEF!
WH-DROOL? OH!
EW! SORRY...
AH- GOT ONE!
YUCK ~ GROSS. SAY, IS ALL THIS SOME SORT OF JOKE OR~
~OOP!
FWAMP!
AH HA HA HA HA!!! OH EXCUSE ME! YOU MUST BE THE MAGICIAN FOR TONIGHTS SHOW.
A COMEDIC MAGICIAN? WHAT AN EXCELLENT ACT!
ENOUGH OF THE FUN! I'LL SHOW YOU WHERE TO PREPARE.
UM... WHERE AM I? WHAT IS THIS!?
ER~
THIS IS NOT GOOD.
OH MAN.

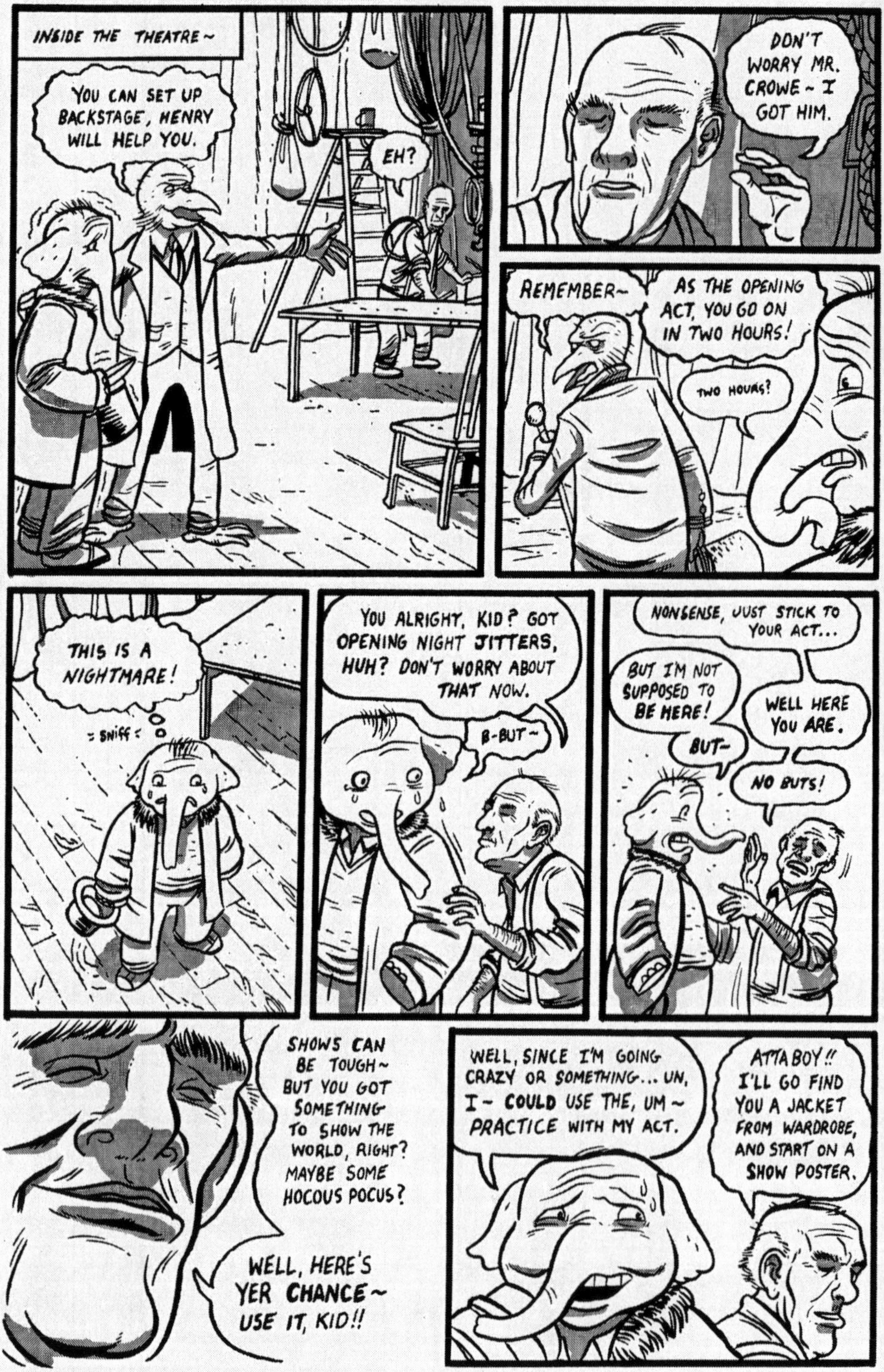
INSIDE THE THEATRE~
YOU CAN SET UP BACKSTAGE, HENRY WILL HELP YOU.
EH?
DON'T WORRY MR. CROWE ~ I GOT HIM.
REMEMBER~
AS THE OPENING ACT, YOU GO ON IN TWO HOURS!
TWO HOURS?
THIS IS A NIGHTMARE!
SNIFF
YOU ALRIGHT, KID? GOT OPENING NIGHT JITTERS, HUH? DON'T WORRY ABOUT THAT NOW.
B-BUT~
NONSENSE, JUST STICK TO YOUR ACT...
BUT I'M NOT SUPPOSED TO BE HERE!
WELL HERE YOU ARE.
BUT-
NO BUTS!
SHOWS CAN BE TOUGH~ BUT YOU GOT SOMETHING TO SHOW THE WORLD, RIGHT? MAYBE SOME HOCUS POCUS?
WELL, HERE'S YER CHANCE~ USE IT, KID!!
WELL, SINCE I'M GOING CRAZY OR SOMETHING... UN, I~ COULD USE THE, UM~ PRACTICE WITH MY ACT.
ATTABOY!! I'LL GO FIND YOU A JACKET FROM WARDROBE, AND START ON A SHOW POSTER.

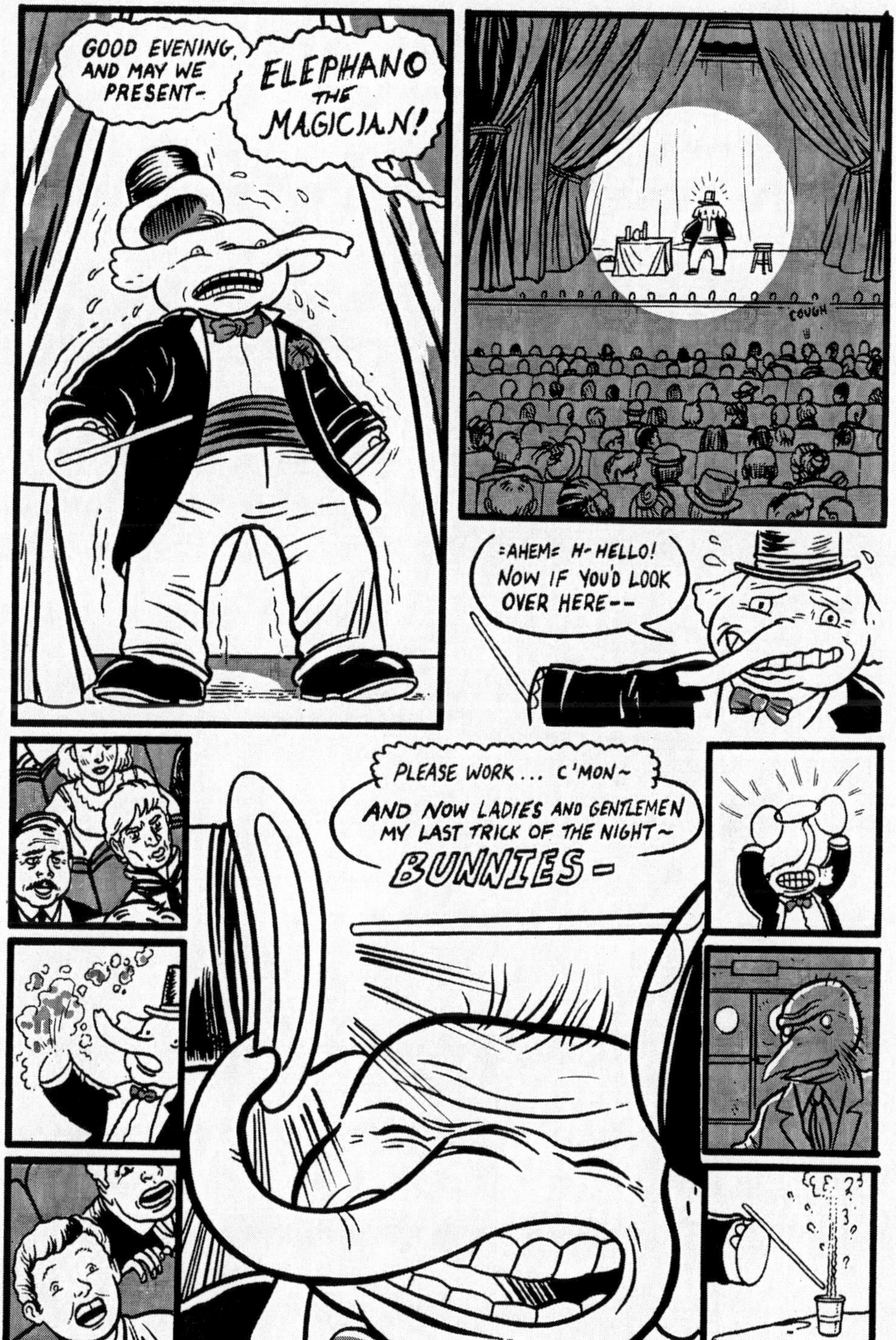
GOOD EVENING, AND MAY WE PRESENT-
ELEPHANO THE MAGICIAN!
COUGH
=AHEM= H-HELLO! NOW IF YOU'D LOOK OVER HERE--
PLEASE WORK... C'MON~
AND NOW LADIES AND GENTLEMEN MY LAST TRICK OF THE NIGHT~
BUNNIES-

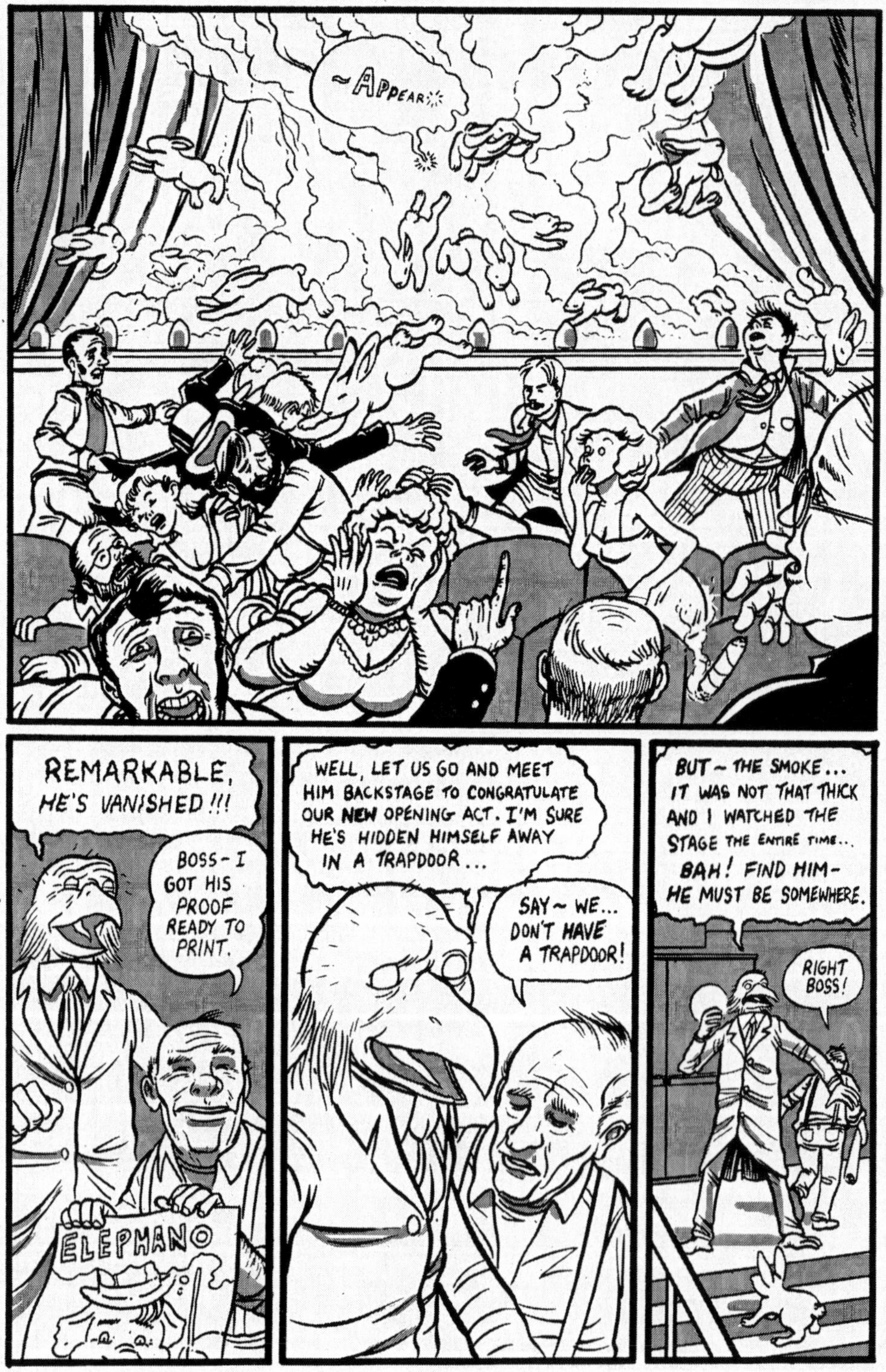
~APPEAR
REMARKABLE, HE'S VANISHED!!!
BOSS - I GOT HIS PROOF READY TO PRINT.
ELEPHANO
WELL, LET US GO AND MEET HIM BACKSTAGE TO CONGRATULATE OUR NEW OPENING ACT. I'M SURE HE'S HIDDEN HIMSELF AWAY IN A TRAPDOOR...
SAY ~ WE... DON'T HAVE A TRAPDOOR!
BUT ~ THE SMOKE... IT WAS NOT THAT THICK AND I WATCHED THE STAGE THE ENTIRE TIME... BAH! FIND HIM- HE MUST BE SOMEWHERE.
RIGHT BOSS!

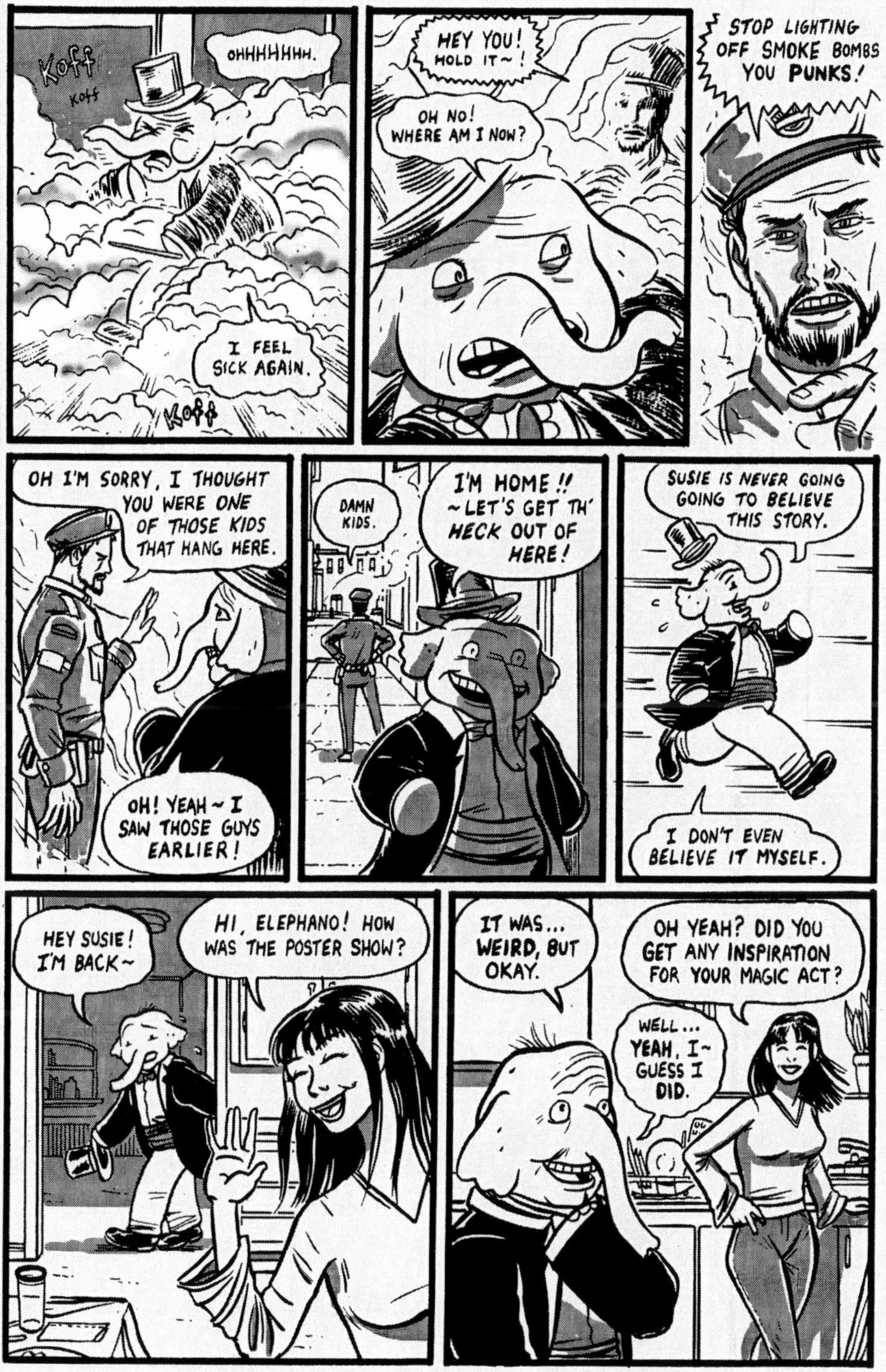
Koff
Koff
OHHHHHHH.
I FEEL SICK AGAIN.
Koff
HEY YOU! HOLD IT~!
OH NO! WHERE AM I NOW?
STOP LIGHTING OFF SMOKE BOMBS YOU PUNKS!
OH I'M SORRY, I THOUGHT YOU WERE ONE OF THOSE KIDS THAT HANG HERE.
OH! YEAH ~ I SAW THOSE GUYS EARLIER!
DAMN KIDS.
I'M HOME!! ~LET'S GET TH' HECK OUT OF HERE!
SUSIE IS NEVER GOING GOING TO BELIEVE THIS STORY.
I DON'T EVEN BELIEVE IT MYSELF.
HEY SUSIE! I'M BACK~
HI, ELEPHANO! HOW WAS THE POSTER SHOW?
IT WAS... WEIRD, BUT OKAY.
OH YEAH? DID YOU GET ANY INSPIRATION FOR YOUR MAGIC ACT?
WELL... YEAH, I~ GUESS I DID.

CONTRIBUTORS' WEBSITES:

CRAIG ARNDT
www.craigarndt.ca
www.nenimo.livejournal.com

ADAM AYLARD
www.adamaylard.com
www.adamaylard.livejournal.com

KEVIN BURKHALTER
www.kevinsjournalcomic.com
www.kar2nist.livejournal.com

MICHELE CHIDESTER
www.michelechidester.com
www.drogochideseter.livejournal.com

JP COOVERT
www.jpcoovert.com
www.ziel.livejournal.com

BECKY DREISTADT
www.owlfactory.com
professor-chai.livejournal.com

DOUG FREY
www.darkwaterfrey.deviantart.com
www.darkwaterfrey.livejournal.com

FRANK GIBSON
www.beckyandfrank.com

GRAHAM KAHLER
www.grahamkahler.com
www.grahamtastic.livejournal.com

LUCY KNISLEY
www.stoppayingattention.com
www.lucylou.livejournal.com

MELISSSA MENDES
www.tropist.com/mezilla/

ARLENE O'LEARY
www.oharlene.livejournal.com

JOSE-LUIS OLIVARES
www.joseluisolivares.com
www.jogs600.livejournal.com

JASON RAINEY
www.jae.imperialotter.com
www.jasonism_wow.livejournal.com

CHRIS SCHWEIZER
www.curiousoldlibrary.com
www.chrisschweizer.livejournal.com

MICHAEL SKATTUM
www.diamondrudge.livejournal.com

JEREMY SORESE
www.derbyartist.livejournal.com

ROSEMARY TRAVALE
www.rosemarytravale.ca
www.piratecore.livejournal.com

JOEY WEISER
www.tragic-planet.com
www.joeyweiser.livejournal.com

CHRIS WRIGHT
www.godbuckle.com
www.cwright.livejournal.com

DAVID YODER
www.davidyoderisawesome.com
www.awesomeyoder.livejournal.com

THANKS

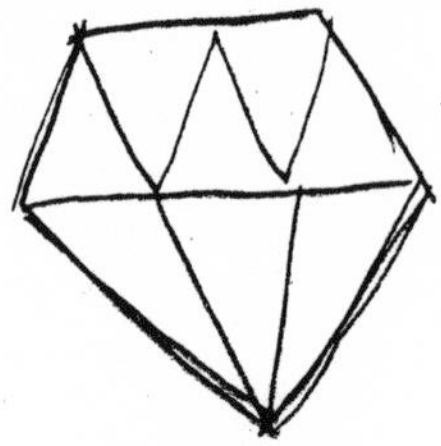

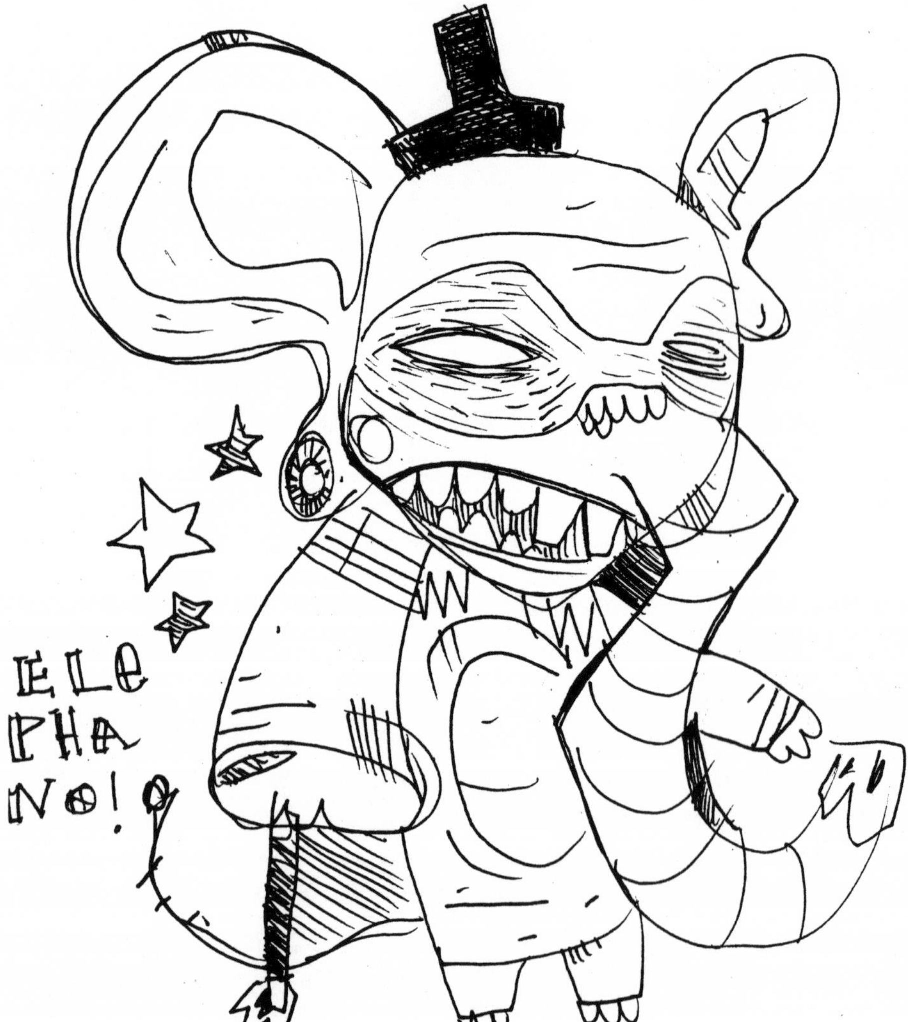
ELE
PHA
NO!